DEVELOPING WRITING SKILLS FOR IELTS

An essential companion for IELTS writing instructors and students, Developing Writing Skills for IELTS provides IELTS test-takers with the necessary skills to succeed in the two academic writing tasks in IELTS.

Adopting an original exemplar-based writing instructional approach, this text offers an in-depth and reader-friendly analysis of the assessment standards of the two academic writing tasks in IELTS. Authentic exemplars written by EFL university students are included to illustrate high (Bands 8-9), average (Bands 6-7), and low (Bands 4-5) performances in IELTS writing.

Key Features:

- Diagrammatical representation of assessment standards of the two academic writing tasks by experienced IELTS writing examiners and instructors.
- 100 writing questions modelled after the IELTS format, designed by the authors, and categorised according to question types and topics that emerge from an analysis of over 400 IELTS writing questions.
- Over 100 writing exemplars by EFL university students, accompanied by guided activities and suggested answers.

Designed as a classroom text, a resource for workshops and consultations, or a self-study material, *Developing Writing Skills for IELTS: A Research-based Approach* will support IELTS writing instructors and test-takers with a variety of writing proficiencies.

Sin Wang Chong is Lecturer (Assistant Professor) in TESOL in the School of Social Sciences, Education and Social Work at Queen's University Belfast in the UK. His research interests include language and educational assessment, research synthesis, and computer-assisted language learning. He is Associate Editor of two journals, Higher Education Research & Development (T&F) and Innovation in Language Learning and Teaching (T&F).

Xuejun Ye is a doctoral candidate in Applied Language Sciences at the Hong Kong Polytechnic University and a former research assistant at the Education University of Hong Kong.

DEVELOPING WRITING SKILLS FOR IELTS

A Research-Based Approach

Sin Wang Chong and
Xuejun Ye

Routledge
Taylor & Francis Group

NEW YORK AND LONDON

First published 2021
by Routledge
52 Vanderbilt Avenue, New York, NY 10017

and by Routledge
2 Park Square, Milton Park, Abingdon, Oxon, OX14 4RN

Routledge is an imprint of the Taylor & Francis Group, an informa business

Library of Congress Cataloging-in-Publication Data
A catalog record for this title has been requested

ISBN: 978-0-367-25839-9 (hbk)
ISBN: 978-0-367-25837-5 (pbk)
ISBN: 978-0-429-29016-9 (ebk)

Typeset in Interstate
by KnowledgeWorks Global Ltd.

Visit the eResources: www.routledge.com/9780367258375

CONTENTS

Part II

SUPPORT MATERIAL

The answer chapters in Part II can be downloaded for personal use. You can access these downloads by visiting the book product page on our website: http://www.routledge.com/9780367258375. Then click on the tab that says "Support Material" and select the files. They will begin downloading to your computer.

ACKNOWLEDGEMENTS

The authors would like to acknowledge the support of the Education University of Hong Kong who funded the project *Developing an Exemplar Anthology and Online Exemplar Platform for IELTS Writing* through the Teaching Development Grant (T0203).

We would like to express our gratitude to the scholars, researchers, teachers, and students whose contributions have made this textbook a more useful resource to IELTS teachers and test-takers. First, we would like to thank the two external reviewers of this project, Prof Hayo Reinders, TESOL Professor at Anaheim University and Dr Jessica To, Post-doctoral Fellow at the Faculty of Education, the University of Hong Kong, for their valuable comments on this textbook. Our heartfelt appreciation also goes to former colleagues of the first author at the Centre for Language in Education, the Education University of Hong Kong, for sharing their expert knowledge in teaching and assessing IELTS Writing. In particular, we would like to thank Miss Blanche Chu, Mr David Brown, and Mr Stephen Holyoak for participating in lengthy individual interviews which consolidated our understanding of the assessment standards of IELTS Writing. Last but not least, we would like to thank all the undergraduate and postgraduate students at the Education University of Hong Kong who participated in this project and provided their written consent for us to use their writing as textbook materials.

The first author would like to acknowledge that Chapter 2 is written based on an article published in *Assessment & Evaluation in Higher Education* (Taylor & Francis):

Chong, S. W. (2019). The use of exemplars in English writing classrooms: From theory to practice. *Assessment & Evaluation in Higher Education, 44*(5), 748-763.

Finally, we would like to acknowledge that a version of the materials presented in this textbook is stored on the Intranet of the Education University of Hong Kong for free usage by the university's staff and students. A note was added to this electronic version of the materials indicating that its final version will be published in the form of a textbook by Routledge. This arrangement was an agreement made between the publisher and the authors.

Sin Wang Chong
School of Social Sciences, Education and Social Work
Queen's University Belfast, UK

Xuejun Ye
Faculty of Humanities
The Hong Kong Polytechnic University

Part I

1 Introduction to IELTS and IELTS Writing

What is IELTS?

IELTS, the International English Language Testing System, managed by the University of Cambridge Local Examinations Syndicate (UCLES), the British Council, and the Australian International Development Programme (IDP), is designed to measure the language proficiency of candidates who need entry to study or work in the United Kingdom and other English-speaking countries.

What are the Two IELTS Test Types?

The IELTS test consists of two forms: the Academic test (or module) and the General Training test (or module). Test-takers choose the module according to the purpose of taking the test. Generally speaking, people take the Academic module in order to satisfy the language entrance requirement of academic programmes offered by post-secondary institutions and universities which use English as the medium of instruction or fulfil the professional requirements in their workplace. For people who expect to join professional associations in nursing, medicine, law, or engineering, they may also be required to take this academic version of IELTS to become a member of a professional body in an English-speaking country. However, for people who aspire to enrol in vocational courses, secondary schools or, for immigration purposes, these individuals are required to take the General Training module. The government authorities of English-speaking countries, including Australia, Canada, New Zealand, the United States, and the United Kingdom, often demand and accept an IELTS score of the General Training certificate to prove the language competence of the applicants.

Diverse levels of English are required by different bodies such as governments, tertiary education institutions, and companies around the globe, depending on their specific objectives. Candidates can get a score between 1 and 9. Half scores such as 5.5 can be given. University applicants often need an IELTS score of 6 or above to guarantee a successful admission to a tertiary programme. Some university programmes may also require a minimum score in each of the four parts, especially in speaking and writing. It is therefore very significant to make full preparations before taking the Academic IELTS exam. The IELTS test scores of both Academic and General Training modules are valid for two years from the day the results are released to the candidates.

What are the Four Parts of an IELTS Test?

The IELTS test (both Academic and General Training modules) is divided into four parts: reading, writing, listening, and speaking. The Academic and General Training modules have both similarities and differences: the format and content of listening and speaking tests are precisely the same but the reading and writing tests are different. The total test time is approximately 2 hours and 45 minutes. Test-takers need to complete Listening, Reading, and Writing on one day, while they can choose to take the Speaking test on the same day or a few days before or after the other tests. For detailed information regarding IELTS test format, you can refer to the official IELTS website: https://www.ielts.org/about-the-test/test-format.

What is the Academic Writing Test?

The Academic Writing test, which comprises two separate tasks, is 60 minutes long in total. Candidates are expected to write at least 150 words for Task 1 within around 20 minutes and at least 250 words for Task 2 within about 40 minutes. In IELTS Academic Task 1, candidates are normally asked to employ their own words to describe stages of a process, describe and explain data, describe a mechanism (e.g., a manufacturing process), or write about an object or event, according to the materials presented. In IELTS Academic Task 2, test-takers are usually required to discuss a point of view, an argument or a problem. Candidates may sometimes be asked to give solutions to a problem, present and justify an opinion, compare and contrast opinions, and evaluate arguments depending on the question type.

Introduction to IELTS Rubrics

The IELTS writing rubrics for Academic module Tasks 1 and 2 are made freely available on the internet.[1] According to the rubrics, there are four domains: task achievement, coherence and cohesion, lexical resource, and grammatical range and accuracy. Comparing the descriptors of the four domains of the two tasks, descriptors of two of the domains are identical, namely 'lexical resource' and 'grammatical range and accuracy', while slight differences are noted in the domains 'task achievement' and 'coherence and cohesion'.

In this section, a brief introduction to each of the four domains will be given in accordance with the key words generated from a word cloud website. A more detailed explanation of the descriptors of each domain will be provided from Chapter 3 to Chapter 10.

1 **Task Achievement (Task 1)**
   In Task 1, candidates are required to report information presented in a graph or diagram by highlighting and comparing the key features. Candidates are required to start their data report by providing an overview, which includes an introduction of what the graph or diagram is about (usually by paraphrasing the question) and a description of the most salient piece of information presented in the graph or diagram. In terms of format, candidates are reminded to refrain from writing in bullet points but in paragraph(s) and complete sentences. The content presented in Task 1 will be evaluated according to its accuracy, clarity, appropriacy, and relevance.

2 Task Achievement (Task 2)

In Task 2, the requirements in this domain are largely identical to those of Task 1. Nevertheless, given the more argumentative nature of the task, candidates are expected to present their position (i.e. their standpoint) clearly at the beginning of the essay (e.g., to what extent do they agree or disagree with a statement). In addition, the arguments included in the body paragraphs should fully address the task (e.g., if there are two parts in the question, the essay should respond to both parts). Moreover, sufficient elaboration and examples should be provided to support and develop the main ideas. Extended and relevant response to the task should be accompanied by an appropriate essay format with an introduction paragraph, at least one body paragraph, and a conclusion.

3 Coherence and Cohesion (Task 1)

When attempting Task 1, another area of concern of the examiners is coherence and cohesion of candidates' writing. Coherence is defined as the logical progression of ideas and information, while cohesion refers to connection of ideas and relationships between sentences. Coherence is achieved through effective paragraphing. To improve cohesion of writing, candidates are expected to utilise a range of cohesive devices and strategies (e.g., connectives, conjunctions, referencing) accurately.

4 Coherence and Cohesion (Task 2)

In Task 2, there are similar requirements to develop arguments coherently and cohesively. In addition to the above, there is a strong emphasis on the importance of managing paragraphing skillfully and appropriately. This implies test-takers should be able to construct well-structured paragraphs with a clearly identified central idea and supporting details. In terms of inter-paragraph relationship, the order of the paragraphs should demonstrate a logical development of thought.

5 Lexical Resource (Tasks 1 and 2)

'Lexical resource' refers to the effective and accurate use of vocabulary. In terms of effectiveness, candidates are required to have a sophisticated control over the range of lexical items (vocabulary) used in their writing. A more competent candidate in this domain demonstrates the ability to use a wide range of common and rare words. Regarding accuracy of vocabulary use, candidates should be able to demonstrate accurate use of collocation, word formation, and spelling.

6 Grammatical Range and Accuracy (Tasks 1 and 2)

In the IELTS writing descriptors, the word 'grammar' concerns two aspects of candidates' use of sentence structures, which are range of sentence structures and accuracy of sentence structures. As far as the range of sentence structures is concerned, there is an expectation for candidates to use both simple and complex sentence structures.

Regarding accuracy of sentence structures, examiners are looking for accurate use of punctuations (e.g., avoid comma splices) and error-free sentences.

IELTS Writing Question Analysis

Sample units of 25 IELTS writing textbooks available at the Centre for Language in Education, the Education University of Hong Kong were analysed and writing questions included in the textbooks were collated in a Word file. In total, 231 Task 1 questions and 222 Task 2 questions were collected. These 453 questions were inputted into *NVivo 12*, a qualitative research software, for inductive coding to identify the common question types and themes of IELTS writing tasks. In total, four types of questions and 29 themes were identified for Task 1; as for Task 2, five question types and 22 themes were identified. Informed by the data analysis above, 50 IELTS writing questions for Tasks 1 and 50 IELTS writing questions for Task 2 were developed by the authors. The 100 IELTS writing questions can be found in Chapter 13.

1. Question analysis of Task 1

In total, four question types and 29 question themes were identified based on the analysis of the 231 Task 1 writing questions. The four question types include:

- chart/graph
- table
- charts/graphs
- map/diagram/infographics

An example of a chart/graph question

T1-01

You should spend about 20 minutes on this task.

The graph below gives information about the number of academic jobs in some humanities and social sciences disciplines between 2012 and 2014.

Summarise the information by selecting and reporting the main features, and make comparisons where relevant.

Write at least 150 words.

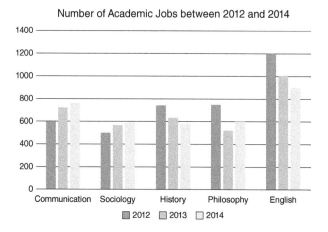

Number of Academic Jobs between 2012 and 2014

An example of a table question

T1-35

You should spend about 20 minutes on this task.

The table below gives information about languages which can be learned through participating in online courses.

Summarise the information by selecting and reporting the main features, and make comparisons where relevant.

Write at least 150 words.

Language	Number of courses on Online Platform A	Number of courses on Online Platform B	Total number of courses
English	92	21	113
Chinese	34	61	95
French	37	12	49
Italian	35	7	42
Korean	21	2	23
French	20	1	21

An example of a charts/graphs question

T1-26

You should spend about 20 minutes on this task.

The charts below show information about different types of social welfare benefits between 1995 and 2015.

Summarise the information by selecting and reporting the main features, and make comparisons where relevant.

Write at least 150 words.

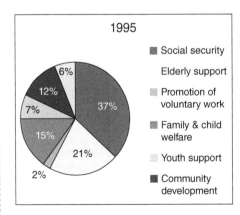
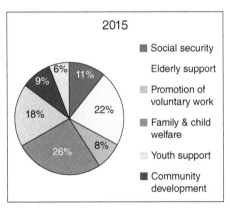

An example of a map/diagram/infographics question

T1-09

You should spend about 20 minutes on this task.

The diagram below gives information about the process of making soap and detergent.

Summarise the information by selecting and reporting the main features, and make comparisons where relevant.

Write at least 150 words.

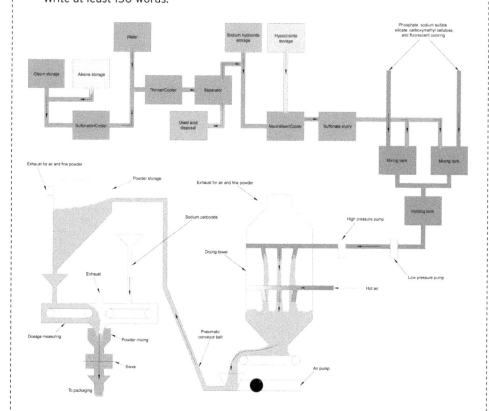

Source: https://commons.wikimedia.org/wiki/File:Soap_and_Detergent_manufacturing_process_03.png

Table 1.1 presents the 29 themes identified from the question analysis according to their number of instances.

Table 1.1 Question themes, example topics, and number of instances of Task 1 questions[2]

	Question Theme	Example Topic	Number of Instances
1	Economy	global sale of hybrid vehicles	36
2	Age and gender	male and female workers in several employment sectors	25
3	Manufacturing	manufacture frozen fish pies	22
4	Education	overseas and local students in Australian universities	18
5	Science and technology	the number of people using the internet	13
6	City development	development plan of a town centre	11
7	Environment	the consequences of deforestation	11
8	Tourism	Japanese tourists travelling abroad	11
9	Work	unemployment rates in the US and Japan	11
10	Socio-cultural issues	marriage and divorce rates	10
11	Resources	the sources of generated electricity	9
12	Population	changes in world population	8
13	Traffic	underground railway systems	8
14	Health	overweight rates	7
15	Language	foreign languages learning	7
16	Climate	average monthly rainfall and temperature	5
17	Public's opinions	survey results about visitors' satisfactory rates	5
18	Sales	sales at a small restaurant	4
19	Crime	injuries resulted from gun and knife crimes	3
20	Leisure	concert, cinema, and theatre tickets	3
21	Media	social media businesses	3
22	Agriculture	grain harvested	2
23	Communication	total number of minutes of telephone calls	2
24	Food	fast food consumption of men and women	2
25	Social responsibility	giving money to charity	2
26	Airline Business	airlines and aspects of air travel	1
27	Animals	life cycle of salmon	1
28	Art	art museum before and after renovation	1
29	Location	location of a village	1

2. Question analysis of Task 2

Based on the question analysis of Task 2, five question types and 22 themes were identified. The five question types are presented in Table 1.2.

Table 1.3 presents the 22 themes identified from the question analysis according to their number of instances.

Why This Book?

Unlike a wide range of published IELTS writing textbooks on the market, which largely focus on the development of students' writing skills (especially grammatical accuracy), this book is intended to foster students' understanding and evaluative judgment of IELTS writing assessment standards, which serves as a complement to the existing IELTS writing resources. It is the authors' belief that test-takers can achieve a more satisfactory score in IELTS writing if they have internalised IELTS writing assessment standards (in addition to a firm language foundation). Therefore, it is suggested that both teachers and students combine the two types of writing resources when preparing for IELTS. Specifically, readers can benefit tremendously from the book's clear categorisation of question types and its inclusion of authentic exemplars written by university students. Through incorporating more and less successful writing samples, readers can sharpen their understanding of what good quality writing looks like. Moreover, they are expected to make targeted improvements by referring to the comments provided by the authors (e.g., in Chapters 11–12).

Table 1.2 Question types and example questions of Task 2

Question Type	Example Question
Opinion (agree or disagree)	Family friendly measures (e.g., flexible working hours) should be adopted by companies to ensure the work-life balance of their employees. To what extent do you agree or disagree with this opinion? (T2-06)
Discuss views	Some people argue that heredity exerts a greater influence on an individual's development than a person's later experiences. Discuss the view and give your opinion. (T2-16)
Two-part question	Women's status has improved dramatically both in the society and in the family as a result of the development of the society. However, they are still faced with inequalities. What are some of the inequalities? What measures should be adopted to solve the problems? (T2-21)
Advantages and disadvantages	Some people favor the use of private cars as they bring people much convenience. However, some people think that private cars cause air pollution which is harmful to the environment. Do the advantages of using private cars outweigh the disadvantages? (T2-30)
Problem and solutions	It seems that traffic congestion is becoming more serious than ever. Some people think that the problem can be solved by raising the price of petrol to discourage people from using private cars. Others believe that the government should provide more public transportation to ease the situation. Are the above suggestions feasible in solving traffic jams? What are other possible measures to solve the problem? (T2-34)

Table 1.3 Question themes, example topics, and number of instances of Task 2 questions[3]

	Question Theme	Example Topic	Number of Instances
1	Education	universities should accept equal numbers of male and female students	36
2	Work	an appropriate retirement age	25
3	Food and health	junk food advertising contributes to the problem of obesity	23
4	Socio-cultural and global issues	raising animals for human consumption is cruel	23
5	Age, generation, and gender	insufficient respect shown to older people	21
6	Science, technology, and innovation	modern technology has made it easier to download copyrighted music and books without charge	18
7	Media and communication	mass media have great influence on shaping people's ideas	15
8	Government, politics, and diplomacy	many governments think that economic progress is their most important goal	14
9	Environment	recycle household waste	12
10	Lifestyle	modern lifestyle makes parents spend little time with their children	11
11	Traffic	the use of private motor vehicles	11
12	Economy, money, and trade	money spent on space research	10
13	Crime, punishment, and law	capital punishment is necessary	9
14	Leisure, sports, and hobbies	popular events like the Word Cup are essential	9
15	Language	learn foreign languages in order to travel or work	8
16	Travelling and tourism	eco-tourism is expanding	7
17	Population	population living in cities has increased substantially	4
18	Art and museums	creative artists should be given the freedom to express their ideas	2
19	City development	migration from rural areas to cities	2
20	Climate	the government's responsibility to deal with climate change	2
21	Ethics	testing drugs and new products on animals	2
22	Animals	many people keep dogs and cats as companions	1

Notes

1 Assessment standards of IELTS writing Tasks 1 and 2 (Academic module) can be retrieved at https://www.britishcouncil.it/sites/default/files/ielts_guide_for_teachers_italy.pdf.
2 The same question may be coded under more than one theme.
3 The same question may be coded under more than one theme.

2 Use of Exemplars
Q&A on Theory and Research

Q: What is an 'exemplar' and 'exemplar-based instruction'?

Exemplars are examples of work produced by students (and sometimes teachers) which are used to 'illustrate dimensions of quality' (Carless et al, 2018, p 108).

'Exemplar-based instruction' means the use of exemplars by teachers to illustrate 'a "quality continuum" of authentic student work [or sometimes student work modified by the teacher] to help them make judgements about what constitutes quality' (Scoles et al, 2013, p 632; words in brackets are by authors).

The use of exemplars is regarded as one of the promising ways to develop students' understanding of the ambiguous criteria of 'good work'. Recent literature on the use of exemplars in the context of higher education has shown that exemplar-based instruction is implemented in various disciplines, including life sciences, teacher education, design education, animal science, and English for Academic Purposes (EAP).

Q: What are the theoretical underpinnings of 'exemplar-based instruction'?

'Exemplar-based instruction' is informed by a number of notions:

- 'Tacit knowledge': Tacit knowledge refers to aspects of knowledge that are difficult to transmit through speaking and writing (e.g., descriptors in IELTS writing rubrics) (Sadler, 2010; Carless et al, 2018). The notions of the 'tacit' and 'explicit' facets of knowledge were first thoroughly discussed in Polanyi's (1958, 1962) work on personal knowledge. To Polanyi (ibid), tacit knowledge is compared to 'connoisseurship', which 'can be communicated only by example, not by percept' (p 56). In other words, it is not effective for teachers to explain tacit knowledge, such as the assessment standards of IELTS writing, in the forms of lectures and handouts, because the wordings and expressions used in the assessment standards remain abstract to students. Instead, it is argued that students acquire tacit knowledge through their active involvement in dialogic and reflective activities (e.g., discussion of writing exemplars with peers and teacher with reference to the assessment standards) (Bloxham and Campbell, 2010).
- 'Assessment as learning': Assessment as learning (AaL) is 'a subset of assessment for learning that emphasises using assessment as a process of developing and supporting metacognition for students' (Earl, 2013, p 3). Adhering to the spirit of student-centredness of assessment for learning (AfL), AaL aims to promote 'the active engagement of students in setting goals for their learning and growth, monitoring their progress toward these goals, and determining how to address any gaps' (Andrade et al, 2012, p 8). Instead of the teacher, students take up the role of 'the critical connector

between assessment and their own learning' (Earl, 2013, p 3). 'Exemplar-based instruction' is an example of AaL operationalised with students being the assessors of writing samples by applying their understanding of assessment standards and reflecting on their own performance.

- 'Dialogic feedback': In the context of higher education, there has been an exponential growth in the number of assessment and feedback studies which conceptualise feedback from a constructivist and sociocultural point of view (Carless, 2016; Chong, 2018). Such conceptualisation of feedback is often referred to as 'dialogic feedback'. The notion of dialogic feedback is built upon the tenet of sociocultural theory (SCT) (Vygotsky, 1987). SCT suggests that human cognitive development takes place during social interactions and is mediated by material and symbolic tools. The notion of mediation is further developed by Feuerstein and his associates in their theory of mediated learning experience:

Feuerstein, Rand, and Rynders (1988) suggest four criteria for interactions to be qualified as mediated learning interaction: (1) *intentionality*; (2) *reciprocity*; (3) *transcendence*; and (4) *meaning*. Lee (2014; 2017) explains these criteria in relation to teacher's feedback:

- *Intentionality*: Feedback should be intentional in directing students' attention to particular areas (e.g., content, coherence, language) rather than giving feedback in an unfocused manner.
- *Reciprocity*: Feedback *should* be interactional rather than unidirectional in which students play a passive role.
- *Transcendence*: Feedback *should* facilitate 'feed-up' and 'feed-forward' in which students are able to transfer what they have gained from the feedback to their future writing tasks (Hattie and Timperley, 2007).
- *Meaning*: Feedback should *provide* students with a clear understanding of their strengths and weaknesses in a piece of writing and actions that can be done to close the feedback loop.

Dialogic use of exemplars is regarded as a kind of mediated learning experience where students analyze the given exemplars with reference to the given assessment standards (intentionality), discuss the strengths and weaknesses of the exemplars with their peers and teacher (reciprocity), reflect on ways that the strengths and weaknesses of the exemplars could inform their own writing (transcendence and meaning). Through the provision of dialogic feedback on the given exemplars, teachers develop a better understanding of students' current state of knowledge of the assessment standards which helps teachers provide more effective scaffolding to expand students' understanding of assessment standards (zone of proximal development).

- 'Evaluative judgement': It is defined as 'the capacity to make decisions about the quality of work of oneself and others' (Tai et al, 2018, p 467). The notion has received a revived attention in higher education literature. It was originally developed by Sadler (1989) and known as 'evaluative knowledge' (p 135) and 'evaluative expertise' (p 138). Using exemplars is a promising way to develop students' evaluative judgement because they develop this important cognitive ability through making informed decisions about quality of work they undertake in a self-directed manner (Cowan, 2010).

Q: What are the benefits of using exemplars?

Benefits for students:

- Recent assessment research in higher education has found that understanding of assessment standards, which is a type of 'tacit knowledge', is 'difficult to transfer verbally or in writing' (Carless and Chan, 2017), but is best illustrated through the use of exemplars.

- Research has found that exemplar-based instruction in the higher education context helps clarify teacher expectations to students, simplify the process of assignment preparation (Carless, 2015), illustrate different approaches to tackle an assignment (Orsmond, Merry, and Reiling, 2002), minimise students' assessment-related stress (Yucel, Bird, Young, and Blanksby, 2014), and make students more confident in completing an assignment (Hendry and Anderson, 2013).

- From my own research, students find reading and analysing writing exemplars useful in the following ways:

  1 Using exemplars to promote students' understanding of rubrics
     - *"I learn how to understand the descriptors in a more detailed way, and I now know how to write to gain a higher mark."*
     - *"I think it could be better if we talk about these [requirements in rubrics] while reading the exemplars, integrating these two, and no need to explain them separately. It is meaningless to explain them separately. For example, when we talked about pronouns, we might not know how to place the pronouns in a sentence. We need to learn how to use."*
  2 Using exemplars to facilitate comparison of standards through self-assessment
     - *"When we use exemplar, we would automatically compare our own writing with the exemplar, think about the differences between our articles and the exemplar, then I know what I should improve on."*
     - *"When our group looked through the bad exemplar, which was of 5.5 points to 6 points, we know that is at the same level as ours, then we know what our problems are."*
  3 Using exemplars to facilitate comparison of standards through peer assessment
     - *"You can compare, because he (the teacher) gave two passages. So, while you are comparing the two passages, you can consider why one gets higher marks, or somehow, to learn the... how to say... to learn from this comparison, and to improve your writing skills."*
     - *"The exemplars can let me know more about the differences between a piece of higher-scored and lower-scored writing."*

Benefits for teachers:

- The use of exemplars is a student-centred pedagogical approach which requires little preparation (Smith et al, 2013).
- The use of exemplars contributes to standardising teachers' understanding of the assessment standards, which is likely to lead to fairer and more objective grading.

Table 2.1 Three approaches to using exemplars

Approaches to Using Exemplars	Description
Inductive use of exemplars	• Students are involved in judging the quality of the exemplars by using a marking rubric provided by the teacher. Teachers then explain the assessment standards in relation to the rubric and the exemplars (Hendry et al, 2016).
Scaffolded use of exemplars	• Students are involved in a pre-task (e.g., producing a part of a writing task reminiscent of the exemplar) before being introduced to high quality exemplars (Carless et al, 2018).
Dialogic use of exemplars	• Students' opinions are elicited and divergent viewpoints are encouraged (Carless et al, 2018). • Students are encouraged to discuss their viewpoints with their classmates before teachers explicate the assessment standards (Hendry et al, 2016). • Students are asked to verbalise their judgements and provide suggestions for improving the exemplars (Sadler, 2010). • Students compare exemplars with their own work and reflect on their own performance through self-reflective questioning (Hounsell, 2008).

Q: Why should we use exemplars to prepare students for IELTS writing?

When used in IELTS writing courses and workshops, exemplars can be used to exemplify a spectrum of quality (high, mediocre, low) described in the assessment standards or rubrics.

The use of exemplars facilitates students' understanding of the assessment standards of the four domains: task achievement, coherence and cohesion, lexical resource, and grammatical range and accuracy, which are often expressed in a generic and opaque manner. Through the analysis of and discussion on the exemplars, students can 'engage in feedforward to better understand the disciplinary discourse and its expectations' (Scoles et al, 2013, p 632).

Q: How can teachers use exemplars?

There are three approaches to using exemplars: *inductive*, *scaffolded*, and *dialogic (Table 2.1)*.

In particular, it is important for teachers to share their understanding of assessment standards (e.g., descriptions in writing rubrics) by using exemplars. O'Donovan et al (2008) suggested four approaches for doing so: the 'laissez faire' approach, the 'explicit' approach, the 'social constructivist' approach, and the 'community of practice' approach (Table 2.2).

Q: What online resources do you recommend if I would like to know more about using exemplars in my own classroom?

Resources related to the use of exemplars in higher education

1 Academic journals
   • *Assessment & Evaluation in Higher Education* (Taylor & Francis) https://www.tandfonline.com/toc/caeh20/current
   • *Active Learning in Higher Education* (Sage) http://journals.sagepub.com/home/alh
   • *Higher Education* (Springer) https://link.springer.com/journal/10734
   • *Teaching in Higher Education* (Taylor & Francis) https://www.tandfonline.com/loi/cthe20

Table 2.2 A framework of approaches to sharing meaningful knowledge of assessment standards with students in higher education (adapted from O'Donovan et al, 2008)

	The 'Laissez-faire' Approach	The 'Explicit' Approach	The 'Social Constructivist' Approach	The 'Community of Practice' Approach
Role of the teacher	*Passive* (wait for students to approach them)	*Active* (explicitly explain to students the assessment standards)	*Active* (lead dialogues with students to develop their understanding of assessment standards)	*Active* (facilitate dialogues amongst students to develop their understanding of assessment standards)
Role of the student	*Passive* (wait for opportunities to approach the teacher)	*Passive* (listen to teachers' explanations of assessment standards)	*Active* (engage in dialogues with teachers to better understand assessment standards)	*Active* (engage in dialogues with peers to better understand assessment standards)
The use of exemplars in IELTS writing	Exemplars distributed in the form of model essays without teacher input or discussions with students	Exemplars distributed in the form of model essays with teachers highlighting the strengths of the exemplars with reference to the IELTS writing descriptors	Essays and IELTS writing descriptors are distributed to students. The teacher guides students' understanding of the 'quality' of the exemplars through the use of a range of interactive and questioning strategies (e.g., Carless and Chan, 2017)	Essays and IELTS writing descriptors are distributed to students. Students discuss with peers in small groups (sometimes with the teacher's facilitation) about the 'quality' of the exemplars interactively.

2   Journal articles

- Carless, D., and Chan, K. K. H. (2017). *Managing dialogic use of exemplars. Assessment & Evaluation in Higher Education, 42*(6), 930–941.
- Chong, S. W. (2019). The use of exemplars in English writing classrooms: From theory to practice. *Assessment & Evaluation in Higher Education, 44*(5), 748–763.
- Grainger, P. R., Heck, D., and Carey, M. D. (2018). Are assessment exemplars perceived to support self-regulated learning in teacher education? *Assessment, Testing and Applied Measurement, 60*(3), 1–9.
- Hendry, G. D., and Tomitsch, M. (2014). Implementing an exemplar-based approach in an interaction design subject: Enhancing students' awareness of the need to be creative. *International Journal of Technology and Design Education, 24*(3), 337–348.

- Hendry, G. D., White, P., and Herbert, C. (2016). Providing exemplar-based 'feedforward' before an assessment: The role of teacher explanation. *Active Learning in Higher Education, 17*(2), 99-109.
- O'Donovan, B., Price, M., and Rust, C. (2008). Developing student understanding of assessment standards: A nested hierarchy of approaches. *Teaching in Higher Education, 13*(2), 205-217.
- Orsmond, P., S. Merry, and Reiling, K. (2002). The use of exemplars and formative feedback when using student derived marking criteria in peer and self-assessment. *Assessment & Evaluation in Higher Education, 27*(4), 309-323.
- Sadler, D. R. (2010). Beyond feedback: Developing student capability in complex appraisal. *Assessment & Evaluation in Higher Education, 35*(5), 535-550.
- Tai, J., Ajjawi, R., Boud, D., Dawson, P., and Panadero, E. (2018). Developing evaluative judgement: Enabling students to make decisions about the quality of work. *Higher Education, 76*(3), 467-481.
- Yucel, R., Bird, F., Young, J., and Blanksby, T. (2014). The road to self-assessment: Exemplar marking before peer review develops first year students' capacity to judge the quality of a scientific report. *Assessment & Evaluation in Higher Education, 39*(8), 971-986.

3 Scholarly books
- Boud, D., and Molloy, E. (Eds.) (2012). *Feedback in higher and professional education: Understanding it and doing it well*. London: Routledge.
- Boud, D., Ajjawi, R., Dawson, P., and Tai, J. (Eds.) (2018). *Developing evaluative judgement in higher education*. London: Routledge.
- Merry, S., Price, M., Carless, D., and Raras, M. (Eds.) (2013). *Reconceptualising feedback in higher education*. London: Routledge.

Resources related to IELTS and IELTS writing

1 Websites
- IELTS Exam Writing Samples: https://www.ielts-exam.net/IELTS-Writing-Samples/ielts-writing.htm
- Prepare for IELTS (British Council) https://takeielts.britishcouncil.org/prepare
- Road to IELTS (British Council) https://www.roadtoielts.com

References

Andrade, H., Huff, K., and Brooke, G. (2012). *Assessing learning: The students at the center series*. New England: The Nellie Mae Education Foundation.

Bloxham, S., and Campbell, L. (2010). Generating dialogue in assessment feedback: Exploring the use of interactive cover sheets. *Assessment & Evaluation in Higher Education, 35*(3), 291-300.

Carless, D. (2015). *Excellence in university assessment: Learning from award-winning practice*. London: Routledge.

Carless, D. (2016). Feedback as Dialogue. *Encyclopaedia of Educational Philosophy and Theory*, 1-6. Retrieved at http://link.springer.com/referenceworkentry/10.1007/978-981-287-532-7_389-1

Carless, D., and Chan, K. K. H. (2017). Managing dialogic use of exemplars. *Assessment & Evaluation in Higher Education, 42*(6), 930-941.

Carless, D., Chan, K. K. H., To, J., Lo, M., and Barrett, E. (2018). Developing students' capacities for evaluative judgement through analysing exemplars. In D. Boud, R. Ajjawi, P. Dawson, and J. Tai (Eds.), *Developing evaluative judgement in higher education: Assessment for knowing and producing quality work* (pp 1–18). London: Routledge.

Chong, I. (2018). Interplay among technical, socio-emotional and personal factors in written feedback research. *Assessment & Evaluation in Higher Education*, *43*(2), 185-196.

Cowan, J. (2010). Developing the ability for making evaluative judgements. *Teaching in Higher Education*, *15*(3), 323-334.

Earl, L. M. (2013). Assessment for learning; Assessment as learning: Changing practices means changing beliefs. In Hong Kong Education Bureau (Ed.), *Assessment and learning* (Issue 2) (pp 1-5). Hong Kong: The Hong Kong Government Printer.

Feuerstein, R., Rand, Y., and Rynders, J. (1988). *Don't accept me as I am*. New York, NY: Plenum.

Hattie, J., and Timperley, H. (2007). The power of feedback. *Review of Educational Research, 77*(1), 81-112.

Hendry, G., and Anderson, J. (2013). Helping students understand the standards of work expected in an essay: Using exemplars in mathematics pre-service education classes. *Assessment & Evaluation in Higher Education, 38*(6), 754-768.

Hendry, G. D., White, P., and Herbert, C. (2016). Providing exemplar-based 'feedforward' before an assessment: The role of teacher explanation. *Active Learning in Higher Education, 17*(2), 99-109.

Hounsell, D. (2008). *The trouble with feedback: New challenges, emerging strategies*. International change, Spring. www.tla.ed.ac.uk/interchange.

Lee, I. (2014). Revisiting teacher feedback in EFL writing from sociocultural perspectives. *TESOL Quarterly, 48*(1), 201-213.

Lee, I. (2017). *Classroom writing assessment and feedback in L2 school contexts*. Singapore: Springer.

O'Donovan, B., Price, M., and Rust, C. (2008). Developing student understanding of assessment standards: A nested hierarchy of approaches. *Teaching in Higher Education, 13*(2), 205-217.

Orsmond, P., Merry, S., and Reiling, K. (2002). The use of exemplars and formative feedback when using student derived marking criteria in peer and self- assessment. *Assessment & Evaluation in Higher Education, 27*(4), 309-323.

Polanyi, M. (1958, 1962). *Personal knowledge: Towards a post-critical philosophy*. London: Routledge.

Sadler, D. R. (1989). Formative assessment and the design of instructional systems. *Instructional Science, 18*(2), 119-144.

Sadler, D. R. (2010). Beyond feedback: Developing student capability in complex appraisal. *Assessment & Evaluation in Higher Education, 35*(5), 535-550.

Scoles, J., Huxham, M., and McArthur, J. (2013). No longer exempt from good practice: Using exemplars to close the feedback gap for exams. *Assessment & Evaluation in Higher Education, 38*(6), 631-645.

Smith, C., Worsfold, K., Davies, L., Fisher, R., and McPhail, R. (2013). Assessment literacy and student learning: The case for explicitly developing students' 'assessment literacy'. *Assessment & Evaluation in Higher Education, 38*(1), 44-60.

Tai, J., Ajjawi, R., Boud, D., Dawson, P., and Panadero, E. (2018). Developing evaluative judgement: Enabling students to make decisions about the quality of work. *Higher Education, 76*, 467-481.

Vygotsky, L. S. (1987). *Thinking and speech*. New York, NY: Plenum.

Yucel, R., Bird, F., Young, J., and Blanksby, T. (2014). The road to self-assessment: Exemplar marking before peer review develops first year students' capacity to judge the quality of a scientific report. *Assessment & Evaluation in Higher Education, 39*(8), 971-986.

3 Task 1

Task Achievement

In this unit, you will:

- develop a better understanding of the various requirements related to the domain 'Task Achievement';
- read and discuss writing exemplars using the assessment standards of 'Task Achievement';
- evaluate and improve writing exemplars following the assessment standards of 'Task Achievement'.

Check Your Understanding

Read the following statements and determine if they are true or false:

1 I don't have to provide an overview at the beginning of the essay. [True/False]
2 I should report both the similarities and differences I observe in the graphs. [True/False]
3 I can write every detail I find in the graph(s). [True/False]
4 I should highlight the key features in the graph(s). [True/False]
5 I should support my description with data from the graph(s). [True/False]

Activity 1: Understanding the Assessment Standards of 'Task Achievement'

- Read the concept map which summarises the assessment standards of 'Task Achievement' of Task 1.
- Discuss with your partner the meanings of these keywords. Note down any differences in your understanding.
- Match these key words with their definitions.

Task requirements

Summarise	Overview	Select
Grouping	Extremes	Compare
Similarities	Differences	

Key word	Definition
	Report data that represent the extremes in the graph e.g., highest/lowest, oldest/youngest, the most frequent/the least frequent.
	Write a short opening paragraph which tells the reader what the graph or table is about. It is usually done by paraphrasing the writing question.
	Report the trend noted in the graph or table here.
	Categorise data and information into groups.
	Instead of reporting every data point in the graph or table, choose the most important and representative data points to report.
	Report key features, data, and information in the graph or table.
	Highlight contrastive features between data points.
	Highlight similar features between data points.
	Show similarities and differences between data points.

Content development

Format	Clarity	Relevance
Accuracy	Sufficiency	

Key word	Definition
	Report data that are presented in the graph or table; it is not necessary to include explanations of the data.
	Report data by using not only verbs (e.g., increased, decreased) but also adverbs and adjectives to denote the extent of change (e.g., increased drastically, a mild decrease).

The majority of the data points or information presented in the graph or table are reported in the writing.

Include specific numbers to support your data description.

Write in paragraphs and complete sentences, usually with a short introductory paragraph (overview), 1-2 body paragraphs, and an optional concluding paragraph.

Do you know?

In IELTS Writing Task 1, even though you are required to report salient features in the graph or table provided, it is not necessary to explain the data. For example, if a graph is showing an increase in global population, you do not need to offer an explanation for that phenomenon.

Activity 2: Writing an Overview

- Read the following question (T1-01) and Exemplars 3.1–3.3.
- Evaluate how well the exemplars are written by referring to the definition of the term 'overview' in Activity 1. If necessary, use these guiding questions to help your evaluation.

  o Did the student indicate what the graph is about?

  o Did the student use different wordings or did s/he simply copy the question?

  o Did the student summarise the graph in a succinct manner?

T1-01

You should spend about 20 minutes on this task.

The graph below gives information about the number of academic jobs in some humanities and social sciences disciplines between 2012 and 2014.

Summarise the information by selecting and reporting the main features, and make comparisons where relevant.

Write at least 150 words.

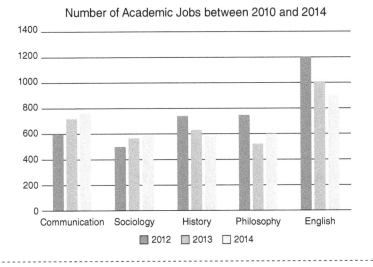

Number of Academic Jobs between 2010 and 2014

Exemplar 3.1

Referring to the graph, it shows the number of academic jobs in some humanities and social sciences disciplines from 2012 to 2014.

Guiding question	Yes/No	Remark
Did the student indicate what the graph is about?		
Did the student use different wordings or did s/he simply copy the question?		
Did the student summarise the graph in a succinct manner?		

Exemplar 3.2

The graph below gives information about the number of academic jobs in some humanities and social sciences disciplines between 2012 and 2014.

Guiding question	Yes/No	Remark
Did the student indicate what the graph is about?		
Did the student use different wordings or did s/he simply copy the question?		
Did the student summarise the graph in a succinct manner?		

Exemplar 3.3

Referring to the graph, it shows the number of academic jobs available in some humanities and social sciences disciplines from 2012 to 2014. Generally speaking, most jobs were available for graduates in the English discipline.

Guiding question	Yes/No	Remark
Did the student indicate what the graph is about?		
Did the student use different wordings or did s/he simply copy the question?		
Did the student summarise the graph in a succinct manner?		

Do you know?

It is important to replace the wordings in the question with your own words. In this way, you are giving a good impression to the examiner that you know a wide range of vocabulary.

Activity 3: Selecting Information to Report

- Refer to the same question in Activity 2 (T1-01) and read Exemplars 3.4–3.6.
- Evaluate how well the exemplars are written by referring to the definitions of the terms 'select', 'grouping', and 'extremes' in Activity 1. If necessary, use these guiding questions to help your evaluation.

o   Did the student choose the most important and representative data points to report?
o   Did the student categorise data and information into groups?
o   Did the student report data that represent the extremes in the graph?

Exemplar 3.4

To start with, the number of academic jobs in English declined gradually from 1200 to 900 between 2012 and 2014; yet, the number of English-related jobs was still the highest compared to other disciplines.

Regarding subjects that showed a steady boom in the number of jobs over the three years, there were approximately 200 more academic jobs in the discipline of communication. Furthermore, the number of jobs in sociology escalated slowly between 2012 and 2014.

Guiding question	Yes/No	Remark
Did the student choose the most important and representative data points?		
Did the student categorise data and information into groups?		
Did the student report data that represent the extremes in the graph?		

Exemplar 3.5

To start with, the number of academic jobs in English declined gradually from 1200 in 2012 to 1000 in 2013, and from 1000 in 2013 to 900 in 2014; yet the number of English-related jobs was still the highest compared to other disciplines.

On the other hand, communication was one of the two subjects that has shown a steady boom in the number of jobs over 3 years. Furthermore, the number of jobs in sociology escalated slowly between 2012 and 2014.

Guiding question	Yes/No	Remark
Did the student choose the most important and representative data points to report?		
Did the student categorise data and information into groups?		
Did the student report data that represent the extremes in the graph?		

Exemplar 3.6

To start with, the number of academic jobs in English declined gradually from 1200 in 2012 to 1000 in 2013, and from 1000 in 2013 to 900 in 2014.

The number of jobs for communication graduates increased from 600 in 2012 to slightly over 700 in 2013, and to almost 800 in 2014. The number of jobs in the sociology discipline also increased from 500 in 2012 to slightly less than 600 in 2013 and 2014.

Guiding question	Yes/No	Remark
Did the student choose the most important and representative data points to report?		
Did the student categorise data and information into groups?		
Did the student report data that represent the extremes in the graph?		

Activity 4: Comparing Data

- Read the following question (T1-O2) and Exemplars 3.7-3.9.
- Evaluate how well the exemplars are written by referring to the definitions of the terms 'compare', 'similarities', 'differences' in Activity 1. If necessary, use these guiding questions to help your evaluation.

    o   Did the student highlight similar features between data points?
    o   Did the student highlight contrastive features between data points?

T1-O2

You should spend about 20 minutes on this task.

The pie chart below gives information about the distribution of sales among products manufactured by an IT product company in 2012.

Summarise the information by selecting and reporting the main features, and make comparisons where relevant.

Write at least 150 words.

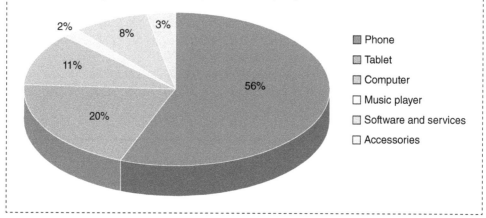

Sales of products of an IT product company

Exemplar 3.7

To begin with, phones occupied the largest distribution of sales among the 6 products in the company, with more than half of the total sales.

Guiding question	Yes/No	Remark
Did the student highlight similar features between data points?		
Did the student highlight contrastive features between data points?		

Exemplar 3.8

To begin with, phones occupied the largest distribution of the total sales among the 6 products in the company, with more than half of the total sales. Specifically, the sale of phones was almost 3 times of that of tablets and approximately 5 times more than that of computers. On the other hand, the percentage of sales of music players and accessories were almost identical.

Guiding question	Yes/No	Remark
Did the student highlight similar features between data points?		
Did the student highlight contrastive features between data points?		

Exemplar 3.9

To begin with, the sale of phones contributed to 56% of the total sales of the company in 2012.

Guiding question	Yes/No	Remark
Did the student highlight similar features between data points?		
Did the student highlight contrastive features between data points?		

Activity 5: Format

- Read the following question (T1-03) and read Exemplars 3.10 and 3.11.
- Evaluate how well the exemplars are written by referring to the definitions of the term 'format' in Activity 1. If necessary, use the following guiding questions to help your evaluation.

  o Did the student write in paragraphs and complete sentences?
  o Did the student include a short introductory paragraph (overview), one or two body paragraphs, and an optional concluding paragraph?

- Try to reach a consensus regarding the performances of these overviews by rating them as 'appropriate format' or 'inappropriate format'.

T1-03

You should spend about 20 minutes on this task.

The pie charts below give information about the distribution of sales of e-books in Country A in 2008 and 2018.

Summarise the information by selecting and reporting the main features, and make comparisons where relevant.

Write at least 150 words.

Online sales of e-books in Country A

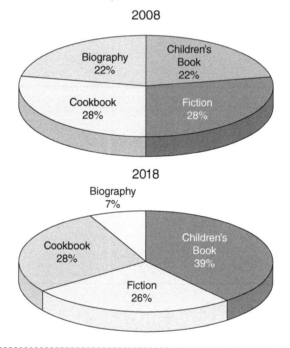

Exemplar 3.10

The pie charts indicate the distribution of online sales for four types of e-books in Country A between 2008 and 2018.

In 2008, all e-book types, including biography, children's book, fiction, and cookbook, occupied more than one-fifth of the sales in Country A. In 2018, children's book dominated the four e-book types with nearly two-fifths of the share. On the other hand, biography had the largest drop in the distribution of sales from one-fifth to less than one-tenth. Besides, the distribution of sales for cookbook remained unchanged at 28%, while fiction showed a slight decline in the distribution of online sales compared to that in 2008.

The e-book sales distributed more evenly in 2008 compared with that in 2018. Moreover, children's book was the only e-book type that demonstrated a greater distribution of sales in this decade.

To conclude, there is a prediction that the distribution of sales for children's book would become bigger and this e-book type would be dominant in the future because children's books are essential for every family. (173 words)

Guiding question	Yes/No	Remark
Did the student write in paragraphs and complete sentences?		
Did the student include a short introductory paragraph (overview), 1-2 body paragraphs, and an optional concluding paragraph?		

Rating: Appropriate format/Inappropriate format

Exemplar 3.11

In 2008, all e-book types, including biography, cookbook, fiction, and children's book, occupied more than one-fifth of the sales in Country A.

In 2018, children's book dominated with nearly two-fifths in the sales distribution.

Sales of biography declined from one-fifth to less than one-tenth.

The distribution of sales for cookbook was 28%; on the other hand, fiction showed a slight decline in the distribution of sales compared to that in 2008.

The e-book sales distributed more evenly in 2008 compared with the situation in 2018.

Children's book was the only e-book type that possessed a greater distribution of online sales in this decade. (103 words)

Guiding question	Yes/No	Remark
Did the student write in paragraphs and complete sentences?		
Did the student include a short introductory paragraph (overview), 1-2 body paragraphs, and an optional concluding paragraph?		

Rating: Appropriate format/Inappropriate format

> **Do you know?**
>
> The concluding paragraph is optional in Task 1. A summary is optional because the text you are asked to write is already very short.

Activity 6: Clarity, Relevance, Accuracy, and Sufficiency

- Refer to the same question in Activity 5 and read Exemplars 3.12-3.14.
- Evaluate how well the exemplars are written by referring to the definitions of the terms 'clarity', 'relevance', 'accuracy', and 'sufficiency' in Activity 1. If necessary, use the following guiding questions to help your evaluation.

o   Did the student report data by using not only verbs (e.g., increased, decreased) but also adverbs and adjectives to denote the extent of change?
o   Did the student report data that are presented in the graph or table and not include explanations of the data?
o   Did the student include specific numbers to support his/her data description?
o   Did the student report the majority of the data points or information presented in the graph?

Exemplar 3.12

The pie charts indicate the distribution of e-book sales in Country A between 2008 and 2018.
*   In 2008, all retail sectors, including biography, children's book, fiction, and cookbook, occupied more than one-fifth of the sales in Country A. In 2018, childrens' book dominated the four e-book types. On the other hand, biography dropped in its distribution of sales. Besides, the distribution of sales for cookbook remained unchanged, while fiction showed a decline in the distribution of sales compared to that in 2008.*
*   The sales for e-books distributed more evenly in 2008 compared with that in 2018. Moreover, children's book was the only e-book type that demonstrated a greater distribution of sales in this decade. (114 words)*

Guiding question	Yes/No	Remark
Did the student report data by using not only verbs (e.g., increased, decreased) but also adverbs and adjectives to denote the extent of change?		
Did the student report data that are presented in the graph or table and not include explanations of the data?		
Did the student include specific numbers to support his/her data description?		
Did the student report the majority of the data points or information presented in the graph?		

Exemplar 3.13

The pie charts indicate the distribution of sales for four types of e-books in Country A between 2008 and 2018.
*   In 2008, all e-book types, including biography, cookbook, fiction, and children's book, occupied more than one-fifth of the sales in Country A. In 2018, children's book dominated the four e-book types with nearly two-fifths of the total share. On the other hand, biography had the most significant drop in the distribution of online sales from one-fifth to less than one-tenth. Besides, the distribution of sales for cookbook remained unchanged at 28%, while fiction showed a slight decline in the distribution of sales compared to that in 2008.*
*   The sales for e-books distributed more evenly in 2008 compared with that in 2018. Moreover, children's book was the only e-book type that demonstrated a greater distribution of sales in this decade. (139 words)*

Guiding question	Yes/No	Remark
Did the student report data by using not only verbs (e.g., increased, decreased) but also adverbs and adjectives to denote the extent of change?		
Did the student report data that are presented in the graph or table and not include explanations of the data?		
Did the student include specific numbers to support his/her data description?		
Did the student report the majority of the data points or information presented in the graph?		

Exemplar 3.14

The pie charts indicate the distribution of sales for four types of e-books in Country A between 2008 and 2018.

In 2008, all e-book types, namely cookbook, biography, children's book, and fiction, occupied the sales in Country A evenly. In 2018, children's book dominated the four e-book types. On the other hand, biography dropped in its distribution of online sales. Besides, the distribution of sales for cookbook remained unchanged, while fiction showed a decline in the distribution of sales compared to that in 2008.

Children's book was the only retail sector that demonstrated a greater distribution of sales in this decade. There is a prediction that the distribution of sales for children's book would be enlarged and this e-book type would dominate in the future because children's books are essential for every family. (150 words)

Guiding question	Yes/No	Remark
Did the student report data by using not only verbs (e.g., increased, decreased) but also adverbs and adjectives to denote the extent of change?		
Did the student report data that are presented in the graph or table and not include explanations of the data?		
Did the student include specific numbers to support his/her data description?		
Did the student report the majority of the data points or information presented in the graph?		

Activity 7: Peer Evaluation

Based on your understanding of the assessment standards of 'task achievement', complete the evaluation form for Exemplar 3.15 written by a university student.

In the evaluation, complete the 'evaluate' section by assessing (1) whether the element concerned is present in the exemplar (the yes/no questions) and (2) how well the element is presented in the exemplar. Complete the 'suggest' section by writing an improved version of the element concerned. This section can be left blank if the exemplar demonstrates a good quality in a certain aspect.

T1-04

You should spend about 20 minutes on this task.

The line graph below gives information about the average tax on salaries paid by residents of two cities between 2004 and 2018.

Summarise the information by selecting and reporting the main features, and make comparisons where relevant.

Write at least 150 words.

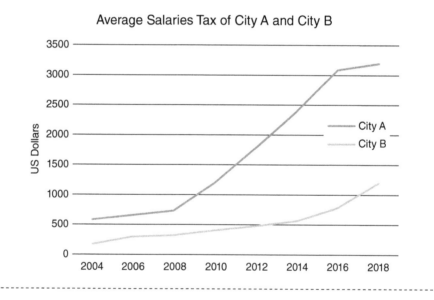

Average Salaries Tax of City A and City B

Exemplar 3.15

The line graph demonstrates the average tax on salaries of City A and City B from 2004 to 2018.

In City A, the average tax on salaries rose steadily between 2004 and 2018 during which the average tax on salaries boomed from $2000 to $12000 approximately. On the other hand, the average tax on salaries in City B had a gradual growth from 2004 to 2008, then swelled rapidly for the next 8 years, followed by another slight increase until 2018, in which the average tax on salaries expanded from $6000 to $32000 approximately.

Apparently, the average tax on salaries in City B was higher. However, the percentage of increase in City A was larger than that in City B. Particularly, the average tax on salaries in City A and City B in 2018 was 6 times and 5 times the average tax on salaries back in 2004 respectively.

To conclude, both City A and City B had experienced boosts in their average tax on salaries between 2004 and 2018. In the future, it is predicted the average tax on salaries of both cities would climb, provided that they have been escalating over the past 14 years. (187 words)

Assessment standard	Guiding question	Evaluate	Suggest
Overview	Did the student indicate what the graph is about?	e.g. The student includes information related to graph type (line graph), the topic of the graph (average tax on salaries in two cities), and the period of time concerned (from 2004 to 2018).	N/A
	Did the student use different wordings or did s/he simply copy the question?	e.g., Yes, the student used the verb 'demonstrates' instead of 'gives information about'. The student replaced the prepositions 'between... and...' with 'from... to...'.	The verb 'demonstrates' was not used appropriately here because of the wrong collocation between 'graph' and 'demonstrates'. The student can consider using 'shows' or 'reports'.
	Did the student summarise the graph in a succinct manner?		
Selecting information	Did the student choose the most important and representative data points to report or report every data point?		
	Did the student categorise data and information into groups?		
	Did the student report data that represent the extremes in the graph?		
Comparing information	Did the student highlight similar features between data points?		
	Did the student highlight contrastive features between data points?		
Format	Did the student write in paragraphs and complete sentences?		
	Did the student include a short introductory paragraph (overview), 1-2 body paragraphs, and an optional concluding paragraph?		

Clarity	Did the student report data by using not only verbs (e.g., increased, decreased) but also adverbs and adjectives to denote the extent of change?
Relevance	Did the student report data that are presented in the graph or table and not include explanations of the data?
Accuracy	Did the student include specific numbers to support his/her data description?
Sufficiency	Did the student report the majority of the data points or information presented in the graph?

Activity 8: Writing Practice

Based on your understanding of 'task achievement', write an overview for the following student's work.

T1-12

You should spend about 20 minutes on this task.

The bar chart below gives information about different undergraduate courses chosen at three universities in Auckland by gender in 2017.

Summarise the information by selecting and reporting the main features, and make comparisons where relevant.

Write at least 150 words.

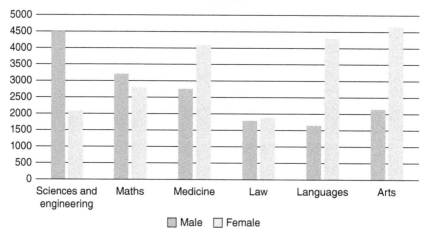

Undergraduate courses chosen at three universities in Auckland

The most significant difference between male and female students' choice was shown in two courses – sciences and engineering and arts. On the other hand, the number of male and female students who chose law was almost the same.

Arts was chosen by approximately 2,000 male students and 4,500 female students in 2017. In other words, the number of female students who chose arts is around double of that of male students. Similarly, about 6,500 students chose sciences and engineering in 2017, including 4,500 male students and around 2,000 female students. Both the number of male and female students who chose law in 2017 was about 2,000.

Do you know?

Remember to provide a summary of the chart by rephrasing the question. You may refer to Activity 2 if you find it difficult to complete this task.

4 Task 1
Coherence and Cohesion

In this unit, you will:

- develop a better understanding of the various requirements related to the domain 'coherence and cohesion';
- read and discuss writing exemplars using the assessment standards of 'coherence and cohesion';
- evaluate and improve writing exemplars following the assessment standards of 'coherence and cohesion'.

Check Your Understanding

Read the following statements and determine if they are true or false.

1. It is a good idea to use as many connections as I can. [True/False]
2. Using only basic and repetitive connectives may lead to an unsatisfactory score in the domain 'coherence and cohesion'. [True/False]
3. I can use some other words that have similar meanings (i.e., synonyms). [True/False]
4. I should divide my essay into paragraphs. [True/False]

Activity 1: Understanding the Assessment Standards of 'Coherence and Cohesion'

What is meant to be 'coherent' and 'cohesive' in writing? What techniques do you usually adopt to achieve the above?

- Read the concept map which summarises the assessment standards of 'coherence and cohesion' of Task 1.
- Discuss with your partner the meanings of these keywords. Note down any differences in your understanding.
- Match these key words with their definitions.

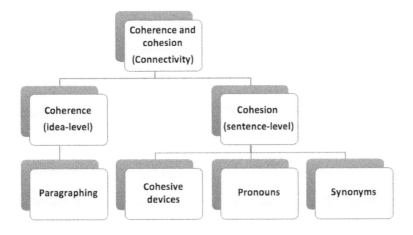

Coherence	Cohesion	Paragraphing
Cohesive devices	Pronouns	Synonyms

Key word	Definition
	Ways a writer employ to organise information thoughtfully and logically into paragraphs
	Words which have similar meanings
	Words which function as nouns or noun phrases mentioned in the previous sentences
	Linking words used to connect ideas and sentences logically and meaningfully
	Connection of ideas at the idea level
	Connection of ideas at the sentence level

Activity 2: Achieving Coherence through Paragraphing

- Read the following question (T1-05) and Exemplars 4.1–4.3.
- Evaluate how well the exemplars are written by referring to the definitions of the terms 'coherence' and 'paragraphing' in Activity 1. If necessary, use these guiding questions to help your evaluation:

  o   Did the students connect ideas by organising information thoughtfully and logically within a paragraph?

  o   Did the students connect ideas by organising information thoughtfully and logically between paragraphs?

T1-05

You should spend about 20 minutes on this task.

The table below gives information about the gross domestic product (GDP) ranking between 2013 and 2014.

Summarise the information by selecting and reporting the main features, and make comparisons where relevant.

Write at least 150 words.

	2013			2014	
Rank	Country	GDP (US$ billion)	Rank	Country	GDP (US$ billion)
1	United States	17,000	1	United States	17,500
2	China	9,000	2	China	10,100
3	Japan	4,900	3	Japan	4,800
4	Germany	3,600	4	Germany	3,700
5	France	2,700	5	United Kingdom	2,800
6	United Kingdom	2,500	6	France	2,750
7	Brazil	2,200	7	Brazil	2,150
8	Russia	2,100	8	Italy	2,100
9	Italy	2,000	9	India	1,950
10	India	1,900	10	Russia	1,930

Exemplar 4.1

In 2013, the US had the highest GDP -17000 billion US dollars. China was second place while Japan and Germany ranked the third and forth by having a GDP of 9000, 4900 and 3600 billion respectively. They are followed by France, the UK and Brazil where GDP reached 2700, 2500 and 2200 billion. Russia ranked the eighth and Italy and India were in the ninth and the tenth place.

Although GDP in Japan dropped from 4900 to 4800 billion in 2014, the top 4 in GDP ranking of the year remained unchanged. They were the US where GDP grew from 17000 to 17500, China where it raised from 9000 to 10100 and Germany where it increased from 3600 to 3700 billion. GDP in both the UK and France raised in 2014; however, their ranking switched to the fifth and the sixth with 2800 and 2750 billion US dollars respectively. Brazil remained in the seventh place, followed by Italy, India and Russia.

Guiding question	Yes/No	Evidence
Did the students connect ideas by organising information thoughtfully and logically within a paragraph?		
Did the students connect ideas by organising information thoughtfully and logically between paragraphs?		

Exemplar 4.2

The highest increase in GDP from 2013 to 2014 was China. It had increased US$1100 billion. Although China had increased the most GDP from 2013 to 2014, United States was still the top of the GDP ranking in 2013 and 2014. It was US$17000 billion in 2013 and US$17500 billion in 2014. It had increased US$500 billion.

The countries of the top four GDP ranking also remained unchanged. However, France and Russia fell in the GDP ranking from 2013 to 2014. Although France's GDP increased, its ranking decreased because the rise of United Kingdom was higher.

Guiding question	Yes/No	Evidence
Did the students connect ideas by organising information thoughtfully and logically within a paragraph?		
Did the students connect ideas by organising information thoughtfully and logically between paragraphs?		

Exemplar 4.3

In 2014, alterations in the GDP in some countries were noted, when compared to the situation in 2013. The United States still had the highest GDP, which was US$17500 billion; however, Russia had the lowest GDP, which was US$1930 billion. The GDP of India became the second lowest in 2014. China was the second highest country with GDP increasing from US$9000 billion to US$10100 billion. Also, Japan ranked third with the GDP decreasing from US$4900 billion to US$4800 billion.

While most of the countries' GDP increased or remained the same from 2013 to 2014, GDP of Japan, Brazil, Italy did not. The GDP of Japan decreased US$100 billion; the GDP of Brazil and Italy decreased US50 billion. In general, the ranking of these countries with GDP did not fluctuate too much from 2013 to 2014.

Guiding question	Yes/No	Evidence
Did the students connect ideas by organising information thoughtfully and logically within a paragraph?		
Did the students connect ideas by organising information thoughtfully and logically between paragraphs?		

Activity 3: Achieving Cohesion through using Cohesive Devices

- Read the following question (T1-06) and Exemplars 4.4–4.5.
- Evaluate how well the exemplars are written by referring to the definitions of the terms 'cohesion' and 'cohesive devices' in Activity 1. If necessary, use these guiding questions to help your evaluation:

  o   What cohesive devices did the students use in the paragraphs?
  o   Were the cohesive devices used meaningfully and accurately?
  o   Were there a variety of cohesive devices used?

T1-06

You should spend about 20 minutes on this task.

The table below gives information about people's attitudes towards gender roles categorised by age.

Summarise the information by selecting and reporting the main features, and make comparisons where relevant.

Write at least 150 words.

'A man's duty is to earn money while a woman's duty is to look after her family'.

	18-25	26-35	36-45	46-55	56-65
Agree	5%	13%	10%	6%	12%
Neutral	13%	13%	19%	29%	21%
Disagree	82%	74%	71%	65%	67%

Exemplar 4.4

It is seen that relatively younger interviewees felt negative about the stated gender roles. The 18-25 age group had the highest percentage against the statement. In contrast, less supporters were found among people who are between 45 and 55 than the 18-25 group regarding the statement 'A man's duty is to earn money while a woman's duty is to look after her family.'

On the contrary, three age groups, 26-35, 36-45 and 56-65, are recorded with more than one-tenth of support on the attitudes towards gender role. Around one third of the people aged 45-55 interviewed responded neutrally towards the statement. Only 13 per cent of the respondents under 35 held a neutral view towards the gender role description.

Guiding question	Yes/No	Response
What cohesive devices did the students use in the paragraphs?		
Were the cohesive devices used meaningfully and accurately?		
Was there a variety of cohesive devices used?		

Exemplar 4.5

As for the positive responses, no more than 6% of the interviewees of two age groups, 18-25 and 46-55, agreed with the statement. On the other hand, around one out of ten of the interviewees of the other age groups agreed with it.

Finally, for the neutral stance, 13% of the interviewees of age groups 18-25 and 26-35 voted for it. Moreover, one out of five of the 36-45 and 56-65 age groups held a neutral stance. The age group which voted the most in the neutral stance is 46-55, with almost 30%.

Guiding question	Yes/No	Response
What cohesive devices did the students use in the paragraphs?		
Were the cohesive devices used meaningfully and accurately?		
Was there a variety of cohesive devices used?		

Learn online

You can find out more about cohesive devices at this website: https://www.smart-words.org/linking-words/

Activity 4: Achieving Cohesion through using Pronouns

- Read the following question (T1-07) and Exemplar 4.6.
- Evaluate how well the exemplars are written by referring to the definitions of the terms 'cohesion' and 'pronouns' in Activity 1. If necessary, use these guiding questions to help your evaluation:

  o What pronouns did the students use in the paragraphs?
  o What did the pronouns refer to?
  o Were the pronouns used accurately?

T1-07

You should spend about 20 minutes on this task.

The graph below gives information about birth rate and death rate in China in every 1000 people between 1950 and 2015.

Summarise the information by selecting and reporting the main features, and make comparisons where relevant.

Write at least 150 words.

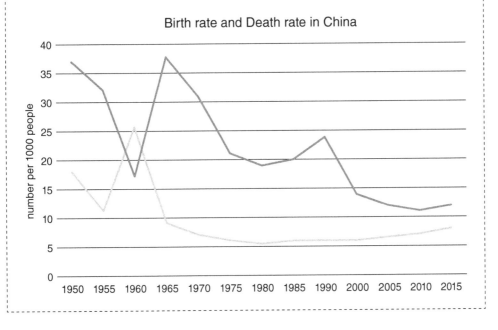

Exemplar 4.6

The birth rate in China per 1000 people stood at around 37% in 1950 and dramatically decreased to approximately 17% in 1960, after which it experienced a sharp rise, peaking at about 38% in 1965. Then, the birth rate in China per 1000 people fell again considerably to about 12% in 2015, with a fluctuation between 1975 and 1995.

The death rate in China in every 1000 people was about 17% in 1950. It increased by around 5% in the next five years. After that, it went up significantly and overtook the birth rate, reaching its peak at about 26% in 1960. But it started to decline again to about 9% in 1965, and then remained stable and was lower than the birth rate per 1000 people in China in the next 50 years, finally reaching at 8% in 2015.

Guiding question	Response
What pronouns did the students use in the paragraph? What did the pronoun refer to? Were the pronouns used accurately?	

Do you know?

In English, pronouns are used to avoid repetitions. At the same time, anaphoric pronouns (i.e., pronouns which refer to the precedent sentence) are used to strengthen linkage between sentences.

Activity 5: Achieving Cohesion through using Synonyms

- Read the following question (T1-08) and Exemplars 4.7–4.8.
- Evaluate how well the exemplars are written by referring to the definitions of the terms 'cohesion' and 'synonyms' in Activity 1 and respond to the guiding questions under each exemplar.

T1-08

You should spend about 20 minutes on this task.

The chart below shows information about suicide methods of middle-aged people in the US by gender in a year.

Summarise the information by selecting and reporting the main features, and make comparisons where relevant.

Write at least 150 words.

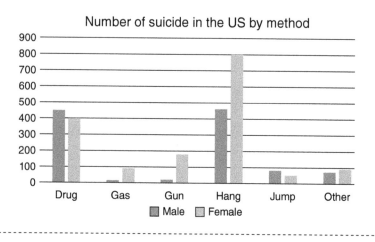

Exemplar 4.7

Two main suicide methods in the US are drug abuse and hanging. Referring to the chart, there is 1 person who dies by hanging and taking drugs every day in the US.

Guiding question	Response
Did the student use any synonyms? Which words could be replaced by synonyms? What synonyms do you suggest the students use?	

Exemplar 4.8

From the above chart, it shows some statistics of middle-aged people's suicide methods in the United States. It is displayed by gender. Firstly, we can observe that the most common suicide method for both male and female is by hanging. There are 450 males and 900 females committing suicide by hanging respectively. At the same time, taking drug is also another most common suicide way for males. There are also 450 males taking drugs to commit suicide.

Guiding question	Response
Did the student use any synonyms? Which words could be replaced by synonyms? What synonyms do you suggest the students use?	

Learn online

wordandphrase.info is a great resource for you to find synonyms which match the sense of the word you want to use. Alternatively, Collins has a decent thesaurus (https://www.collinsdictionary.com/dictionary/english-thesaurus) with synonyms, antonyms (words with opposite meanings), and real-life examples from search engines.

Activity 6: Peer Evaluation

Based on your understanding of the assessment standards of 'Coherence and Cohesion', complete the evaluation forms for Exemplars 4.9–4.10.

In the evaluation, complete the 'evaluate' section by assessing: (1) whether the element concerned is present in the exemplar (the yes/no questions); and (2) how well the element is presented in the exemplar. Complete the 'suggest' section by writing an improved version of the element concerned. This section can be left blank if the exemplar demonstrates a good quality in an aspect.

T1-09

You should spend about 20 minutes on this task.

The diagram below gives information about the process of making detergent.

Summarise the information by selecting and reporting the main features, and make comparisons where relevant.

Write at least 150 words.

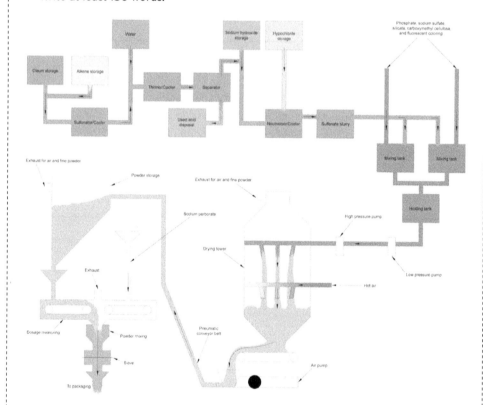

Source: https://commons.wikimedia.org/wiki/File:Soap_and_Detergent_manufacturing_process_03.png

Exemplar 4.9

The diagram demonstrates the process of making detergent.

The process contains three major stages. In the first stage, Oleum and Alkene are cooled down and sulfonated by adding water. Next, the processed materials are processed first in the thinner or cooler and then the separator to produce sodium hydroxide and remove used acid. Then, the stored sodium hydroxide is added into the neutralizer or cooler together with hyochlorite to produce sulfonate slurry. When it comes to the second phase, the sulfonate slurry is mixed with phosphate, sodium sulfate, silicate, carboxymethyl cellulose, and fluorescent colouring. Then, the mixed chemicals in the holding bank are pumped into the drying tower where they interact with the hot air. After the drying process, the powder is air pumped via a pneumatic conveyor belt into the powder storage tank. In the final stage, sodium perborate is added to the powder for mixing. Having been sieved, the detergent is ready for packaging. *(156 words)*

Assessment standard	Guiding question	Yes/No	Evaluate	Suggest
Paragraphing	Did the students connect ideas by organising information thoughtfully and logically within a paragraph?			
	Did the students connect ideas by organising information thoughtfully and logically between paragraphs?			
Cohesive devices	Were the cohesive devices used meaningfully and accurately?			
	Was there a variety of cohesive devices used?			
Pronouns	Did the student use any pronouns?			
	Were the pronouns used accurately?			
Synonyms	Did the student use any synonyms?			

T1-12

You should spend about 20 minutes on this task.

The bar chart below gives information about different undergraduate courses chosen at three universities in Auckland by gender in 2017.

Summarise the information by selecting and reporting the main features, and make comparisons where relevant.

Write at least 150 words.

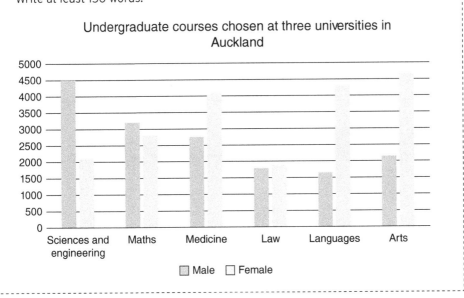

Undergraduate courses chosen at three universities in Auckland

Exemplar 4.10

The result of the bar chart reveals the proportion of male and female undergraduates and their choice of undergraduate courses. For the proportion of male and female undergraduates, there were more female undergraduates than male in the three universities in Auckland. According to the bar chart, there were around 19000 female undergraduates while there were only around 13000 male undergraduates, which reveals that more femalse receive tertiary education than males. For the choice of undergraduate courses, female undergraduates were found to choose courses related to Languages, Arts and Medicine. For the Arts course, there were 4600 females in the course while 2100 males took the same course, which was less than half of the female population. Male undergraduates tended to choose courses related to logic like Sciences and engineering and maths. There were 4500 males who took Science and engineering when there were only 2100 females taking the course. The result reveals that female undergraduates tended to study Language-related courses while males tended to take Science-related courses. (167 words)

Assessment standard	Guiding question	Yes/No	Evaluate	Suggest
Paragraphing	Did the students connect ideas by organising information thoughtfully and logically within a paragraph?			
	Did the students connect ideas by organising information thoughtfully and logically between paragraphs?			
Cohesive devices	Were the cohesive devices used meaningfully and accurately?			
	Was there a variety of cohesive devices used?			
Pronouns	Did the student use any pronouns?			
	Were the pronouns used accurately?			
Synonyms	Did the student use any synonyms?			

Activity 7: Writing Practice

Based on your understanding of 'coherence and cohesion', evaluate an example of paragraphs of T1-16.

T1-16

You should spend about 20 minutes on this task.

The chart below shows information about a report made by a European newspaper about the internet users in 2010 and the expected numbers in 2025 in six European countries.

Summarise the information by selecting and reporting the main features, and make comparisons where relevant.

Write at least 150 words.

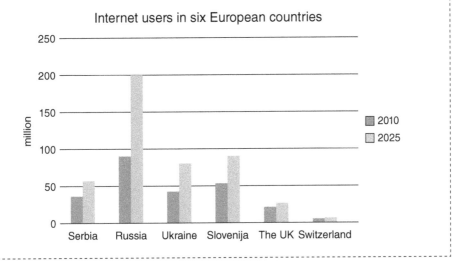

The bar graph illustrates the data of internet users and the expected numbers in six European countries in 2010 and 2025 respectively from an Asian newspaper.

As can be perceived from the chart, the highest numbers of internet users in 2010 and 2025 are noted in Russia, while Swiss netizens remain the lowest in number in both years. Even so, the expected internet users in 2025 are higher than those in 2010 in all six European countries.

Guiding question	Response
Did the student use any synonyms?	
Were there some well-written cohesive devices?	
Did the student use any pronouns?	

Write one to two paragraphs by describing the graph of T1-48 by using the good features in the above example.

T1-48

You should spend about 20 minutes on this task.

The chart below shows information about the percentage of endangered animal species by taxonomy in 2014.

Summarise the information by selecting and reporting the main features, and make comparisons where relevant.

Write at least 150 words.

The percentage of endangered species by taxonomy in 2014

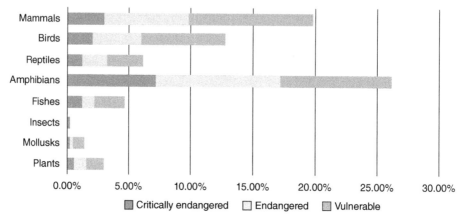

5 Task 1

Lexical Resource

In this unit, you will:

- develop a better understanding of the various requirements related to the domain 'lexical resource';
- read and discuss writing exemplars using the assessment standards of 'lexical resource';
- evaluate and improve writing exemplars following the assessment standards of 'lexical resource'.

Check Your Understanding

Discuss these questions with a partner:

1 What techniques have you used to achieve a better score in the 'lexical resource' domain?
2 Is it preferrable to overuse less common academic vocabulary? Why?
3 What are some ways to enrich your vocabulary?

Activity 1: Understanding the Assessment Standards of 'Lexical Resource'

- Read the concept map which summarises the assessment standards of 'lexical resource'.
- Discuss with your partner the meanings of these keywords. Note down any differences in your understanding.

The term 'lexical resource' is used in the IELTS writing assessment standards to denote 'vocabulary'. Three aspects of use of vocabulary are considered by IELTS writing examiners, which include: (1) variety of vocabulary; (2) difficulty of vocabulary; and (3) accuracy of vocabulary.

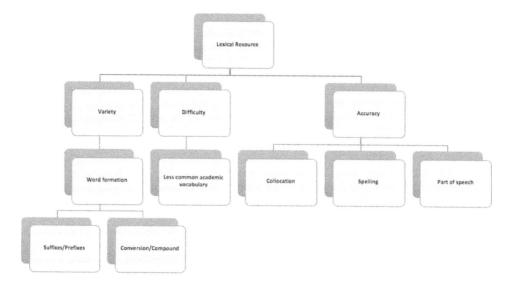

Aspect 1: Variety of Vocabulary

Variety of vocabulary is achieved through word formation. There are four major types of word formation: **prefixes**, **suffixes**, **compounds**, and **conversion**.

Learning online

The following websites can help you learn more about prefixes, suffixes, and compounds.

http://www.prefixsuffix.com/

https://www.enchantedlearning.com/grammar/compoundwords/

https://www.spellingcity.com/compound-words.html

Write down the type of word formation next to the corresponding definition and example.

Type of word formation	Definition	Example
	It connects two or more base words to form a new word.	foremost
	It is a group of letters that are placed before the root of a word. It usually changes the meaning of the word, but not the part of speech of the word.	in-disputably
	It is the change of a word from one part of speech to another.	process (n.) → process (v.)
	It is a group of letters that are placed at the end of the root of a word. It usually changes the part of speech of the word, but not the meaning of the word.	second-ly

Aspect 2: Difficulty of Vocabulary

Writing in an academic context requires the use of a set of more sophisticated and formal words than we would normally use in our daily life.

Learn online

For examples of commonly used academic vocabulary, you can refer to Dr. Averil Cox-head's Academic Word List (https://www.victoria.ac.nz/lals/resources/academicwordlist).

Complete the following table.

Word in a less academic style	Word in a more academic style
The process of making white wine is growing and harvesting grapes, pressing grapes to extract juice . . . Since grapes are important to making white wine, growing grapes in good soil is . . . For it is key to start with the clear juice, the particles need to form sediment at the bottom of the tanks, also called settling, as the next step. Afterwards, it should go through racking process to remove the clear wine from the sediment.	The process of making white wine _____ ____ growing and harvesting grapes, pressing grapes to extract juice . . . Since grapes are to making white wine, growing grapes in good soil is . . . For it is key to start with the clear juice, the particles need to form sediment at the bottom of the tanks, also _____ settling, as the next step. Afterwards, it should _____ racking process to remove the clear wine from the sediment.

Aspect 3: Accuracy of Vocabulary

Three types of vocabulary accuracy are mentioned in the IELTS writing assessment standards, including: (1) collocation; (2) spelling; and (3) part of speech.

Write down the type of vocabulary accuracy next to the corresponding definition and example.

Type of vocabulary accuracy	Definition	Example
	The accurate use of word forms in sentences e.g. noun, verb, adjective, adverb.	( ) Thirdly, the harvested grapes are pressed to extraction (n.) the pulp of juice and skins also known as the must. (✓)Thirdly, the harvested grapes are pressed to extract (v.) the pulp of juice and skins also known as the must.
	The accurate alphabetical formation of words.	( ) For it is key to start with the clear juice, the particles need to form sentiment at the bottom of the tanks, also called settling, as the next step. (✓) For it is key to start with the clear juice, the particles need to form sediment at the bottom of the tanks, also called settling, as the next step.
	The accurate combination of words.	( ) After this step, Malolactic conversion process should begin when it is oaked, so as for convert malic acid . . . (✓) After this step, Malolactic conversion process should begin when it is oaked, so as to convert malic acid . . .

Activity 2: Using a Variety of Vocabulary

- Read the following question (T1-14) and read Exemplars 5.1–5.3.
- Evaluate how well the exemplars are written in terms of using a variety of vocabulary by referring to the definitions and examples of the related terms in Activity 1. If necessary, use the following guiding questions to help your evaluation:

  o   Did the student form new words through the use of prefixes?
  o   Did the student form new words through the use of suffixes?
  o   Did the student form new words through the use of conversion?
  o   Did the student form new words through the use of compounding?

T1-14

You should spend about 20 minutes on this task.

The charts below give information about the survey results about people's views towards studying languages. The first chart shows the reasons for studying an additional language. The second pie chart displays the preferred ways of learning a new language.

Summarise the information by selecting and reporting the main features, and make comparisons where relevant.

Write at least 150 words.

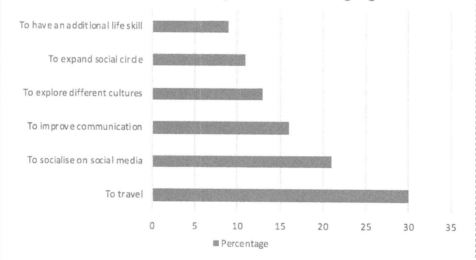

Reasons for learning an additional language

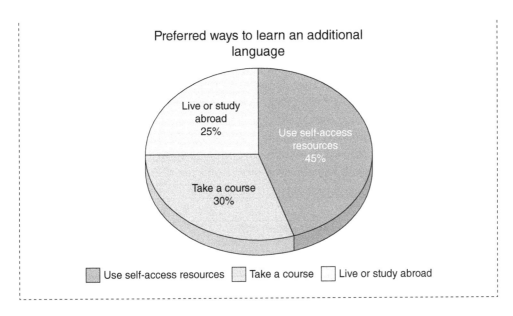

Preferred ways to learn an additional language

Live or study abroad 25%

Use self-access resources 45%

Take a course 30%

☐ Use self-access resources   ☐ Take a course   ☐ Live or study abroad

Exemplar 5.1

As shown by the survey results, the main reason for learning an additional language is due to people's interest in travelling and there are around thirty percent of interviewees who agree with it. To socialise on social media is the second important reason for people to have further study. About one of five people agree with it. Improving communication is the third crucial reason for them to learn a new language as reflected by the chart. On the other hand, around half of the interviewees agree that people should use self-access resources to learn an additional language. The second way to learn another language is to register for a formal course and thirty percent of people agree with it. However, the least effective way to learn a new language is to live or study overseas as only twenty five percent of people agree with it. The percentages of taking a course and go overseas are quite similar but there is no doubt that using online resources remains the most effective means to acquire a new language. (176 words)

Guiding question	Yes/No	Example/Suggestion
Did the student form new words through the use of prefixes?		
Did the student form new words through the use of suffixes?		
Did the student form new words through the use of conversion?		
Did the student form new words through the use of compounding?		

Exemplar 5.2

The graphs illustrate interviewees' opinions on the reasons for learning a new language and preferred ways to do so.

To begin with, in the first chart, it is obvious that most interviewees (30% of the interviewees) think that their own interest to travel is the main reason for learning a new language. 'To have an additional life skill' and 'to explore different cultures' can also be classified as individual reasons, and they are chosen by almost 9% and 13% of interviewees respectively. It seems that more than half of interviewees make decision towards learning an additional language based on their personal factors, and it may be the reason why most people (45% of the interviewees) think that people should make good use of online self-access resources to do so.

Following this, 'to expand social circle', 'to improve communication', and 'to socalise on social media' are chosen by almost 11%, 16% and 21% of interviewees respectively, and they can be grouped as social reasons. Most social reasons have higher ranking than those individual reasons, and it can explain why 30% of interviewees think that they should socialise with other students in a formal language course.

To conclude, more people have the incentive to learn an additional language because of individual reasons rather than social reasons. Also, they mostly think that the most effective way to learn a new language is to get hold of online resources. (235 words)

Guiding question	Yes/No	Example/Suggestion
Did the student form new words through the use of prefixes?		
Did the student form new words through the use of suffixes?		
Did the student form new words through the use of conversion?		
Did the student form new words through the use of compounding?		

Exemplar 5.3

The bar chart illustrates the proportion of six reasons (to have an additional life skill, to expand social circle, to explore different cultures, to improve communication, to socialise on social media, and to travel) why people want to learn an additional language.

Overall, the most significant percentage of why people want to learn a new language was their desire to travel, which accounted for 30%. To network on social media platforms is the second main purpose, making up more than 20%. On the other hand, the percentage of people who learn a foreign language to gain an additional life skill was in stark contrast with those who want to travel and socialise. It was the least important reason for learning a new language and it was less than half of the percentages of the two most popular reasons.

On the other hand, the other pie chart illustrates the proportion of three methods (use self-access resources, take a course, live or study abroad) to learn a foreign language. It shows that 45% of the respondents think that the person who is going to learn a new language should learn it independently through online self-access resources. (194 words)

Guiding question	Yes/No	Example/Suggestion
Did the student form new words through the use of prefixes?		
Did the student form new words through the use of suffixes?		
Did the student form new words through the use of conversion?		
Did the student form new words through the use of compounding?		

Activity 3: Using Academic Vocabulary

- Read the following question (T1-15) and read Exemplar 5.4.
- Evaluate how well the exemplars are written in terms of using academic vocabulary by referring to the definitions and examples of the related terms in Activity 1. If necessary, use the following guiding question to help your evaluation:
  o Did the student use a set of more sophisticated and formal words than we would normally use in our daily life?

T1-15

You should spend about 20 minutes on this task.

The chart below gives information about the respective sales volume of two kinds of printers from 2006 to 2016.

Summarise the information by selecting and reporting the main features, and make comparisons where relevant.

Write at least 150 words.

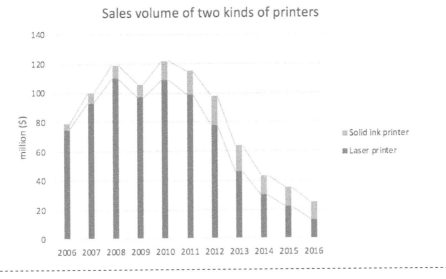

Exemplar 5.4

The bar chart illustrates the sales volume of two different kinds of printers, namely, solid ink printers and laser printers. Generally, the trend of these two kinds of printers increased in the first three or four years and then decreased gradually.

For the solid ink printer, its sales rose for 40 million from 2006 to 2008, and dropped in 2009. After peaking at around 120 million the following year, it turned to a steady decline until 2012, followed by a significant decrease in 2013. In the period of 2014 to 2016, the sales volume dropped continuously. On the other hand, the sales volume of laser printers shared a similar trend with solid ink printers. The main difference is that they peaked in different years.

To sum up, the graph shows the trend of the sales volume of two kinds of printers, and it is likely that the trend of the sales volume of these two printer types would decline in the future. (162 words)

Categorize the following words into "word/expression in a less academic style" and "word/expression in a more academic style" by putting a tick (✓) in the appropriate boxes. Suggest a more formal and sophisticated word for the latter.

Word/expression	Word/expression in a less academic style	Word/expression in a more academic style	Suggestion (if any)
illustrates			
For ...			
rose			
drops			
shows			

Activity 4: Using Accurate Vocabulary

- Read the following question (T1-17) and read Exemplar 5.5.
- Evaluate how well the exemplars are written in terms of using accurate vocabulary by referring to the definitions and examples of the related terms in Activity 1. If necessary, use the following guiding questions to help your evaluation:

  o   Did the student use collocations accurately?
  o   Did the student spell words accurately?
  o   Did the student use parts of speech accurately?

T1-17

You should spend about 20 minutes on this task.
  The diagrams below show floor plans for the first floor of two houses.
  Summarise the information by selecting and reporting the main features, and make comparisons where relevant.
  Write at least 150 words.

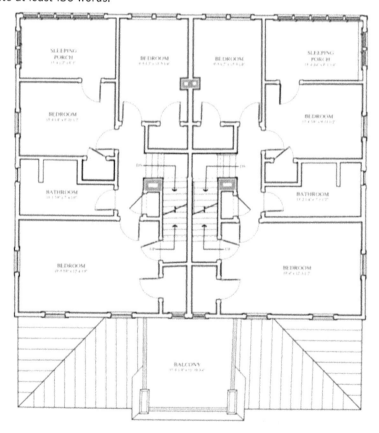

Source: https://commons.wikimedia.org/wiki/File:South_Elevation,_South_Wall_Elevation,_ and_Second_Floor_Plan_-_National_Home_for_Disabled_Volunteer_Soldiers,_Mountain_ Branch,_Duplex_Quarters,_Lamont_and_Veterans_Way,_HABS_TN-254-N_(sheet_3_of_8).tif

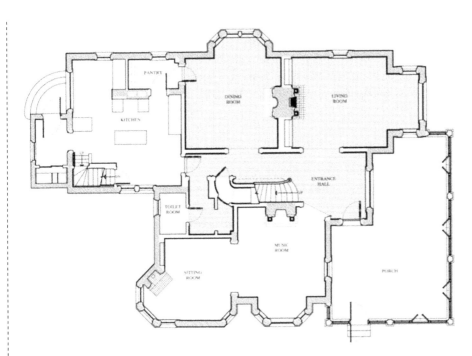

Source: https://commons.wikimedia.org/wiki/File:First_Floor_Plan_-_National_Home_
for_Disabled_Volunteer_Soldiers,_Northwestern_Branch,_Governor%27s_Resi-
dence,_5000_West_National_Avenue,_Milwaukee,_Milwaukee_County,_WI_HABS_WI-
360-C_(sheet_3_of_16).tif

Exemplar 5.5

*There are both similarities and differences from the designs of the two floor plans of the two
houses.*

*One of the major different in the two floor plans is that the first floor plan has five bed-
rooms while the second one does not have any. While both floor plans include bathrooms, the
first one has more bathrooms than the second one. Addition, there are more diverse room
types in the first floor of the second floor plan namely kitchen, pantry, living room, dining
room, music room, and sitting room. In the other hand, the first floor of the first floor plan
mainly comprises bedrooms.*

*As far as similarities are concerned, both floor plans contain an outdoor or semi-outdoor
arena. In the first floor plan, it is the baconly whereas a pouch can be find in the second floor
plan.*

*Correct the lexical errors you find in the following exemplars. Focus on collocation, spell-
ing, and part of speech. Write 'NA' if there are not such errors.*

Type of error	Error	Correction
Collocation		
Spelling		
Part of speech		

Activity 5: Peer Evaluation

Based on your understanding of the assessment standards of 'lexical resource', complete the evaluation form for Exemplar 5.6 written by a university student.

In the evaluation, identify problematic aspects of vocabulary use in relation to: (1) **variety**; (2) **difficulty**; and (3) **accuracy** by responding to the guiding questions.

T1-18

You should spend about 20 minutes on this task.

The line graph below shows information about the urbanisation rate of four countries from 1950 to 2010 and with forecasts for the year 2020 and the year 2030.

Summarise the information by selecting and reporting the main features, and make comparisons where relevant.

Write at least 150 words.

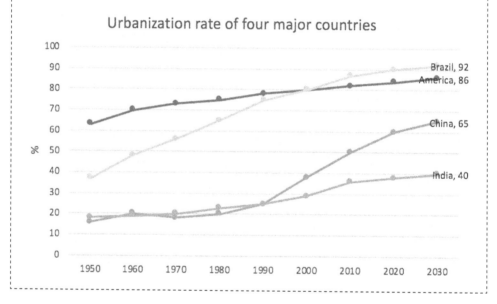

Exemplar 5.6

The line graph shows the urbanization rate of four countries, including America, China, India and Brazil from 1950 to 2030.

From 1950 to 2010, the rate of the country urbanization in America and India followed the same trend. In 1950, the figures were 63% and 18% respectively, rising to 82% and 36% respectively. Thereafter, their urbanization rates are forecast to steady rise to 84% and 38% until 2020, after which it is expected to increase to 86% and 40% respectively in 2030.

Although China's urbanization rate is similar to that of India and shares the same endpoint of 25% from 1950 to 1990, it went up dramatically to 50% in 2010. This increase is forecast to continue until 2030 with an estimated rate of 65%.

The situation in Brazil differs considerably, with a rapid increase of urbanization rate between 1950 (37%) and 1990 (75%), followed by a marked rise until 2010 (87%). This rise is projected to continue until 2030, when the urbanization rate of Brazil is expected to reach 92%.

The overall trend is a rise in the urbanization rate of four major countries between 1950 and 2030.

Question for paragraph 1:

Q1. What is a more formal and academic word to replace 'shows'?

Questions for paragraph 2:

Q1. The word 'respectively' has been used a few times. Can you suggest a synonymous expression for the word?

Q2. The parts of speech of 'steady rise' are wrong. How will you correct them?

Questions for paragraph 3:

Q1. What is a more formal and academic word to replace 'although'?

Q2. What is a more formal and academic word to replace 'went up'?

Q3. Use the conversion technique to rewrite the sentence: *'This increase is forecast to continue until 2030 with an estimated rate of 65%'* by changing the part of speech of 'forecast' from a verb to a noun.

Questions for paragraph 4:

Q1. What is the collocation problem with the phrase 'with a rapid increase of the urbanisation rate . . .'?

Q2. The word 'rise' has been used a few times. Can you suggest a synonymous expression for the word?

Activity 6: Writing Practice

Based on your understanding of 'lexical resource', rewrite the underlined words which are too simple. Replace the simple words with more sophisticated vocabulary. Remember that word changes may result in changes in sentence structures as well. So, modify the sentences if necessary.

T1-24

You should spend about 20 minutes on this task.

The bar chart below shows the percentages of various types of workplace harassment faced by male and female employees.

Summarise the information by selecting and reporting the main features, and make comparisons where relevant.

Write at least 150 words.

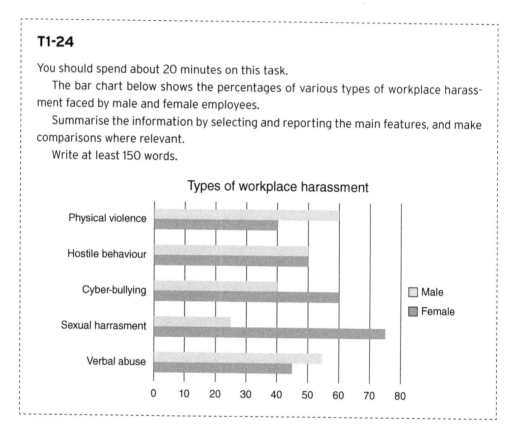

This bar chart shows the different types of workplace harassment affecting employees. For the two gender groups, they have similar experience in hostile behaviour and verbal abuse. But for the other types of workplace harassment, they hold different opinions. More female employees report being sexually harassed.

6 Task 1

Grammatical Range and Accuracy

In this unit, you will:

- develop a better understanding of the various requirements related to the domain 'grammatical range and accuracy';
- read and discuss writing exemplars using the assessment standards of 'grammatical range and accuracy';
- evaluate and improve writing exemplars following the assessment standards of 'grammatical range and accuracy'.

Check Your Understanding

Discuss the following questions in pairs:

1 Are we required to use many complex sentences when attempting IELTS writing?
2 Is accuracy of the sentence patterns used in my writing as important as their variety?

Activity 1: Understanding the Assessment Standards of 'Qrammatical Range and Accuracy'

- Read the concept map which summarises the assessment standards of 'grammatical range and accuracy'.
- Discuss with your partner the meanings of these keywords. Note down any differences in your understanding.

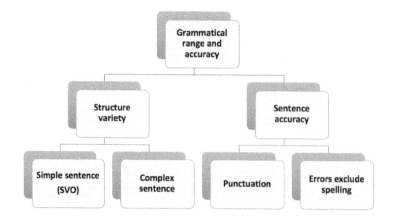

In the grammar domain of IELTS writing descriptors, the major focus is on sentences. Candidates are required to write with a variety of accurate sentence structures. As shown from the concept map, this domain is divided into two aspects: (1) structure variety; and (2) sentence accuracy.

Learn online

You can know more about different types of sentences by visiting this website: https://www.english-grammar-revolution.com/sentence-structure.html.

In the following, definitions and examples of structure variety will be given. The example sentences are taken from student exemplars on the following writing topic:

T1-19

You should spend about 20 minutes on this task.

The pie charts below display information about CO_2 emissions in London. The first pie chart shows CO_2 emissions by different sectors. The second pie chart presents the consumption of different transportation fuels.

Summarise the information by selecting and reporting the main features, and make comparisons where relevant.

Write at least 150 words.

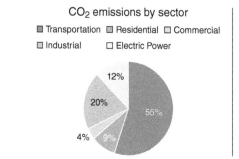

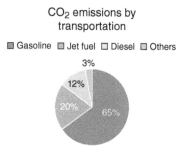

Structure Variety

According to the official IELTS writing descriptors, candidates are expected to 'use a mix of simple and complex sentence forms' at Band 6. For higher achievers, in addition to writing both simple and complex sentence patterns, candidates should be able to demonstrate their ability to 'use a variety of complex structures' (Band 7).

a) *Simple sentences (SVO)*

A simple sentence contains one 'independent clause'. An 'independent clause' has a subject (S) (a noun or noun phrase on which the rest of the clause is predicated), a verb (V) (a word to describe an action or state), and sometimes an object (O) (a noun or noun phrase influenced by an active transitive verb); alternatively, an 'independent clause' can contain a subject (S) and a predicate (P) (a part of a clause which contains a verb and gives information about the subject). They are called 'independent' because these two can stand alone in terms of meaning and syntax.

e.g. The pie charts illustrate the breakdown of CO_2 emissions in London.

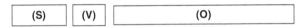

e.g. Gasoline was 65 per cent in the pie chart.

An associated concept of simple sentences is 'compound sentences'. A compound sentence comprises at least two independent clauses (simple sentences) and no dependent clauses (which means clauses which are incomplete in terms of meaning and syntax, and thus, cannot stand alone). These two independent clauses are joined together by a 'coordinating conjunction' such as 'and', 'or', 'but'.

*e.g. The pie charts show the CO_2 emissions by sectors **and** by transportations.*

*e.g. Residential use only consumed 9 per cent of CO_2 emissions **but** it used 20 per cent of jet fuel.*

Note that from the two examples above, the compound sentences could be separated into two independent clauses. However, for the sake of avoiding repetitions and enhancing cohesion, writers usually choose to combine the two clauses by a coordinating conjunction.

Compound sentence	Independent clause
*The pie charts show the CO_2 emissions by sectors **and** by transportations.*	*The pie charts show the CO_2 emissions by sectors.* *The pie charts show the CO_2 emissions by transportations.*
Compound sentence	Independent clause
*Residential use only consumed 9 per cent of CO_2 emissions **but** it used 20 per cent of jet fuel.*	*Residential use only consumed 9 per cent of CO_2 emissions.* *But, it used 20 per cent of jet fuel.*

b) *Complex sentences*

A complex sentence includes an independent clause and at least one dependent clause. A 'dependent clause' (also known as 'subordinate clause') refers to a clause which cannot stand alone regarding its meaning and syntax.

There are three major types of dependent clause:

- Adjective clauses (clauses which function as adjectives by using **relative pronouns** (e.g., which, when, who, where, that), also known as relative clause)

Independent clause	Dependent clause
Electric power consumed 12 per cent of total CO_2 emissions	**which** *was larger than that for residential use.*

- Adverbial clauses (clauses which function as adverbs by using **subordinating conjunctions** e.g., because, although, so)

Independent clause	Dependent clause
Gasoline was the main contributor of CO_2 emissions	**because** *of heavy transportation.*

- Participle clauses (a type of adverbial clause which can be used when the participle and the verb of the main clause share the same subject)

Dependent clause	Independent clause
Contributing the most to CO_2 emissions,	*gasoline was regarded as the major cause of air pollution and global warming.*

Sentence Accuracy

The second aspect of 'grammatical range and accuracy' is related to sentence accuracy, which is further broken down into two sub-categories: (1) punctuation errors and (2) other error types.

a) *Punctuation errors*

- Comma splice: The misuse of a comma instead of a coordinating conjunction to form a compound sentence.

  e.g. According to the diagram, the highest emission in Boston of dinitrous oxide was 100 ug/m³, and for the other kind of pollutant, sulphur dioxide, did not exceed 50 ug/ m3. (incorrect)

  e.g. According to the diagram, the highest emission in Boston of dinitrous oxide was 100 ug/m³. As for the other kind of pollutant, sulphur dioxide, it did not exceed 50 ug/m³. (correct)

- Run-on sentence: A compound sentence which has not been correctly punctuated.

  e.g. Overall, Beijing and Mexico emitted more sulphur dioxide than the other two cities on the other hand Boston and Mexico emitted more dinitrous dioxide than the other two cities. (incorrect)

  e.g. Overall, Beijing and Mexico emitted more sulphur dioxide than the other two cities; on the other hand, Boston and Mexico emitted more dinitrous dioxide than the other two cities. (correct)

- Sentence fragments: This error occurs when a sentence is treated as an independent clause when it is not.

    e.g. For the emission of sulphur dioxide. Beijing and Mexico showed a considerable difference. (incorrect)

    e.g. For the emission of sulphur dioxide, Beijing and Mexico showed a considerable difference. (correct)

Learn online

You can know more about how different punctuations are used by visiting this website: https://www.thepunctuationguide.com/.

---

b) Other error types

According to the IELTS official writing rubric, it mentions 'errors' without clearly defining it. Below is a non-exhaustive list of common sentence-level errors.

- Faulty parallelism: A parallel sentence becomes faulty when one or more than one part of the sentence is not presented to be identical with the rest in terms of grammatical structure.

    *e.g. The differences in the minimum and maximum Sulphur dioxide were **105** and **it was 120** respectively.* (incorrect because of unidentical parts)

    *e.g. The differences in the minimum and maximum Sulphur dioxide were **105** and **120** respectively.* (correct because of identical parts)

- Subject-verb disagreement: This happens when the verb of a sentence or clause does not agree with the subject in terms of singularity/plurality.

    *e.g. The chart **show** the fluctuations in the emissions of two pollutants in four cities, namely, Boston, Calcutta, Beijing and Mexico in 2015.* (incorrect)

    *e.g. e.g. The chart **shows** the fluctuations in the emissions of two pollutants in four cities, namely, Boston, Calcutta, Beijing and Mexico in 2015.* (correct)

- Misplaced modifiers: A 'modifier' is a word or phrase that modifies another word or phrase. A modifier is misplaced if it is used to modify the wrong word or phrase.

    e.g. Despite discharging fewer pollutants than developing cities, the chart shows that developed cities like Boston still had high emission level. (incorrect because the participle ('discharging') and the verb ('shows') do not share the same subject, i.e., while the chart 'shows', the chart does not 'discharge')

    e.g. Despite discharging fewer pollutants than developing cities, developed cities like Boston still had high emission levels. (correct because the participle ('discharging') and the verb ('had') share the same subject)

Learn online

You can learn more about how to avoid different sentence-level errors by reading this online document: Resource: https://www.uts.edu.au/sites/default/files/sentence.pdf.

Activity Two Structure Variety

- Read the following question (T1-21) and read Exemplars 6.1-6.3.
- Evaluate how well the exemplars are written in terms of using a variety of sentence structures by referring to the definitions and examples of the related terms in Activity 1.

T1-21

You should spend about 20 minutes on this task.

The graph below shows information about tourist growth in the last 60 years and the estimates.

Summarise the information by selecting and reporting the main features, and make comparisons where relevant.

Write at least 150 words.

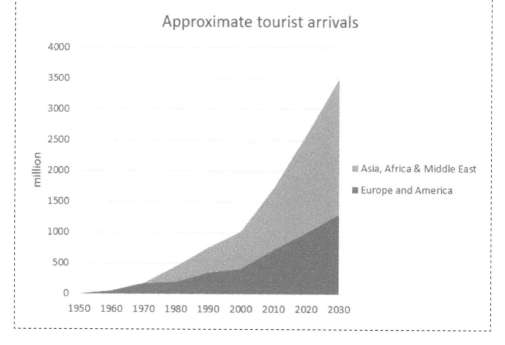

Exemplar 6.1

(1) The graph shows an obvious growing tendency of approximate tourist arrivals. Overall, the number of tourists from Europe and America appeared to be less than those from Asia, Africa and Middle East in the whole process.

In detail, the number of approximate tourist arrivals is increasing. The graph can be divided into three parts according to growth rates. (2) In the first part of the graph, from 1950 to 1970, it can be found that the approximate number of tourists was low, with a slight growth throughout these years. The second part of the graph is the period 1970 to 2000. (3) During this time, the number of tourists who visited Asia, Africa and Middle east started to grow swiftly. In 2000, (4) it witnessed a turning point of the escalation. (5) The number of tourists is predicted to increase dramatically from 2000 to 2030, and reaches 3500 million in 2030. (152 words)

Categorise the underlined sentences into three types: (1) simple sentences; (2) compound sentences; and (3) complex sentences.

Sentence pattern	Sentence number
Simple sentence	
Compound sentence	
Complex sentence	

Exemplar 6.2

(1) The graph demonstrates the statistics of the approximate tourists' arrivals in the last sixty years and the estimation of growth between 2020 and 2030. (2) It includes the arrivals from Europe and America and the arrivals from Asia, Africa and the Middle East.

(3) The figure reveals that there was a gradual increase from zero to 500 million of European and American visitors. (4) From 2000 onwards, there was a relatively rapid rise from 2000 to 2010. (5) Regarding this trend, therefore, it is reasonable to estimate that there will be continuous add-ons from 2020 to 2030.

(6) Compared with the tourists from Europe and America, there was a relatively huge number of visitors from Asia, Africa and the Middle East. (7) During the period 1970 to 2000, the number of tourists had been experiencing a stable gain from 250 million to 1000 million, which was a fourfold increase. (8) From 2000 until the foreseeable future, the number could surge to 3500 million by 2030.

(9) Both arrivals had been increasing from 1950 to 2010 and could be increasing in the twenty years to come. (186 words)

Categorize the underlined sentences into three types: (1) simple sentences, (2) compound sentences, and (3) complex sentences.

Sentence pattern	Sentence number
Simple sentence	
Compound sentence	
Complex sentence	

Exemplar 6.3

The graph unfolds the number of approximate tourist arrivals in Asia, Africa and Middle East area, and Europe and America Area separately. It is clear that ascending patterns were shown in numbers of tourist arrivals in these regions.

(1) The tourist industry started blooming in 1950 for both areas. The number of tourists travelling increased from 0 to approximately 250 million for both areas in 1970. Starting from 1970, the travel industry of Asia, Africa and Middle East countries flourished. (2) It showed a significant increase. It reached 1000 million in 2000.

The trend kept on increasing rapidly. (3) The number of tourists visit Asia, Africa and Middle East countries reached 2000 million in the following 15 years. It is predicted that, it will reach 3500 million people in 2030. Meanwhile, the number of tourists visiting Europe and America will grow steadily by 200% from 500 millions (in 2000) to 1000 millions (in 2030).

To sum up, (4) we can say that the tourism industry shows positive progress all around the world. Asia, Africa and Middle East are relatively more popular destinations than Europe and America. (186 words)

Sentence number	Instruction	Rewritten sentence
1	Combine the two sentences into a compound sentence using the coordinating conjunction 'and'	
2	Combine the two sentences into a complex sentence using the subordinating conjunction 'which'	
3	Correct this complex sentence (relative clause)	
4	Combine the two sentences into a complex sentence by using the subordinating conjunction 'although'	

Activity 3: Sentence Accuracy

- Read the following question (T1-23) and read Exemplars 6.4–6.5.
- Evaluate how well the exemplars are written in terms of using a variety of sentence structures accurately by referring to the definitions and examples of the related terms in Activity 1.

T1-23

You should spend about 20 minutes on this task.

The pie charts below show information about preferred work benefits of employees in Asian and Western societies.

Summarise the information by selecting and reporting the main features, and make comparisons where relevant.

Write at least 150 words.

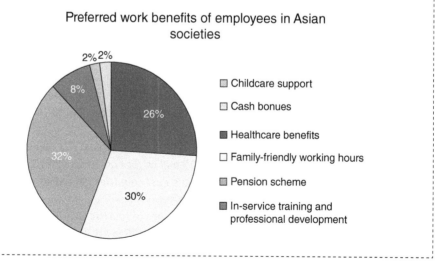

Preferred work benefits of employees in Asian societies

☐ Childcare support
☐ Cash bonues
■ Healthcare benefits
☐ Family-friendly working hours
▨ Pension scheme
■ In-service training and professional development

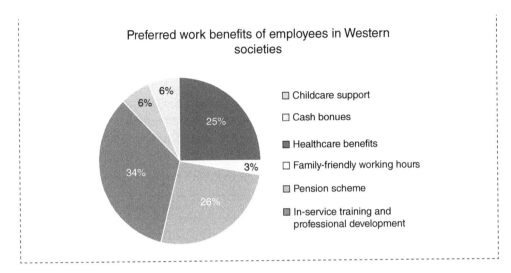

Preferred work benefits of employees in Western societies

- ☐ Childcare support
- ☐ Cash bonues
- ■ Healthcare benefits
- ☐ Family-friendly working hours
- ■ Pension scheme
- ■ In-service training and professional development

Exemplar 6.4

(1) For the pie chart of preferred work benefits of Asian employees, it reveal that 32% of the employees preferred childcare support, which was the highest percentage. There were only 2% who opted for cash bonuses, which was the lowest percentage. (2) On the other hand, as for the preference of western employees, it shows that family-friendly work hours was the most popular option, there were nearly one-third of employees voting for it.

(3) Comparing the two pie charts. Having a flexible working hours appeared to appeal to both Asian and western employees. (4) Moreover the charts display that among various benefits, the percentages of Asian and western workers who preferred intangible benefits were quite high, both with more than 50%. (5) Being at 32%, the charts show that more Asian workers preferred pension scheme than their western counterpart.

(6) Overall, the two pie chats illustrate and discusses the preferences of Asian and western employees towards work benefits. (159 words)

Match sentences (1) to (6) with the six types of errors described at the outset of the chapter. These error types include: comma splice, run-on sentence, sentence fragment, faulty parallelism, subject-verb disagreement, and misplaced modifiers. Rewrite a grammatically correct sentence for each.

Sentence number	Error type	Rewritten sentence
1		
2		
3		
4		
5		
6		

Exemplar 6.5

Asian employees mainly preferred monetary benefits. (1) As the information shows. There were 34% of the Asian employees who preferred monetary benefits, which had a higher percentage than western employees as the latter only had 9% also less than half of the workers who worked in Asian communities opted for healthcare benefits, childcare support, and professional development opportunities, which shows that they did not value non-monetary reward as much.

(2) The most popular benefit option of Asian workers is pension scheme, which had more than 30%, it proves that these employees tend to look for long-term security, especially after they have retired.

(3) The most popular benefit choice of western employees is having flexible and family-friendliness working hours, which was 34%. It had a higher percentage than those who work in Asian.

(4) Being at approximately 30%, the charts show that family-friendly working hours was a popular option among Asian and western employees. (5) It show that striking a balance between work and life is important to both groups. (166 words)

Sentence number	Error type	Rewritten sentence
1		
2		
3		
4		
5		

Activity 4: Peer Evaluation

Based on your understanding of the assessment standards of 'grammatical range and accuracy', complete the evaluation form for Exemplar 6.6 written by a university student.

In the evaluation, identify problematic aspects of sentence use in relation to (1) **variety** and (2) **accuracy** by responding to the guiding questions.

T1-28

You should spend about 20 minutes on this task.

The charts below show information about the energy consumption in the UK in 2017. The first pie chart displays the energy sources. The second pie chart presents different types of renewable energy.

Summarise the information by selecting and reporting the main features, and make comparisons where relevant.

Write at least 150 words.

UK energy consumption by source in 2017

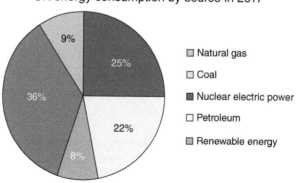

- Natural gas
- Coal
- Nuclear electric power
- Petroleum
- Renewable energy

25%
9%
36%
22%
8%

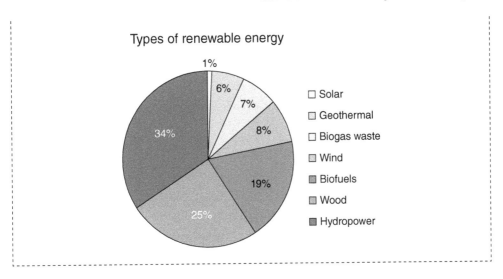

Types of renewable energy

□ Solar
□ Geothermal
□ Biogas waste
▨ Wind
▨ Biofuels
▨ Wood
▨ Hydropower

Exemplar 6.6

(1) The pie charts above illustrate the different sources of UK energy consumption in 2017 and displays the different types of renewable energy, one of the sources that only occupies a relatively small proportion.

(2) In 2017, petroleum as an available resource was the main drive of energy in the United Kingdom. Making up 36% of the total consumption. Natural gas was the second most-used resource, covering 25% while Coal ranked the third, with only 3% less. Renewable energy and nuclear electric power only accounted for 9% and 8% respectively.

(3) As one of the least commonly used energy sources, the charts show that renewable energy is divided into 7 types. (4) The main body consists of three resources: the most popular type of renewable energy was Hydropower (34%), second was Wood (25%), in the third place was Biofuels (19%). Wind resource, Biogas waste and Geothermal accounted for 8%, 7%, and 6% of the total renewable energy consumption respectively while Solar only occupied 1% of renewable energy consumption.

In summary, (5) renewable energy still do not play an important role in energy consumption. (6) Although there are different resources making up renewable energy it is still important to continuously develop resources other than Hydropower. (204 words)

Q1. Identify the types of error of sentences (1) to (6) and correct those errors.

Sentence number	Error type	Rewritten sentence
1		
2		
3		
4		
5		
6		

Q2. Give one example of compound sentence used in the exemplar.

Q3. Give one example of complex sentences used in the exemplar.

___

Activity 5: Writing Practice

Based on your understanding of 'grammatical range and accuracy', try to identify the gram-matical errors and punctuation errors of T1-30. Rewrite the paragraph using some complex sentences.

T1-30

You should spend about 20 minutes on this task.

The charts below show information about the estimates of population change in different continents from 1950 to 2050, according to an official report.

Summarise the information by selecting and reporting the main features, and make comparisons where relevant.

Write at least 150 words.

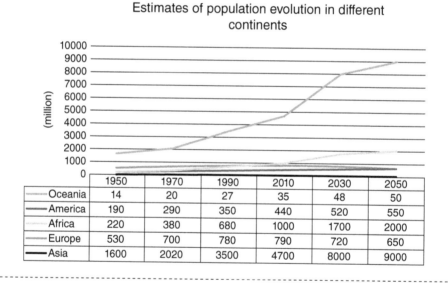

Estimates of population evolution in different continents

(million)	1950	1970	1990	2010	2030	2050
Oceania	14	20	27	35	48	50
America	190	290	350	440	520	550
Africa	220	380	680	1000	1700	2000
Europe	530	700	780	790	720	650
Asia	1600	2020	3500	4700	8000	9000

About the change of population in different continents. From 1990 to 2050, the popula-tion of Asia and Africa increased in a rather fast speed, but more people will bear in Asia and the population of Asia will far exceed the others up to nine billion, and Africa's population will only up to 2000 million. In addition, the population of other continents don't have too big change.

7 Task 2

Task Achievement

In this unit, you will:

- develop a better understanding of the various requirements related to the domain 'task achievement';
- read and discuss writing exemplars using the assessment standards of 'task achievement';
- evaluate and improve writing exemplars following the assessment standards of 'task achievement'.

Check Your Understanding

Discuss the following question with a partner:

> Are there any differences and similarities between Task 1 'task achievement' and Task 2 'task achievement'? How?

Activity 1: Understanding the Assessment Standards of 'Task Achievement'

- Read the concept map which summarises the assessment standards of 'task achievement' of Task 2.
- Discuss with your partner the meanings of these keywords. Note down any differences in your understanding.

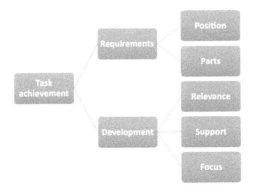

Content Requirements

There are two keywords under the 'requirements' aspect of this domain: (1) position; and (2) parts. Write down the two keywords next to the corresponding definitions.

Keyword	Definition
	The writer's standpoint or thesis statement, usually placed in the introductory paragraph
	The essential components of a Task 2 essay, usually comprises an introduction, two body paragraphs, and a conclusion

Content Development

Three keywords are identified from the official IELTS writing descriptors which help explicate the expectations for candidates to develop their ideas. These keywords include: (1) relevance; (2) support; and (3) focus. Write down the keywords next to the corresponding definitions.

Keyword	Definition
	Explanations, examples, reasons given by the writer to elaborate on or substantiate his/her points
	A clearly defined topic for each paragraph, usually demonstrated by a clear topic sentence at the beginning of each body paragraph
	Ideas discussed in the essay are related to the question and the standpoint

---

Do you know?

'Task achievement' of Task 1 is a little bit different from 'task achievement' of Task 2 because the nature of the writing task is different. In Task 1, you are asked to report data from a graph; thus, you will be assessed based on your ability to summarise and compare data. In Task 2, you are asked to write a short essay on a given topic. Accordingly, your work will be evaluated with reference to the quality of your arguments and how you elaborate and/or support your arguments.

To understand more about these keywords, let's read two writing exemplars (Exemplars 7.1-7.2) written by university students to see what they (should not) look like in action.

T2-09

You should spend about 40 minutes on this task. Write about the following topic:

Due to the rapid technological development, new career options have emerged such as online store owners, and vloggers. People are becoming less willing to work in an office. Do you think the advantages of having a 'virtual' career outweigh its disadvantages?

Give reasons for your answer and include any relevant examples from your own knowledge or experience.

Write at least 250 words.

Exemplar 7.1	Remarks
Recently, there has been a popular trend of being vloggers or online store owners because of the rapid development of the Internet and modernization of lifestyle. Moreover, many people start to consider the aforesaid 'virtual' roles as their full-time jobs and stop working in a physical workplace. Undoubtedly, there must be advantages and disadvantages of having a virtual career. Yet, it is my belief that the advantages outweigh its disadvantages.	Parts: Introduction
To begin with, pursuing a virtual career, namely running an online store, brings flexible working schedule to the owners which enables them to design their personal timetable every day, including day-offs. Moreover, people like vloggers can kill two birds with one stone. In particular, they can videotape their daily matters while enjoying their time, such as, shopping and eating. Furthermore, the number of people who are obsessed with the Internet world continue to surge due to technological advancement which provides a major opportunity for those who have a virtual career to be well-known. In addition, these virtual jobs are not paid monthly; therefore, the "workers" have the ability to earn a lot more by being slash workers.	*Standpoint/thesis statement* Parts: Body 1 *A clear topic sentence focusing on advantages*
On the other hand, opponents to having a virtual career contend that it is risky to have a profession that relies solely on Internet communication. Specifically, while most of the "workers" invest all of their time and money in order to be successful and popular, there is no guarantee that they would succeed; from what is reported on the news and social media, countless people have failed during the journey of becoming "online celebrities".	Parts: Body 2 *A clear topic sentence focusing on disadvantages* *Support through explanation* *Support through providing examples*
To conclude, every coin has two sides. Admittedly, while it is not necessary that being a youtuber or vloggers will bring you fame and glory eventually, I personally consider taking risk as a key to success and it will be worthwhile, especially to teenagers.	*Parts: A concluding paragraph*

Exemplar 7.2	Remarks
For example, Ricky Wong, is a businessman in Hong Kong; after his failure of getting a free TV licence, he changed to open a TV channel and open an online store, he succeeded in attracting young people to buy his products and make a great profit. I think being a successful man do not need to follow the traditional track, but learn how to be innovative. I will take this as a good example.	Irrelevant example because the topic is about virtual career, but the example given is a successful businessman in Hong Kong.

Do you know?

Unlike Task 1, there must be a concluding paragraph for IELTS Writing Task 2.

Activity 2: Writing a Position

- Read the following questions (T2-02 and T2-04) and read Exemplars 7.3-7.4.
- Evaluate how well the exemplars are written by referring to the definitions and examples of the related terms in Activity 1. If necessary, use the following guiding questions to help your evaluation:

  - o Did the student state his/her standpoint or thesis statement of his/her essay clearly?
  - o Did the student present the position in a succinct manner?
  - o Was there enough scaffolding (e.g., background information) before the position statement is introduced?

T2-02

You should spend about 40 minutes on this task. Write about the following topic:

Advocates of high-stakes standardised tests believe that they provide an objective description of students' abilities; on the contrary, some teachers expressly underscore the many problems that these tests bring to the quality of their teaching.

Discuss both these views and give your opinion.

Give reasons for your answer and include any relevant examples from your own knowledge or experience.

Write at least 250 words.

Exemplar 7.3

Supporters of high-stakes standardized tests believe that they provide an objective description of students' abilities while some teachers concern about the quality of their teaching because of these standardized tests.

Guiding question	Yes/No	Explanation
Did the student state his/her standpoint or thesis statement of his/her essay clearly?		
Did the student present the position in a succinct manner?		
Was there enough scaffolding (e.g., background information) before the position statement is introduced?		

T2-04

You should spend about 40 minutes on this task. Write about the following topic

Many university students are required to enrol in a number of general education courses. These courses are usually related to the social, cultural, psychological, and spiritual lives of young people.

What are the advantages of general education courses to university students?

Give reasons for your answer and include any relevant examples from your own knowledge or experience.

Write at least 250 words.

Exemplar 7.4

It is important for university students to take General Education courses and I agree that it should be a compulsory course for the students. It is because General Education courses disseminate different types of information and knowledge which students should learn. For example, social, cultural, psychological and spiritual knowledge. The above knowledge and information are good for student development. I will give reasons and explain my standpoint in this article.

Guiding question	Yes/No	Explanation
Did the student state his/her standpoint or thesis statement of his/her essay clearly?		
Did the student present the position in a succinct manner?		
Was there enough scaffolding (e.g., background information) before the position statement is introduced?		

Activity 3: Writing a Four-Part Essay

- Read the following question (T2-03) and Exemplar 7.5.
- Evaluate how well the exemplar is written by referring to the definitions and examples of the related terms in Activity 1. If necessary, use the following guiding questions to help your evaluation:

  o Did the student include an introduction?
  o Did the student include at least two body paragraphs?
  o Were the body paragraphs organised in a focused and logical manner?
  o Did the student include a conclusion?
  o Do you think the essay is too long? How can it be shortened?

T2-03

You should spend about 40 minutes on this task. Write about the following topic:
  Some parents believe in educating their children themselves and homeschool their children. What are the advantages of homeschooling? Should homeschooling become a regular option for parents?
  Give reasons for your answer and include any relevant examples from your own knowledge or experience.
  Write at least 250 words.

Exemplar 7.5

Homeschooling has become an increasingly hot topic among parents. Parents might have seen failures in their children at standard schools, or might have seen talents in their children which could not be developed in schools, and start to wonder if homeschooling is their right option.

While it is still widely recognized as an unlawful act for parents to deprive their children from the right to receive formal education, more and more parents realize that there are exceptional situations which can be accepted by government authorities as legitimate cases for homeschooling.

However, there are both advantages and disadvantages arisen from the homeschooling practice which we shall discuss below.

One size doesn't fit all. If we appreciate that each student is a special individual, how can we not question if the standard curriculum is suitable for all children? Even in a class of 40, there are students who are good at mathematics and students who are good at music. Standard curriculum is designed for "average" children. For example, when 80% of the students in Grade 3 are ready to learn how to do the multiplication 3 x 3, the standard curriculum neglects the need of those who can do 1+1 only, and those who are doing 33 x 33 at the same age. Schools teach these standard curriculums to build our children like a gear in the mechanism of the society, like a clerk, an accountant, a doctor. It is not flexible enough to fit every student's need.

Homeschooling can be advantageous to students who have individual strength that cannot be developed at school, and those with special education needs whose needs cannot be addressed at school as well. Moreover, during homeschooling, parents can develop their relationship with their children and build a harmonious family.

On the other hand, parents have to be very careful if they adopt homeschooling. Currently, there are insufficient supports and lack of resources for parents to homeschool their children. If the parents have not received sufficient education themselves, it is questionable how the effect of their homeschooling would be. Also, there is no standard assessment for the parents to understand the developmental levels of their children. Parents could not provide the best teaching to their children based on the results.

It is also important for parents to understand that schools are not only a place to develop their children's academic abilities, but also a place to teach children social skills, ethical values, physical strength, in order to ensure students' whole person development. Children who receive education at home lack the chance to socialize with fellow classmates and are deprived of the chance to develop social skills. Someday, when they are back to school or when they go to work, they will have a hard time cooperating with others if they did not develop their social skills at an early stage.

Homeschooling can be advantageous to some students, but there are lots of things that parents have to be careful of. If parents decide to take this route, they must be well advised of all the advantages and disadvantages of homeschooling, and make the right choice for their children. (521 words)

Guiding question	Yes/No	Explanation
Did the student include an introduction?		
Did the student include at least two body paragraphs?		
Were the body paragraphs organised in a focused and logical manner?		
Did the student include a conclusion?		
Do you think the essay is too long? How can it be shortened?		

Activity 4: Writing with Relevant Ideas

- Read the following question (T2-05) and Exemplars 7.6–7.8.
- Evaluate how well the exemplars are written by referring to the definitions and examples of the related terms in Activity 1. If necessary, use the following guiding questions to help your evaluation:

  o   Were the ideas relevant to the topic?
  o   Were the ideas relevant to the position?

T2-05

You should spend about 40 minutes on this task. Write about the following topic:

Distance education enables students to study at their own pace. Nevertheless, it also creates problems including a high withdrawal rate and a lack of interaction between teachers and students. Explain some possible reasons for these problems and suggest some solutions.

Give reasons for your answer and include any relevant examples from your own knowledge or experience.

Write at least 250 words.

Exemplar 7.6

Distance education allows students to study wherever they want. However, it also creates problems including high withdrawal rate and lack of interaction between teachers and students. I reckon that inadequate monitoring and time-consuming student-teacher communication between are the causes of the above problems.

First and foremost, inadequate monitoring brought by distance education will cause high withdrawal rate. By adopting distance education, teachers and students are no longer sitting in the same classroom in class - students are required to watch pre-recorded video lessons instead. In view of the phenomenon that most parents need to work in daytime, there will not be any authorities to supervise students in classes. As a result, this may contribute to a high withdrawal rate. Offering a tutor for every student is clearly unaffordable. Therefore, assigning after-lesson quizzes to students is a way to solve the problem. If all students are required to take a test regarding teaching content after each lesson, they will be more willing to attend online lessons with a view to get a pass. The pupils will attend and concentrate in online classes.

Guiding question	Yes/No	Explanation
Were the ideas relevant to the topic?		
Were the ideas relevant to the position?		

Exemplar 7.7

Distance education is advantageous because students can study at their own pace. They can choose the time and the place to study. Technology is an important element in distance education. Online education is the focus of distance education.

...

Moreover, distance education causes the lack of interactions between teachers and students. As distance education is not face-to-face study, students do not have time to communicate with teachers. They only need to finish the task and learn by themselves. When they do not have much time to interact with teachers, their relationships are not close. It makes students feel alienated because their teachers do not know them. It is difficult to help them to make an efficient teaching plan. Students cannot get the efficient way to learn too.

Guiding question	Yes/No	Explanation
Were the ideas relevant to the topic?		
Were the ideas relevant to the position?		

Exemplar 7.8

As technology develops, many students learn by themselves in distance education. However, students who study in front of the computer lack interactions with teachers and it causes high withdrawal rate. In this article, I will provide some reasons and solutions to solve these problems.

The main reason is that students lack supervision in distance education. It is good that students can dominate their own study and learn flexibly. However, it requires students to have high self-regulated skill, which is challenging for some students. For example, students may play with their phones during the class. Also, it is hard for teachers to assess students' real performance because students can search for answers online. The solution is that parents can be the supervisors to supervise their children's learning to ensure the effectiveness of distance education.

Guiding question	Yes/No	Explanation
Were the ideas relevant to the topic?		
Were the ideas relevant to the position?		

Activity 5: Writing with Support

- Read the following question (T2-06) and Exemplars 7.8-7.9.
- Evaluate how well the exemplars are written by referring to the definitions and examples of the related terms in Activity 1. If necessary, use the following guiding questions to help your evaluation:

    o   How are the ideas elaborated (e.g., giving examples, explanations)?
    o   Are the supports provided effective and adequate? Why/why not?
    o   If your answer is 'no' for Q2, how can the support be strengthened?

T2-06

You should spend about 40 minutes on this task. Write about the following topic:

Family-friendly measures (e.g., flexible working hours) should be adopted by companies to ensure the work-life balance of their employees.

To what extent do you agree or disagree with this opinion?

Give reasons for your answer and include any relevant examples from your own knowledge or experience.

Write at least 250 words.

Exemplar 7.9

First and foremost, some caring initiatives commonly implemented by companies, namely the change of working environment from office to home, could bring a range of benefits to employees which ultimately lead to the rise of productivity. Parents could make use of the extra time to be with their children which undoubtedly strengthen their relationship and help relieve pressure from work. Meanwhile, staff could concentrate on their projects in a less crowded environment. While the mental wellbeing of staff is becoming positive, companies which offer similar flexible measures would definitely enjoy relatively higher productivity than those without family caring policies.

Q1. How are the ideas elaborated (e.g., giving examples, explanations)?

_____

Q2 Are the supports provided effective and adequate? Why/why not?

_____

Q3. If your answer is 'no' for Q2, how can the support be strengthened?

_____

Exemplar 7.10

Without doubt, long working hours have been a major source of discontent for almost all the employees. The reason for insisting on pushing them to beat their brains out and work until the last moment of the day is to ensure a high level of productivity of the company. Surprisingly, the weekly working hours in Germany are 30 hours while those in Hong Kong are 50 hours. However, the former leads to greater productivity than the latter. This demonstrates that working quality should be the key to a company's high productivity instead of long working hours. Therefore, companies should take good care of their employees by implementing measures like flexible working hours, instead of simply prolonging their employees' working hours.

Q1. How are the ideas elaborated (e.g., giving examples, explanations)?

_____

Q2. Are the supports provided effective and adequate? Why/why not?

_____

Q3. If your answer is 'no' for Q2, how can the support be strengthened?

_____

Activity 6: Writing with a Clear Focus

- Read the following question (T2-07) and Exemplars 7.10–7.11.
- Evaluate how well the exemplars are written by referring to the definitions and examples of the related terms in Activity 1. If necessary, use the following guiding questions to help your evaluation:
    o   What is the topic sentence of the paragraph?
    o   Is the topic sentence focused and clear?

T2-07

You should spend about 40 minutes on this task. Write about the following topic:

It is not uncommon nowadays for people to work overseas. Working overseas allows people to experience different cultures and extend their social and professional connections. However, some find it hard to adapt due to nostalgia and acculturation.

Discuss both these views and give your opinion.

Give reasons for your answer and include any relevant examples from your own knowledge or experience.

Write at least 250 words.

Exemplar 7.11

However, working overseas is a double-edged sword, which could lead to pros and cons, because people from different countries have distinctive cultures. For example, westerners and Chinese treat their co-workers differently. As a result, foreign people may feel awkward when interacting with local people. At the end, it may result in positive or negative effects. For instance, I used to work in Beijing for my internship. I was an administrator assistant in a corporation. Because of the language barrier, it caused me to miss Hong Kong. Luckily, the local people were pleasant enough to take care of every colleague, and I convinced myself to adapt to the new environment in order to learn new working skills. Hence, no matter what people learn by working overseas, having an open mind is the key.

Q1. What is the topic sentence of the paragraph?

Q2. Is the topic sentence focused and clear?

Exemplar 7.12

On one side of the argument, oversea working experience enables people to have cultural explorations. People who work abroad might face the challenges of new languages, customs and lifestyles. All of these cultural aspects provide them with valuable cultural experiences in both professional and personal life in other countries. Apart from the cultural experience, working abroad facilitates people's expansion of their social and professional connections. They can meet and work with local people and people from all walks of life in their workplace, which allows them to establish friendships and partnerships. Therefore, working abroad provides chances to enrich people's cultural experiences and helps the formation of international relationships in their professional lives.

Q1. What is the topic sentence of the paragraph?

Q2. Is the topic sentence focused and clear?

Activity 7: Peer Evaluation

Based on your understanding of the assessment standards of 'task achievement', provide feedback to Exemplar 7.12 written by a university student. The guiding questions at the end of each paragraph focus on the different facets of the 'task achievement' domain we discussed in this chapter.

T2-12

You should spend about 40 minutes on this task. Write about the following topic:

It is popular nowadays for people to order takeaway food (e.g., lunch) from their workplace because they are too busy to prepare meals. However, there are still many people who bring home-made food to eat in their workplace because they think DIY food is healthier.

Discuss both these views.

Give reasons for your answer and include any relevant examples from your own knowledge or experience.

Write at least 250 words.

Exemplar 7.13

Nowadays, it is common for people to order takeaway food (e.g. lunch) from their workplace because they are too busy to prepare meals. Yet, there are numerous people who bring home-made food to eat at workplace as they consider DIY food is healthier. In this essay, both advantages and disadvantages of the two methods will be discussed.

Questions for paragraph 1:

Q1. What is the position given by the writer?

_____

Q2. Is the position given in a concise manner?

_____

Q3. Is the position scaffolded by background information?

_____

Q4. Is the position relevant to the question?

_____

To begin with, ordering takeaway is undoubtedly convenient for people as it only takes a short time for people to decide what they want to have for lunch and pay for it. The whole process does not take more than three minutes; so this way helps to save time, which is vitally important in a hectic and fast-paced society. However, the food is believed to be less healthy as lots of sugar, salt, oil, and seasoning would be added into most of the dishes.

Questions for paragraph 2:

Q1. What is the topic sentence?

_____

Q2. Is the topic sentence focused and clear?

_____

Q3. How does the writer provide support to his/her topic sentence?

_____

Q4. Is the support in the paragraph adequate and relevant to the topic sentence? If not, give suggestions.

_____

On the other hand, making homemade food means that one can design the most suitable recipe for oneself. For example, if a person is allergic to specific kinds of ingredients or food, he is able to avoid it when he cooks his lunch. Moreover, cooking at home saves money. Furthermore, making DIY food can ensure the hygiene of the food. However, people will have less time to take a rest as they need extra time to prepare a meal every day at night.

Questions for paragraph 3:

Q1. What is the topic sentence?

_____

Q2. Is the topic sentence focused and clear?

_____

Q3. How does the writer provide support to his/her topic sentence?

_____

Q4. Is the support in the paragraph adequate and relevant to the topic sentence? If not, give suggestions.

_____

To sum up, ordering takeaway or bringing home-made food has its merits and drawbacks. What matters is that the person has extra time and knows his food preference.

Questions for paragraph 4:

Q1. How many parts are there in this exemplar? What are the parts?

_____

Activity 8: Writing Practice

Based on your understanding of 'task achievement', evaluate the essay of T2-10 using the guiding questions in the form. Try to imitate the exemplar when responding to T2-29.

T2-10

You should spend about 40 minutes on this task. Write about the following topic:

Given the greater longevity of people these days, some argue that people should retire at a later stage. What are some of the problems if people's retirement is delayed?

Give reasons for your answer and include any relevant examples from your own knowledge or experience.

Write at least 250 words.

People have a longer life expectancy nowadays so some may suggest retirement can be delayed, since they believe that older citizens can still enjoy a meaningful life. However, others think the retirement age should not be delayed as it may pose a threat to social mobility and to the long-term development of a company.

On the one hand, delaying retirement age may affect social mobility because it obstructs the younger generation from enhancing their social status and financial capability. As the older generation started their careers earlier than the younger generation, the former is much more experienced and sophisticated. Thus, it is conceivable that the older generation is usually at a higher position in the workplace. When they decide to retire, those who are younger and capable enough would be promoted. However, if the society encourages people to retire at a later stage, there would be insufficient vacancies to raise the social status of the younger generation. Despite the numerous attempts of the younger generation, they may still fail to improve their social status.

On the other hand, postponing the retirement age can be detrimental to the development of an institution. To demonstrate, as people begin to age, they are destined to experience slower metabolism, which exerts an undesirable influence on both their body and mind. As a consequence, they tend to act slowly in their job position, having a negative effect on their working efficiency and quality. In addition, elderly people are also inclined to show less commitment to their career. This is attributed to the fact that the older generation face fewer challenges and difficulties in their work. Therefore, they are likely to focus more on their family and leisure life, which may lead to them under-performing.

The later people retire, the lower the social mobility and the worse the institution develops. This probably is the concern of both the young generation and the decision-makers of those corporations. (320 words)

Guiding question	Yes/No	Explanation
Did the student state the standpoint clearly?		
Did the student include at least two body paragraphs?		
Was there a topic sentence in each body paragraph?		
Were the ideas relevant to the topic?		
Were the ideas elaborated by giving sufficient and appropriate examples and explanations?		

T2-29

You should spend about 40 minutes on this task. Write about the following topic:

   An increasing number of domestic appliances (e.g., air purifiers and water purifiers) are on the market to tackle water pollution and air pollution. Why is this the case? Is this a positive indicator of the development of human beings? Give reasons for your answer and include any relevant examples from your own knowledge or experience.

   Write at least 250 words.

Tip

If you don't remember the requirements of 'task achievement' of Task 2, you can refer to Activity 1 in this chapter before writing.

8 Task 2

Coherence and Cohesion

In this unit, you will:

- develop a better understanding of the various requirements related to the domain 'coherence and cohesion';
- read and discuss writing exemplars using the assessment standards of 'coherence and cohesion';
- evaluate and improve writing exemplars following the assessment standards of 'coherence and cohesion'.

Check Your Understanding

According to what you have learnt in Chapter 4, choose the elements that are essential to 'coherence and cohesion' from the following choices:

1. Paragraphs
2. Collocation
3. Punctuation
4. Pronouns
5. Various sentence structures
6. Cohesive devices
7. Synonyms
8. Supporting ideas

Activity 1: Understanding the Assessment Standards of 'Coherence and Cohesion'

Since the assessment standards of this domain in Task 2 are identical to those in Task 1, refer to Activity 1 in Chapter 4 for definitions of keywords of the assessment standards.

Activity 2: Achieving Coherence through Paragraphing

- Read the following question (T2-13) and Exemplars 8.1–8.3.
- Evaluate how well the exemplars are written by referring to the definitions of the terms 'coherence' and 'paragraphing'. If necessary, use these guiding questions to help your evaluation.

  o   Did the students connect ideas by organising information thoughtfully and logically within a paragraph?

  o   Did the students connect ideas by organising information thoughtfully and logically between paragraphs?

Do you know?

When writing a body paragraph, it is important to bear in mind that there is a 'subject' and a 'controlling idea' in each paragraph. A 'subject' can be 'national health care insurance' and a 'controlling idea' can be an advantage of having a national health insurance (e.g., improve the health of residents).

T2-13

You should spend about 40 minutes on this task. Write about the following topic:

In some countries, health care expenditure is covered by the government, while in other countries, the cost is undertaken by both the public and the government. Do you think the advantages of 'sharing the cost' outweigh the disadvantages?

Give reasons for your answer and include any relevant examples from your own knowledge or experience.

Write at least 250 words.

Exemplar 8.1

So important is social productivity that it is reflected in the gross domestic product (GDP) of a country. A sound health care system does not only improve the wellbeing of its citizens, but also boosts the country's productivity, and, by the same token, its economy. Therefore, the government should not be penny-pinching on medical care from a bird's eye view.

Furthermore, tackling inequality is one of the major goals for most of the governments in the world. Having paid taxes, citizens are excepted to receive basic public services - health care, to name but a few. From the perspective of citizen rights, it is the government's responsibility that no one be turned a blind eye to by medical practitioners because of a lack of money.

Guiding question	Yes/No	Evidence
Did the students connect ideas by organising information thoughtfully and logically within a paragraph?		
Did the students connect ideas by organising information thoughtfully and logically between paragraphs?		

Exemplar 8.2

First and foremost, "sharing the cost" reduces financial burden of the government. Even the government pays for the medical cost, it does not mean that there is nothing to do with citizens financially. There is no magic money tree. Looking at the UK, the financial issue of NHS has been discussed for decades. To cover the rising amount of health care expenditure, the so-called "solutions" carried out by the government are either cutting the budget of another area or increasing tax rates, sometimes both. On façade, people do not need to pay a penny for the services they received. They may even pay more than they expect at the end of the day. "Sharing the cost reduces the financial burden of both the government and the citizens, to a certain extent.

In addition to solving financial problems, the fact that the public share the medical cost can somehow increase the quality of health care services. "Sharing the cost" means that more money can be spent on national health services and more money means a better quality of services. Take nurses as an example, the inadequate number of nurses working in public hospitals is not a new topic to Hong Kongers. Nurses have always suffered from heavy workload and stressful working environment. If more financial resources for professional employment are available, public hospitals are able to employ more nurses to provide a better service for patients. Therefore, it is not difficult to find that sharing of cost by the public can contribute to higher service quality in return.

Guiding question	Yes/No	Evidence
Did the students connect ideas by organising information thoughtfully and logically within a paragraph?		
Did the students connect ideas by organising information thoughtfully and logically between paragraphs?		

Exemplar 8.3

To begin with, fresh graduates couldn't afford to pay the medical cost annually, not to mention that many are unemployed or are still paying the student loan. If Hong Kong is planning to propose the 'sharing cost' plan, many students and fresh graduates, especially for those who suffer financially, will surely struggle to pay an extra cost for social welfare. Being a year-three undergraduate, I have to work hard to repay my own school fee. After completing the four-year program, the government loan will start rolling like a snowball, with the interest rate gradually increasing over years; I am therefore determined to put an end to it as quickly as I can. However, once implementing the new medical policy, every student on loan like me is given no choice but to delay the government loan payment. This could be bad news for us all, not to mention that fresh graduates could hardly earn a promising income when they first embark on a new career. Hence, being a soon-to-be fresh graduate carrying heavy loans, I urge the authority to consider whether "sharing the cost" is applicable to all of their people or not.

In addition, the notion of "sharing cost" is mostly distributed to the elderly care or those with serious illness; healthy individuals are likely to be excluded from getting the welfare. Unlike medical insurance, the expenditure on health care protection mainly concerns those with very urgent medical needs, but do not necessarily guarantee every taxpayer's access to the service. Helping others in need should be a voluntary act out of sincerity, but not a kind of responsibility enforced by the authority. I wouldn't want to feel unwanted to help those in dire emergencies, but it could feel like a burden with big responsibility to "share the cost" with strangers. Doing kind acts is everyone's moral responsibility, but they should never come from obeying the commands of the authority.

Guiding question	Yes/No	Evidence
Did the students connect ideas by organising information thoughtfully and logically within a paragraph?		
Did the students connect ideas by organising information thoughtfully and logically between paragraphs?		

Activity 3: Achieving Cohesion through using Cohesive Devices

- Read the following question (T2-14) and Exemplars 8.4–8.6.
- Evaluate how well the exemplars are written by referring to the definitions of the terms 'cohesion' and 'cohesive devices'. If necessary, use these guiding questions to help your evaluation.

    o   What cohesive devices did the students use in the paragraphs?
    o   Were the cohesive devices used meaningfully and accurately?
    o   Was there a variety of cohesive devices used?

T2-14

You should spend about 40 minutes on this task. Write about the following topic:

Despite the enhancement of medical care, modern people are still tortured by various physical and psychological problems. What are some of the causes of the above phenomena? What can be done to improve people's health?

Give reasons for your answer and include any relevant examples from your own knowledge or experience.

Write at least 250 words.

Exemplar 8.4

Secondly, lack of leisure time also affects the physical health and mental health of people. For the working population, most of them need to work more than ten hours a day because there is no law or regulation to regulate the working hours. Long working hours result in the lack of leisure time. People suffer from great pressure from their jobs but they do not have time to relax or do exercise. Thus, the physical and psychological problems exist. To solve the problem, the government need to have regulations on working hours. If people have more leisure time, they may have less pressure.

Guiding question	Yes/No	Response
What cohesive devices did the students use in the paragraphs?		
Were the cohesive devices used meaningfully and accurately?		
Was there a variety of cohesive devices used?		

Exemplar 8.5

First, citizens could not deal with the high medical expenses. Along with the improvement of medical care, the cost of existing medical technology may be reduced. However, the cost of new or more effective treatment would be. Although the government has set up some welfare policies, such as providing public medical service and medical subsidies to the elderly, the expenditure on medical treatment is still high. So, many patients, especially those who suffer from serious illness, such as cancer, are still tortured by the sickness.

Guiding question	Yes/No	Response
What cohesive devices did the students use in the paragraphs?		
Were the cohesive devices used meaningfully and accurately?		
Was there a variety of cohesive devices used?		

Exemplar 8.6

Undoubtedly, more sports facilities would enhance the public's motivation to exercise. Even more and more people like to work out at fitness clubs, it is still too expensive for the low-income people to afford this kind of sport facility. Therefore, if the government provides more open areas for recreation, it would definitely give the public a great chance to do exercises and stay healthy without spending too much money on joining a fitness club. According to the news reports, a person could lose about 5 kg in three weeks if he exercises for 30 minutes a day regularly. Some health problems could be avoided like high blood pressure. Also, doing exercises could make us happy and relaxed. We could stay away from depression.

Guiding question	Yes/No	Response
What cohesive devices did the students use in the paragraphs?		
Were the cohesive devices used meaningfully and accurately?		
Was there a variety of cohesive devices used?		

Learn online

If you want to learn more about different cohesive devices (e.g., connectives, conjunctions, transitional phrases), visit this website: https://www.smart-words.org/linking-words/.

Activity 4: Achieving cohesion through using pronouns

- Read the following question (T2-15) and Exemplar 8.7–8.8.
- Evaluate how well the exemplars are written by referring to the definitions of the terms 'cohesion' and 'pronouns'. If necessary, use these guiding questions to help your evaluation.

o   What pronouns did the students use in the paragraphs?
o   What did the pronouns refer to?
o   Were the pronouns used accurately?

T2-15

You should spend about 40 minutes on this task. Write about the following topic:
   Investors are more important than teachers in that they usually make more money.
   To what extent do you agree or disagree with this opinion?
   Give reasons for your answer and include any relevant examples from your own knowledge or experience.
   Write at least 250 words.

Exemplar 8.7

Though investors might make more money than teachers, there are many factors in determining the importance of a job, such as the contributions and impacts on the society. Teachers are important as they make tremendous contribution to the society - educating new generations continuously. Although knowledge is intangible, it is long-lasting. Comparatively, earning money is temporary, as we exchange money for the product or service we want. For the contributions teachers made to the society, it could be seen that a lot of successful people are well-educated, such as professors in the university. These people are continually nurturing the young generations before they enter the society. People learn, use their knowledge and teach. These people are needed in a healthy and progressive society. Hence, teachers are very important in the society.

Guiding question	Response
What pronouns did the students use in the paragraph? What did the pronouns refer to? Were the pronouns used accurately?	

Exemplar 8.8

From the economic perspective, investors improve our quality of life. Through different investments and technological advancements, investors make our life much easier and more convenient. As for the teachers, they may have indirect contribution to the economy. As mentioned, teachers help to build up the ability of investors in dealing with different problems including human management, technological innovation etc. The investors may not be successful without receiving education.

Guiding question	Response
What pronouns did the students use in the paragraph? What did the pronouns refer to? Were the pronouns used accurately?	

Activity 5: Achieving Cohesion through using Synonyms

- Read the following question (T2-17) and Exemplars 8.9–8.11.
- Evaluate how well the exemplars are written by referring to the definitions of the terms 'cohesion' and 'synonyms' and responding to the guiding questions under each exemplar.

T2-17

You should spend about 40 minutes on this task. Write about the following topic:

Some countries donate large sums of money to help other countries in need, while some citizens of these countries are still starving. Why would these countries take the above action? What can be done to help the starving people?

Give reasons for your answer and include any relevant examples from your own knowledge or experience.

Write at least 250 words.

Exemplar 8.9

I think the main reason for some countries to donate money to other countries is that they want to get a bigger influence in the world. They give other countries resources to build schools and rails. And their names may be the name of the school or the station. This is one of the ways for them to be popular in the world. Their countries will be praised by other countries, and their power in the world may be bigger, since they show that they have enough resources and they are willing to help others. It is a way for them to make friends with other countries and they may have a bigger influence in the world; on the contrary, helping their local people may not get this effect. Therefore, they neglect their citizens' needs.

Guiding question	Response
Did the student use any synonyms? Which words could be replaced by synonyms? What synonyms do you suggest the students use?	

Exemplar 8.10

Unfortunately, the wealth gap is enlarging in lots of places in the world, including these countries. To help the starving people, there are mainly two approaches. In order to solve the problem from the root, the government should embrace equity in the society. For example, ensuring a better access to tertiary education. On the other hand, the government can provide subsidies or allowances to people living below the poverty line.

Guiding question	Response
Did the student use any synonyms? Which words could be replaced by synonyms? What synonyms do you suggest the students use?	

Exemplar 8.11

Some countries donate a large amount of money to help the suffering countries. The former are usually developed countries while the latter are less developed countries. Food products in poor countries are usually exported to other countries for profit, even if people in the poor country are in need of food. More developed countries benefit from the export of these food products, but the countries that produce the food may experience food scarcity and higher food prices with no proper interventions from the corrupted government. As a result, most developed countries, which put emphasis on human rights and morality, would help the poor countries.

Guiding question	Response
Did the student use any synonyms? Which words could be replaced by synonyms? What synonyms do you suggest the students use?	

Activity 6: Peer Evaluation

Based on your understanding of the assessment standards of 'coherence and cohesion', complete the evaluation form for Exemplar 8.12.

In the evaluation, complete the 'evaluate' section by assessing (1) whether the element concerned is present in the exemplar (the yes/no question) and (2) how well the element is presented in the exemplar. Complete the 'suggest' section by writing an improved version of the element concerned. The 'suggest' section can be left blank if the exemplar demonstrates a good quality in an aspect.

T2-18

You should spend about 40 minutes on this task. Write about the following topic:

It is important for travellers to develop adequate understanding of the culture of the destination country. What are some of the advantages of understanding the culture beforehand?

Give reasons for your answer and include any relevant examples from your own knowledge or experience.

Write at least 250 words.

Exemplar 8.12

There are many different cultural differences that travelers can be aware of when traveling to different nations. Cultures can sometimes vary drastically from one's own. So, it is advised that travelers research the local conventions and try to understand the culture of the area prior to departure.

Having a basic idea of the region's culture can help travelers to form a deeper understanding of the local people and can prevent them from offending anyone. Sometimes, traditions are deeply rooted within a culture. People take things very seriously that outsiders aren't typically aware of or understand. For example, in America, the 'OK' gesture is a kind of standard communication for daily use; however, in Japan, it means 'money'; in Brazil, it's akin to extending the middle finger in the U.S. People in China may think that touching children's head would be a normal behavior, which, in Myanmar, is regarded to be a very disrespectful behavior. Without knowing the actual meaning of such cross-cultural gesture in different countries, it will not only cause misunderstanding but also conflicts. If travelers get well-prepared and search for the cultural differences beforehand, they will avoid causing faux-pas and embarrassing situations.

Another advantage for having some fundamental grasp of local cultures is that it's a great way to open doors and gain access to experiences that other travelers may not get to enjoy. Imagine, there are two travelers visiting the Arc de Triomphe now. One of them knows its history and local people's view about it, the other does not. It is easy to foresee that the former will have a better understanding of the architecture and immerse successfully into the environment; the latter one will probably view it as a building and quickly take a photo to have it 'instagramed'. Knowing the cultural and historical background of a country and its architectures will give travelers more colorful and memorable experiences.

To conclude, developing the understanding of the culture of the traveling destination will bring benefits to travelers as they are able to avoid offences and gain more fruitful experiences. (339 words)

Assessment standard	Guiding question	Yes/No	Evaluate	Suggest
Paragraphing	Did the students connect ideas by organising information thoughtfully and logically within a paragraph? Did the students connect ideas by organising information thoughtfully and logically between paragraphs?			
Cohesive devices	Were the cohesive devices used meaningfully and accurately? Was there a variety of cohesive devices used?			
Pronouns	Did the student use any pronouns? Were the pronouns used accurately?			
Synonyms	Did the student use any synonyms?			

Activity 7: Writing Practice

Based on your understanding of 'coherence and cohesion', try to use the underlined cohesive devices in the response to T2-23 to finish writing two body paragraphs of T2-28.

T2-23

You should spend about 40 minutes on this task. Write about the following topic:

Some people think that the development of science and technology has led to a decrease in privacy (e.g., being monitored of speeches and actions). However, others regard the development of science and technology as positive because they feel more secure. Discuss both views and give your opinion.

Give reasons for your answer and include any relevant examples from your own knowledge or experience.

Write at least 250 words.

Regarding the advantages, the development of science and technology enables us to feel more secure. One of the examples is the use of iPhones. In the past, we used to use the 4-digit passcode to prevent others from using our phone. However, it is not a very reliable method of security. Nowadays, we can use fingerprints as passwords instead of the 4-digit passcode. Since we all have our unique fingerprints, it will be more difficult for others to get the important information from our phones. Hence, it is more secure for us.

In terms of disadvantages, it has led to a decrease in privacy. According to some news reports, with the use of some software and IT skills, not only the words that we type, but also the activities that we do on our electronic devices can be easily monitored by some professionals. To exemplify, when we look for some hotel information on computers, social media like Facebook can show us some recommended hotels *because* they can 'read' what we have read before. Therefore, it is true that our privacy becomes vulnerable with such scientific and technological development.

T2-28

You should spend about 40 minutes on this task. Write about the following topic:

Governments are more concerned about creating economic benefits for people while they overlook the actions they should take to control pollution resulting from economic development.

Discuss the above view and give your opinion.

Give reasons for your answer and include any relevant examples from your own knowledge or experience.

Write at least 250 words.

---

9 Task 2

Lexical Resource

In this unit, you will:

- develop a better understanding of the various requirements related to the domain 'lexical resource';
- read and discuss writing exemplars using the assessment standards of 'lexical resource';
- evaluate and improve writing exemplars following the assessment standards of 'lexical resource'.

Check Your Understanding

In Activity 1 in Chapter 5, three important aspects of the 'lexical resource' domain were defined and discussed, which are: (1) variety of vocabulary; (2) difficulty of vocabulary; and (3) accuracy of vocabulary.

Check your understanding of these three aspects of the 'lexical resource' domain by indicating whether the following statements are 'True' or 'False'.

1. There are four major types of word formation, which are prefixes, suffixes, compounds, and conversion. [True/False]
2. We are required to use formal and sophisticated vocabulary to express our ideas. [True/False]
3. Accuracy of vocabulary is assessed with reference to collocation use, spelling and parts of speech. [True/False]

Activity 1: Understanding the Assessment Standards of 'Lexical Resource'

Since the assessment standards of this domain in Task 2 are identical to those in Task 1, refer to Activity 1 in Chapter 5 for definitions of keywords of the assessment standards.

Activity 2: Using a Variety of Vocabulary

- Read the following question (T2-05) and read Exemplars 9.1–9.3.
- Evaluate how well the exemplars are written in terms of using a variety of vocabulary by referring to the definitions and examples of the related terms. If necessary, use the following guiding questions to help your evaluation:

    o   Did the student form new words through the use of prefixes?
    o   Did the student form new words through the use of suffixes?
    o   Did the student form new words through the use of conversion?
    o   Did the student form new words through the use of compounds?

T2-05

You should spend about 40 minutes on this task. Write about the following topic:

Distance education enables students to study at their own pace. Nevertheless, it also creates problems including a high withdrawal rate and a lack of interaction be-tween teachers and students. Explain some possible reasons for these problems and suggest some solutions.

Give reasons for your answer and include any relevant examples.

Exemplar 9.1

First and foremost, inadequate monitoring in distance education will cause high withdraw rate. By adopting distance education, teachers and student are no longer sitting in the same classroom in class - students are required to watch pre-recorded video lesson instead. In view of the phenomenon that most parents need to work in daytime, there will not be any authorities to supervise students in classes. As a result, this may contribute to a high withdrawal rate. Offering a tutor for every student is clearly unaffordable. Therefore, assigning after-lesson quiz for students is a way to solve the problem. If all students are required to take a test regarding teaching content after each lesson, they will be more willing to attend online lessons with a view to get a pass. The pupils will attend and concentrate in online classes.

Guiding question	Yes/No	Example/Suggestion
Did the student form new words through the use of prefixes?		
Did the student form new words through the use of suffixes?		
Did the student form new words through the use of conversion?		
Did the student form new words through the use of compounds?		

Exemplar 9.2

Communication between teachers and students wastes much time and will lead to lack of interaction between teachers and students. Students can not only raise their hands and ask questions verbally but also seek help from teachers by visiting the staff room after class in traditional schooling. In contrast, students can only email their teachers and probably wait for a couple of hours for reply in distance schooling. The long waiting time will discourage students to ask questions and interact with teachers in the long run. The issue can be addressed by launching live lessons in distance education. Unlike pre-recorded videos, students can leave comments which will be seen by the tutor immediately and discuss with the tutor in live lessons. As a result, interactions between teachers and students can be preserved in live teaching.

Guiding question	Yes/No	Example/Suggestion
Did the student form new words through the use of prefixes?		
Did the student form new words through the use of suffixes?		
Did the student form new words through the use of conversion?		
Did the student form new words through the use of compounding?		

Exemplar 9.3

Distance education allows students to study wherever they want. But, it also creates problems because many students give up and students and teachers cannot communicate. I reckon that teacher-student miscommunication is the cause of the above problems.

Guiding question	Yes/No	Example/Suggestion
Did the student form new words through the use of prefixes?		
Did the student form new words through the use of suffixes?		
Did the student form new words through the use of conversion?		
Did the student form new words through the use of compounding?		

Activity 3: Using Academic Vocabulary

- Read the following question (T2-06) and read Exemplars 9.4 and 9.6.
- Evaluate how well the exemplars are written in terms of using academic vocabulary by referring to the definitions and examples of the related terms. If necessary, use the following guiding questions to help your evaluation:

  o   Did the student use a set of more sophisticated and formal words than we would normally use in our daily life?

T2-06

You should spend about 40 minutes on this task. Write about the following topic:
    Family friendly measures (e.g., flexible working hours) should be adopted by companies to ensure the work-life balance of their employees. To what extent do you agree or disagree with this opinion?
    Give reasons for your answer and include any relevant examples.

Exemplar 9.4

First and foremost, flexible working hours should be implemented as it can benefit employee while not harming the interest of the company. Imagine that you are an office lady who wakes up at 7 am and return home at 7 pm on weekdays. How can you have adequate time to accompany your children who go to bed at 9 pm? When working hours become more flexible, workers can have discretion over their working hours. Then, more time can be reserved for their family.

Categorise the following words into 'word/expression in a less academic style' and 'word/expression in a more academic style' by putting a tick (✓) in the appropriate boxes. Suggest a more formal and sophisticated word for the latter.

Word/expression	Word/expression in a less academic style	Word/expression in a more academic style	Suggestion (if any)
first and foremost			
implemented			
benefit			
adequate			
accompany			
have discretion over			
reserved			

Compare Exemplar 9.4 with Exemplar 9.4(a).

Exemplar 9.4(a) - words/expressions in a less academic style

There must be flexible working hours as it is good for employees while not harming the interest of the company. Imagine that you are an office lady who wake up at 7 am and return home at 7 pm on weekdays. How can you have enough time to be with your children who go to bed at 9 pm? When working hours become more flexible, workers can work earlier and finish their work earlier. Then, they can spend their evening with family.

Exemplar 9.5

Moreover, childcare money should be given to workers for promoting working efficiency. For employers, the money is worth-spending as employees do not need to worry about their children while working. Thus, they can put more emphasis on work and working efficiency can be promoted. Besides, parents can obtain more leisure time after launching the scheme. This makes working-parents receive other training or further their studies which can also raise their working efficiency.

Categorise the following words into 'word/expression in a less academic style' and 'word/expression in a more academic style' by putting a tick (✓) in the appropriate boxes. Suggest a more formal and sophisticated word for the latter.

Word/expression	Word/expression in a less academic style	Word/expression in a more academic style	Suggestion (if any)
moreover			
money			
working efficiency			
for employers			
do not need to worry about			
put more emphasis on			
makes			

Compare Exemplar 9.5 with Exemplar 9.5(a).

Exemplar 9.5(a) - words/expressions in a more academic style

Moreover, childcare subsidy should be given to workers for promoting working efficiency. From the perspective of the employers, the money is worth-spending as employees can stop agonizing over their children's needs while working. Thus, they can put more emphasis on work and working efficiency can be promoted. Besides, parents can obtain more leisure time after launching the scheme. This motivates working parents to receive other training or further their studies which can in turn raise their working efficiency.

Exemplar 9.6

Equal amount of time should be spent by employees on work and family. Working is important to them because they need the salary to support their family. Also, family is important because people need support from those who are close to them. So, it is important for the employers to give employees flexible working hours. It will make the company strong.

Categorise the following words into 'word/expression in a less academic style' and 'word/ expression in a more academic style' by putting a tick (✓) in the appropriate boxes. Suggest a more formal and sophisticated word for the latter.

Word/expression	Word/expression in a less academic style	Word/expression in a more academic style	Suggestion (if any)
equal amount of time should be spent			
working			
important			
need the salary			
also			
give			
make the company strong			

Compare Exemplar 9.6 with Exemplar 9.6(a).

Exemplar 9.6(a) - words/expressions in a more academic style

Employees should strike a balance between work and family. It is crucial to secure a stable job because it is their responsibility to provide financial support to their family. In addition, family is indispensable because people need support from those who are close to them. So, it is of paramount importance for the employers to foster a flexible working environment. The adoption of such policy would empower and motivate the employees to contribute significantly to the company.

Activity 4: Using Accurate Vocabulary

- Read the following question (T2-07) and read Exemplars 9.7–9.9.
- Evaluate how well the exemplars are written in terms of using accurate vocabulary by referring to the definitions and examples of the related terms. If necessary, use the following guiding questions to help your evaluation:

  o   Did the student use collocations accurately?
  o   Did the student spell words accurately?
  o   Did the student use part of speech accurately?

T2-07

You should spend about 40 minutes on this task. Write about the following topic:

It is not uncommon nowadays for people to work overseas. Working overseas allows people to experience different cultures and extend their social and professional connections. However, some find it hard to adapt due to nostalgia and acculturation.

Give reasons for your answer and include any relevant examples.

Correct the lexical errors you find in the following exemplars. Focus on collocation, spelling, and part of speech.

Exemplar 9.7

First and foremost, working overseas enables us to experience different cultures and extend our social and professional circles. For instance, you will know more about Japanese cuisine and customs when you are working and living in Japan. In addition, your social and professional networks will be strength by making Japanese friends and aquiring knowledge in a new working environment. You can reap from working in other countries in different aspects.

Type of error	Error	Correction
Collocation		
Spelling		
Part of speech		

Exemplar 9.8

In spite to these, some people find it difficult to fit into a new environment and reluctant to leave their hometown because of homesick and acculturation. I understand that foreign workers may miss their family and do not want to follow foreign cultures. I reckon that these difficulties can be eased. For curing homesickness, you can cook Chinese dishes by yourself, call your family when you miss them, even go home on holidays. For acculturation, I prefer to adapt to local culture and do not violent local customs. If you could not, you should still treat local culture in respect.

Type of error	Error	Correction
Collocation		
Spelling		
Part of speech		

Exemplar 9.9

All and all, not only do we gain experiences when living in different cultures, but we also expand our social and professional circle. Though we will still face some challenges, it is believed that these challenges can be overcomed and we will be hugely benefited by working overseas.

Type of error	Error	Correction
Collocation		
Spelling		

Activity 5: Peer Evaluation

Based on your understanding of the assessment standards of 'lexical resource', complete the evaluation form for Exemplar 9.10 written by a university student.

In the evaluation, identify problematic aspects of vocabulary use in relation to (1) **variety**, (2) **difficulty**, and (3) **accuracy** by responding to the guiding questions.

T2-08

You should spend about 40 minutes on this task. Write about the following topic:

The number of slash workers (people with multiple careers) is on the rise. It is less likely for young people these days to settle on one job for a long time. Why would young people want to be slash workers? What are the social consequences of having more slash workers?

Give reasons for your answer and include any relevant examples from your own knowledge or experience.

Write at least 250 words.

Exemplar 9.10 (paragraph 1)

The number of slash workers is rising in recent years. Youngsters would like to be slash work-ers because they want to broaden their horizon. There are bad impacts brought by slash work-ers such as shortage of full-time workers and low salary tax revenue.

Questions for paragraph 1:

Q1. What is a more formal and academic word to replace 'rising'?

Q2. What is a more formal and academic expression to replace 'would like to be'?

Q3. What is the spelling mistake of 'horizon'?

Q4. What is a more formal and academic word to replace 'bad impacts'?

Q5. What is a more formal and academic expression to replace 'such as'?

Exemplar 9.10 (paragraph 2)

First and foremost, youngsters want to be slash workers because they would like to broaden their horizon. Take my friend Jack as an example, he works as an English tutor, a secretary and a photographer at the same time. Having several jobs allows him to experience both flexible and regular workplace cultures. Being slash workers can also enable Jack to broaden their horizons by offering him more opportunities to make new friends. He meets colleagues in each job and people in different backgrounds.

Questions for paragraph 2:

Q1. The same expression 'broaden one's horizons' has been used in the first paragraph. Can you suggest another synonymous expression?

_____

Q2. The collocation between 'regular' and 'workplace cultures' is wrong. Can you suggest an alternative to 'regular'?

_____

Q3. What is a more formal and academic word/expression to replace 'also'?

_____

Q4. The same expression 'broaden one's horizons' has been used in the first paragraph. Can you suggest another synonymous expression?

_____

Q5. In the expression 'in different backgrounds', the collocation between the preposition 'in' and the noun 'backgrounds' is wrong. Can you suggest another preposition?

_____

Exemplar 9.10 (paragraph 3)

The social consequences of having more slash workers are shortage of full-time workers and low salary tax revenue. When full-time jobs become less appealing for youngsters and the full-time places remain unchanged, a shortage of full-time workers may emerge in the labour market. Also, income received from some of the part-time jobs will not be reported to the authorities. As a results, many slash workers can avoid salary tax and salary tax revenue may become less in the long run.

Questions for paragraph 3:

Q1. The collocation between 'appealing' and 'for' is wrong. Can you suggest another preposition?

_____

Q2. What is a more formal and academic word to replace 'places'?

_____

Q3. What is a more formal and academic word to replace 'also'?

_____

Q4. What is the spelling mistake in the expression 'as a results'?

_____

Q5. What is a more formal and academic word to replace 'become less'?

_____

Exemplar 9.10 (paragraph 4)

In conclusion, wanting to broaden their horizons would be a reason for young people to become slash workers. Disadvantages of the glowing number of slash workers may lead in full-time worker shortage and a drop in salary tax revenue.

Q1. What is a more formal and academic expression to replace 'wanting'?

_____

Q2. The same expression 'broaden one's horizons' has been used multiple times. Can you suggest another synonymous expression?

_____

Q3. What is a more formal and academic expression to replace 'a reason'?

_____

Q4. What is the spelling mistake of 'glowing'?

_____

Q5. The collocation between 'lead' and 'in' is wrong. Can you suggest another preposition?

_____

Activity 5: Writing Practice

Based on your understanding of 'lexical resource', replace the words in italics with more formal words in the following paragraph of T2-30.

T2-30

You should spend about 40 minutes on this task. Write about the following topic:

Some people favor the use of private cars as they bring people much convenience. However, some people think that private cars cause air pollution which is harmful to the environment. Do the advantages of using private cars outweigh the disadvantages?

Give reasons for your answer and include any relevant examples from your own knowledge or experience.

Write at least 250 words.

It cannot be *denied* that using private cars can *save time* when we go outside and it is *easier* for us to *go* to different destinations. However, the public transportation is also *good*, because it can help *mange* our commuting time and it is *cheap* to go around *different destinations*. It has similar functions as driving cars. For example, the underground train follows a routine schedule and there is *no* traffic *jam*, especially in peak hours.

10 Task 2
Grammatical Range and Accuracy

In this unit, you will:

- develop a better understanding of the various requirements related to the domain 'grammatical range and accuracy';
- read and discuss writing exemplars using the assessment standards of 'grammatical range and accuracy';
- evaluate and improve writing exemplars following the assessment standards of 'grammatical range and accuracy'.

Check Your Understanding

In Activity 1 in Chapter 6, two important aspects of the 'lexical resource' domain were defined and discussed, which are (1) structure variety and (2) sentence accuracy.

Check your understanding of these two aspects of the 'grammatical range and accuracy' domain by indicating whether the following statements are 'True' or 'False':

1 We have to use both simple and complex sentence structures in Task 2. [True/False]
2 Complex sentences are formed by a combination of an independent clause with one or more dependent clauses. [True/False]
3 Comma splices, run-on sentences, and sentence fragments will not affect the accuracy of sentences. [True/False]

Activity 1: Understanding the Assessment Standards of 'Qrammatical Range and Accuracy'

Since the assessment standards of this domain in Task 2 are identical to those in Task 1, refer to Activity 1 in Chapter 6 for definitions of keywords of the assessment standards.

Activity 2: Structure Variety

- Read the following question (T2-19) and read Exemplars 10.1-10.3.
- Evaluate how well the exemplars are written in terms of using a variety of sentence structures by referring to the definitions and examples of the related terms.

T2-19

You should spend about 40 minutes on this task. Write about the following topic:

It seems that people over 40 are difficult to find a satisfactory job. What are the causes? Are there any possible solutions to this problem?

Give reasons for your answer and include any relevant examples from your own knowledge or experience.

Write at least 250 words.

Exemplar 10.1

Firstly, (1) people over forty generally work for a long time. (2) Most of them have ample expe-rience. They have a great CV. Therefore, (3) they always aim high when they are looking for a new employment. (4) They cannot accept any position because they find the salary too low. (5) They may have many job requests but there are few jobs which can satisfy them. It is why they are difficult to find a satisfactory job.

Categorise the underlined sentences into three types: (1) simple sentences, (2) compound sentences, and (3) complex sentences.

Sentence pattern	Sentence number
Simple sentence	
Compound sentence	
Complex sentence	

Exemplar 10.2

Firstly, (1) people who are more than 40 years old have been working in the workplace for a long time. It is depressing to be in a job for a long time. (2) They lost the power to work when they are old. When they were young, (3) they had the incentive to work, they wanted to get promotion, or the boss recognized their effort. However, when they get older and do not get promoted, people get lost in front of work. Also, (4) people will be dissatisfied with their work.

Categorise the underlined sentences into three types: (1) simple sentences; (2) compound sentences; and (3) complex sentences.

Sentence pattern	Sentence number
Simple sentence	
Compound sentence	
Complex sentence	

Exemplar 10.3

Secondly, (1) people feel dissatisfied with their job. People think that busy working can affect health, family and life. In some cases, some people choose to divorce because their partners are too busy working. From the above, it is shown that long working hours can make people dissatisfied with their work. (2) Long hours can affect people's health. They lack time to rest. In some serious cases, (3) people spend all their time on work. They lose the chance to meet their friends.

Sentence number	Instruction	Rewritten sentence
1	Combine the two sentences with a subordinating conjunction 'which' to form a complex sentence	
2	Combine the two sentences with a subordinating conjunction to form a complex sentence	
3	Combine the two sentences with a coordinating conjunction to form a compound sentence	

Activity 3: Sentence Accuracy

- Read the following question (T2-20) and read Exemplars 10.4-10.5.
- Evaluate how well the exemplars are written in terms of using a variety of sentence structures accurately by referring to the definitions and examples of the related terms.

T2-20

You should spend about 40 minutes on this task. Write about the following topic:

When it comes to children's leisure activities, they prefer to stay indoors for computer games rather than go outside for sports.

Discuss the view and give your opinion.

Give reasons for your answer and include any relevant examples from your own knowledge or experience.

Write at least 250 words.

Exemplar 10.4

(1) Being more comfortable, the first reason why children love playing computers and stay indoor is because it is too hot outside. (2) Because of the influence of global warming. the scorching sun and suffocating air lead to the fact that city dwellers would like to get into an air-conditioned room, (3) only few, if any, people would like to stay outdoor and enjoy playing sports. (4) Therefore it is not difficult to understand why children these day enjoy playing computer games more. Who would opt for suffering and sweating under the sun instead of playing computer games with comfortable air conditioners operating 24 hours? A similar circumstance is noted in physical education lessons. (5) Most of the girls chooses to sit aside under the shade of building to wait until the end of the lesson instead of going to play sports and games even they are bored and dull. (6) The major reason they would like to sit aside is because of they hate sweat and being hot.

Match sentences (1) to (6) with the six types of errors described in Chapter 6. These error types include: comma splice, run-on sentence, sentence fragment, faulty parallelism, subject-verb disagreement, and misplaced modifiers. Rewrite a grammatically correct sentence for each.

Sentence number	Error type	Rewritten sentence
1		
2		
3		
4		
5		
6		

Exemplar 10.5

Firstly, (1) doing outdoor sports are good for the children's health. The majority of the students have packed schedules. Other than the normal school time, (2) many of them may need to attend various tutorial lessons and participating in extra-curricular activities after school. Therefore, they spend most of their time doing indoor activities without sunlight. (3) However, it is reported that suitable sunlight is good for health, especially for the kids who enter puberty, their bodies are growing every day. It is believed that absorbing enough sunlight and sweating can foster children's physical growth. Therefore, from the perspective of physical health, doing outdoor sports is better than playing computer games.

Secondly, much money is spent on computer games than sports. It is believed that money is involved in purchasing electronic games. (4) Other than the games themselves money is also paid to buy the extra tools which help play the games. (5) The specialized chairs and joysticks. Also, the more time you spend on the game, the more likely that you will pay more. It is reported that thousands of dollars can be lavished on playing one single video game. In contrast, doing sports is mostly free of charge. (6) Being free of charge, people who can afford the time do common sports like running and swimming. Therefore, doing outdoor sports is better than playing computer games.

Match sentences (1) to (6) with the six types of errors described in Chapter 6. These error types include: comma splice, run-on sentence, sentence fragment, faulty parallelism, subject-verb disagreement, and misplaced modifiers. Rewrite a grammatically correct sentence for each.

Sentence number	Error type	Rewritten sentence
1		
2		
3		
4		
5		
6		

Activity 4: Peer Evaluation

Based on your understanding of the assessment standards of 'grammatical range and accuracy', complete the evaluation form for Exemplar 10.6 written by a university student.

In the evaluation, identify problematic aspects of sentence use in relation to (1) **variety** and (2) **accuracy** by responding to the guiding questions.

T2-21

You should spend about 40 minutes on this task. Write about the following topic:

Women's status has improved dramatically both in the society and in the family as a result of the development of society. However, they still face the problem of inequalities. What are some of the inequalities? What measures should be adopted to solve the problems?

Give reasons for your answer and include any relevant examples from your own knowledge or experience.

Write at least 250 words.

Exemplar 10.6

Women have long been underestimated with their capacities which causes gender inequality in the past decades. They were unreasonably treated in the society and also in the family. (1) This situation has been improving with liberal education and social movements, yet, there are still room for improvement.

In the social aspect, take Hong Kong as an example, ladies enjoy equal job opportunities as gentlemen. (2) Both genders could have fair competitions they could take legal action if they have evidence showing the recruitment is unfair. Sex discrimination is less serious comparing to the past because of improvement in legislations. However, there are still discriminations in job applications (3) if the employer knows the applicant is pregnant or birth to baby. This could hardly collect concrete clues demonstrating there are sexually unfair treatments as employers could find many other excuses, such as there is physical workload or overtime work. Women applicant might not be treated fairly in this sense. This could be solved with a clear job advertisement with listed duties which prevents any arguments about eligibility.

(4) Another social point of view. people treat divorced men and women differently. People usually believe women should only marry a man once in a life. (5) If the women is divorced, people would still have the traditional thoughts, saying that the women are "unwanted" and no one would think the men are "unwanted". Unfortunately, this faulty belief could hardly be changed. This concerns how others perceive divorced women who are pursuing a second marriage, especially the parents and relatives of the men. These ridiculous thoughts create a burden for divorced women and put them under stress and pressure which affects their personal and social life. (6) This problem could hardly be solved by media or education, it takes time to improve.

Wives are still facing inequalities in family as they are often labelled as 'housewives' and they are relying on their husbands. (7) Having an unscientific belief, the wives are perceived as merely helping with the housework and children's work, which barely have any economic contribution to the family. According to a Japanese study, if we calculate a housewife's workload in the family, they could earn a fortune. Wives' contributions are usually minimized when compared to those of husbands. This biased interpretation reveals the unbalanced family role and expectations of the spouses. Similar to the previous problem, it could hardly be solved.

To conclude, the society is changing and is becoming a better place for men and women. (8) An equal treatment regarding to sexes. This requires the effort of the entire society with the willingness to change which might take a few decades. (441 words)

Q1. Match sentences (1) to (8) with one of the six types of errors described in Chapter 6. These error types include: comma splice, run-on sentence, sentence fragment, faulty parallelism, subject-verb disagreement, and misplaced modifiers. Rewrite a grammatically correct sentence for each.

Sentence number	Error type	Rewritten sentence
1		
2		
3		
4		
5		
6		
7		
8		

Q2. Give one example of compound sentence used in the exemplar.

Q3. Give one example of complex sentences used in the exemplar.

Activity 5: Writing Practice

Based on your understanding of 'grammatical range and accuracy', try to rewrite the paragraph of T2-33 with complex sentence structures and correct punctuation.

T2-33

You should spend about 40 minutes on this task. Write about the following topic:

Electric cars are becoming more popular nowadays because they are more environmentally friendly. Moreover, electric cars have become an emblem for tech-savvy people.

To what extent do you agree or disagree with this opinion?

Give reasons for your answer and include any relevant examples from your own knowledge or experience.

Write at least 250 words.

Secondly, electric cars are a popular choice among car lovers. Especially those wealthy ones. They represent status and power. For example, you own an electric car manufactured by Tesla. You will be highly regarded in your peer groups. Because you embrace technology to enhance quality of life. Moreover, people will hold the perception that you are technology-savvy. For instance, you will definitely impress your friends. By showing them how you can control your electric car using a touchscreen.

11 Task 1
Exemplar Analysis by Question Types

> **In this unit, you will:**
>
> - analyse exemplars of the four most popular Task 1 question types (chart/graph, charts/graphs, table, diagram/map) of different bands, and
> - develop a better understanding of the various requirements related to the four domains of Task 1 assessment standards in general.

Do You Remember?

Discuss the following questions with your partner:

1 What kinds of graphs are tested in IELTS Writing Task 1?
2 What are some assessment standards related to IELTS Writing Task 1?

Before you read the analysis of each exemplar, you can attempt to evaluate the quality of each exemplar by using the Peer Evaluation Checklist (Task 1) at the end of this chapter. Please note that these writing samples are authentic and are written by EFL university students. **Language errors in these samples are only corrected if they impede meaning because these samples intend to showcase a spectrum of writing abilities.** You are advised not to memorise these samples because they are not 'model essays'. In fact, you will benefit a lot more from critically analysing these exemplars using the evaluation checklist and reading the comments at the end of the exemplars.

Chart/graph

> **T1-43**
>
> You should spend about 20 minutes on this task.
>   The chart below shows information about the crop yields of three nations in 2016.
>   Summarise the information by selecting and reporting the main features, and make comparisons where relevant.
>   Write at least 150 words.

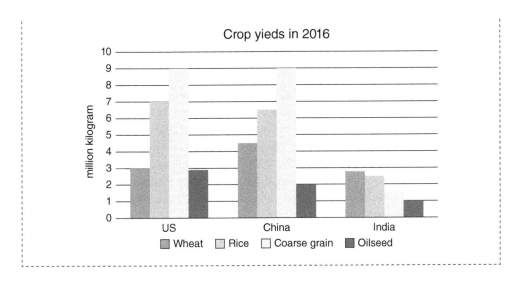

High (Bands 7+)

The following bar graph illustrates different crop productivities of three countries (US, China, and India) in 2016.

According to the chart, both the US and China reaped 9 million kilograms of coarse grain, which was 7.5 more than that of India. The US also harvested rice with 7 million kilograms, ranking the top among the three nations. China had 0.5 million kilograms less than the US, being the second, while India was reported to yield only 2.5 million kilograms rice, ranking last. The nation procuring the greatest amount of oilseed is the US, having almost 3 million kilograms, followed by China, with 2 million kilograms. With 1 million kilograms of oilseed less, India ranked bottom. The quantity of wheat harvested in China (4.5 million kilograms) was more than that in the US with 3 million kilograms only and India with fewer than 3 million kilograms.

From the chart demonstrated, it is indicated that coarse grain is the most abundant in the US and China, followed by, rice, wheat, and oilseed. India did not have much crop yields. Yield in wheat was the richest, followed by rice, coarse grain, and oilseed. India had the least yields of the four crops, compared to those of the US and China. One similarity found from the chart is that oilseed yield is the most limited in all the three nations. (227 words)

Comments

The author presented a clear overview of the main trends and differences of the three countries when describing four types of crop yields. There was a clear progression of ideas throughout. The author used a range of cohesive devices but there was some overuse. The student had the awareness to use less common words such as 'abundant', but she/he produced some occasional errors in word choice, such as 'limited'. The author had a good control of grammar and punctuation but still made a few errors.

Average (Bands 6-7)

In 2016, the US, China, and India had crop yields in wheat, rice, coarse grain, and oilseed. At first glance, coarse grain was the highest amount with 9 million kilograms in the US and China.

Obviously, coarse grain was the highest in US with 9 million kilograms, followed with 7 million kilograms rice. The fewer crops were wheat and oilseed, which were around 3 million kilograms and near 3 million kilograms. In China, the yield of coarse grain shared similarity with US, also the highest with 9 million kilograms. The following was rice with 6.5 million kilograms. The amount of wheat was 4.5 million kilograms. Oilseed was the least which had 2 million kilograms. Wheat was the highest in India with 2.8 million kilograms. The amounts of rice and coarse grain were 2.7 million kilograms and 1.5 million kilograms respectively. Oilseed was the least with 1 million kilograms.

The sequences of US and China were the same which were coarse grain, rice, wheat, and oilseed. Coarse grain was the highest and oilseed was the least. Oilseed was the lowest in the three nations. Surprisingly, wheat was the highest in India. (189 words)

Comments

The author presented an overview with information appropriately selected. She/he described the key features, although some details were not that relevant and necessary. The student could work on cohesive devices, such as using 'while' to show contrast. The student made an attempt to use some less common vocabulary. She/he used a combination of simple and complex sentence structures. She/he made some errors in grammar but they did not affect communication.

Low (Bands 4-5)

About the Crop yields in 2016, the report is reflecting the quantity of output in the different kind of crop in US, China, and India. In general, India was the country with least harvest between them.

First, China was gaining the highest result in wheat. US was slightly better than India.

Regarding the Rice, country with top output is US. China was almost get up the same level. India was the last one. Next, US and China had the same result in Coarse grain. India was 75 per cent less than them, it is also in the lowest level. As for the Oilseed, all of them had the lowest crop yields among other kinds of crop. US was the highest, following with China and lastly India. According to the order, there is 10 per cent of decreasing progressively.

Comments

The author attempted to address the task but failed to cover all key features. The information was not coherently arranged and she/he only employed some basic cohesive devices, such as 'first, next'. The student used only basic vocabulary and the choice of words was sometimes inappropriate, such as 'get up'. She/he used only a very limited range of sentence structures with only rare usage of subordinate clauses. There were lots of sentence-level grammatical errors in the text, such as tense, singular, and plural forms of words.

Charts/graphs

T1-49

You should spend about 20 minutes on this task.

The charts below show information about music preferences of teenager and middle-aged people, respectively.

Summarise the information by selecting and reporting the main features, and make comparisons where relevant.

Write at least 150 words.

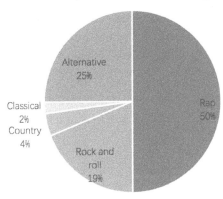

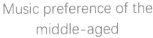

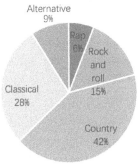

High (Bands 7+)

The pie charts illustrate the details of music favored by adolescents and middle-aged men.

Referring to the first chart, it displays that the majority of teenagers preferred rap as it was chosen by half of the population. From the second chart, however, it indicates that only 6 per cent of the middle-aged men enjoyed listening to rap. The huge discrepancy in music preference between the two age groups is clearly presented by this approximately eight-time difference.

Additionally, the charts picture another significant difference of music choice between two age groups. To exemplify, country music dominates middle-aged men's music preference as around 40 per cent of the population voted for this music type; yet, only 2 per cent of teenagers selected country music as their priority.

Surprisingly, even though quite a few differences regarding music preference are spotted, one type of music was chosen by almost an identical percentage of individuals in the two groups, in which 19 per cent of juveniles and 15 per cent of middle-aged males picked rock and roll as their music preference.

Comments

The author covered all requirements of the task sufficiently. She/he presented, highlighted, and illustrated the key features clearly and appropriately. She/he logically organised the information and ideas with a range of cohesive devices (additionally, to exemplify), and used paragraphing sufficiently and properly. The student also used a wide range of vocabulary, including some less common lexical items (discrepancy, adolescents, juveniles) fluently and flexibly to convey precise meanings. There were also a wide range of sentence structures and the majority of sentences were error-free.

Average (Bands 6-7)

As illustrated by the pie charts above, some distinct characteristics between youngsters and the middle-aged men toward music preference can be easily noted.

Regarding the different genres of music favored by the two groups, over a half of adolescents love rap while only approximately 5 per cent of middle-aged men show interest in rap; moreover, a quarter of teenagers and adults show preference in rock and roll. Furthermore, only 4 per cent of young-aged men demonstrate their passion towards countries music. Regarding alternative music, slightly a quarter of population in adolescent enjoying listening; however, only 10 per cent of adult admire this genre. As for classical music, it is surprising that younger rarely show interest while over a quarter of middle-aged men love this type of music.

When it comes to the comparison of different generation's perspective towards music, over a half of the youngsters enjoy listening rap but loath classical music, showing 2 per cent in the chart; a majority of adult love country music but surprisingly detest rap music, indicating 6 per cent in the diagram.

Comments

The author addressed the requirements of the task and presented an overview with information appropriately selected. She/he presented the key features adequately but there may be some irrelevant and repetitive details. The student arranged information and ideas with an adequate range of cohesive devices (regarding, furthermore) appropriately. The author used a sufficient range of vocabulary for the task, including less common vocabulary (distinct, adolescent). She/he used a mix of simple and complex sentence structures. She/he made some errors in grammar (10 per cent of adult, different generation's perspective, a quarter of population in adolescent) but they rarely made communication ineffective.

Low (Bands 4-5)

These two pie charts indicated the music preference of the teenagers and the middle-aged men for five types of music. The five music types include rap, rock and roll, country, classical, and alternative.

According to the chart of the teenagers, rap is the most popular type which is 50 per cent. However, it is the least popular type of the middle-aged men only 6 per cent. Then, the second and third preference of the teenagers is alternative music and rock and roll. The percentages of these two type music are 25 and 19. Only 4 per cent teenagers prefer country music and 2 per cent of them like classical music.

But the country music and classical music are very popular among the middle-aged men in the second pie chart, which are 42 per cent and 28 per cent for each. The next music preference of them is rock and roll (15 per cent). Alternative music made up 9 per cent in the middle-aged pie chart.

In conclusion, teenagers are more like to listen some dynamic music while middle-aged men prefer to listen the soft music.

Comments

The student generally addressed the task and presented inadequate information of the key features. She/he made comparisons of the two groups but failed to mention the similarity that youngsters and middle-aged men bear. She/he presented information with a range of cohesive devices, but some non-academic connectives (then, but) can be replaced with more academic ones. The author used a limited range of vocabulary (used 'popular' for many times), which is minimally adequate for the task. She/he used only a limited range of sentence structures and made some errors in grammar (two type music, teenagers are more like to listen).

Table

T1-06

You should spend about 20 minutes on this task.

The table below gives information about people's attitudes towards gender roles categorised by age.

Summarise the information by selecting and reporting the main features, and make comparisons where relevant.

Write at least 150 words.

A man's duty is to earn money while a woman's duty is to look after her family	18-25	26-35	36-45	46-55	56-65
Agree	5%	13%	10%	6%	12%
Neutral	13%	13%	19%	29%	21%
Disagree	82%	74%	71%	65%	67%

High (Bands 7+)

Opinions about the attitudes towards gender roles were summarised in the table. It is reflected that the majority of respondents oppose the stereotype of the responsibility that should be shared by males and females, with more than 60 per cent recorded from each age group.

It can be illustrated from the graph that relatively younger interviewees feel more negatively about the stated gender roles. Meanwhile, it is a typical tendency that the older the people, the less they disagree with the statement. To demonstrate, the age group from 18-25 has the highest percentage (82 per cent) against the statement. In contrast, people aged 46-55 and 56-65 have the lowest ratio of disagreement, with 65 per cent and 67 per cent respectively.

On the contrary, more than one-tenth of the respondents of three age groups (26-35, 36-45, 56-65) support the statement, while only a minority of the people who are aged 18-25 and 46-55 (5 per cent and 6 per cent respectively) express a positive response to the denoted gender roles. Significantly, around one-third of the interviewees aged 45-55 gave an ambiguous stand towards the statement. Meanwhile, only 13 per cent of the participants under 35 hold a neutral attitude towards the gender role description. (192 words)

Comments

The author covered all requirements of the task sufficiently. She/he presented, highlighted, and illustrated the key features clearly and appropriately. She/he described the major findings in the introductory paragraph. She/he logically organised the information and ideas with a range of cohesive devices (to illustrate, on the contrary), and used paragraphing sufficiently and properly. The student also used a wide range of vocabulary, including some less common lexical items (oppose, stereotype, ambiguous) fluently and flexibly to convey concise meanings. There were also a wide range of sentence structures.

Average (Bands 6-7)

The table demonstrates data about people's viewpoints on males' and females' responsibilities in a family.

Regardless of age groups, more than half of the interviewees disagree with the conventional view that men are responsible for earning money while women are supposed to look after the family. Among all the negative responses, the age group of 18-25 has the most votes of over 80 per cent.

As for the positive responses, no more than 6 per cent of the participants of age group 18-25 and 46-55 agree with the statement. Around one out of ten of the interviewees of other age groups show positive views on the statement.

Finally, 13 per cent of both interviewees of age group 13-5 and 6-35 vote for the neutral stance. And one out of five of age groups 36-45 and 56-65 hold a neutral viewpoint. Surprisingly, the age group which voted the most for the neutral stance is 46-55 with almost 30 per cent.

To sum up, the majority of the respondents of all age groups disagree with the gender stereotype that bringing home the bacon should be a man's job and looking after the family should be a woman's job. (188 words)

Comments

The author addressed the requirements of the task. She/he presented the key features. The student arranged information and ideas with a wide range of cohesive devices (as for, finally, regardless of) appropriately. The author used a wide range of vocabulary (conventional, stereotype) for the task. She/he used a mix of simple and complex sentence structures. However, the author used an idiomatic expression (bringing home the bacon), which should be avoided in academic writing.

Low (Bands 4-5)

The table below gives information about people's attitudes towards gender roles in different age groups.

Surprisingly, adults who aged 26–35 are the most conservative in gender roles, 13 per cent of them believe that man should be the breadwinner and woman should be housewife, 12 per cent of the middle-aged people who are 56–65 years old and 10 per cent from the age group of 36–45 share the same thought. Only 6 per cent who are aged between 46 to 55 and 5 per cent of young people who are in the age group of 18-25 agree with that.

Thus, 29 per cent of people who are 46-55 years old said that they are neutral toward this gender stereotype. 21 per cent of people who are aged 56-65 and 19 per cent of people who are aged 36-45 said that they are neither agree nor disagree with it. Only 13 per cent from age group of 18-25 and 26-35 hold the same opinion.

Furthermore, more than 80 per cent of young people who are between 18 to 25 years old agree that family role of man and woman should not be limited by traditional mind. More than 70 per cent from the age group of 26-35 and 36-45 support the idea. For the middle age people who are 46-55 and 56-65 years old, only 65 per cent and 67 per cent of them disagree the thought. (210 words)

Comments

The student generally addressed the task. However, she/he presented the information with too many figures. Instead, she/he could select the most important information to report and pay more attention to comparing the figures. She/he presented information with cohesive devices, but there might be some inappropriate use (thus). The author used a range of vocabulary, but it is minimally adequate for the task. She/he used a limited range of sentence structures; and made some errors in grammar (disagree the thought) and punctuation; in particular, the problem of comma splices is evident.

Diagram/map

T1-09

You should spend about 20 minutes on this task.

The diagram below gives information about the process of making detergent.

Summarise the information by selecting and reporting the main features, and make comparisons where relevant.

Write at least 150 words.

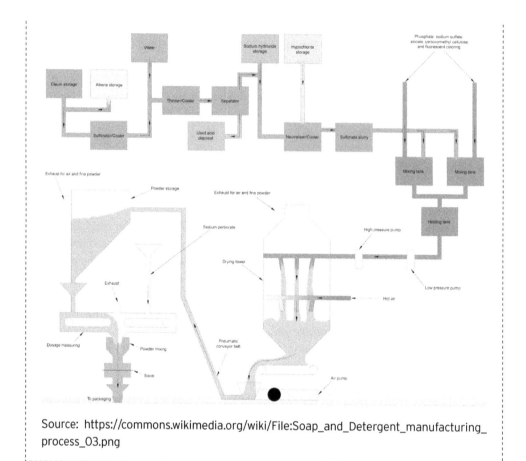

Source: https://commons.wikimedia.org/wiki/File:Soap_and_Detergent_manufacturing_process_03.png

High (Bands 7+)

The diagram demonstrates the process of making detergent. The process contains three major stages.

In the first stage, Oleum and Alkene are cooled down and sulfonated by adding water. Next, the processed materials are processed first in the thinner or cooler and then the separator to produce sodium hydroxide and remove used acid. Then, the stored sodium hydroxide is added into the neutraliser or cooler together with hypochlorite to produce sulfonate slurry.

When it comes to the second phase, the sulfonate slurry is mixed with phosphate, sodium sulfate, silicate, carboxymethyl cellulose, and fluorescent colouring. Then, the mixed chemicals in the holding bank are pumped into the drying tower where they interact with the hot air. After the drying process, the powder is air pumped via a pneumatic conveyor belt into the powder storage tank.

In the final stage, sodium perborate is added to the powder for mixing. Having been sieved, the detergent is ready for packaging. (156 words)

Comments

This student adequately addressed all aspects of the task by describing the procedure of manufacturing detergent in a systematic and orderly manner. Overall, the writing is coherent and cohesive. The student was able to divide the production process of detergent into three stages and effectively use a range of cohesive devices (e.g., in the first stage, then, after) to show the sequence of the process. In terms of vocabulary, the student demonstrated his/her ability to paraphrase the words given in the question by changing their parts of speech. As for the construction of sentences, a good mix of simple, compound, and complex sentences was used appropriately and accurately.

Average (Bands 6-7)

The diagram shows how detergent is made.

First, Oleum and Alkene are cooled down and sulfonated. Water is added. Second, it is put into the thinner/cooler before being separated. This process forms sodium hydroxide and remove used acid. Sodium hydroxide is put into the neutraliser/cooler with hypochlorite to form sulfonate slurry. The sulfonate slurry is mixed with phosphate, sodium sulfate, silicate, carboxymethyl cellulose, and fluorescent colouring. The mixed things are put into the drying tower. Hot air is used there. The powder is put into a pneumatic conveyor belt and then the powder storage tank. Sodium perborate is put into the powder, mixed and sieved. The detergent is ready.

Comments

Generally, this student fulfilled the task requirements, although some specific steps were missing. This student managed to use some cohesive devices (e.g., first, second) to present the procedure in a chronological manner. In terms of word choice, this student appeared to struggle with using a variety of verbs. This is evidenced in his/her repeated use of 'put'. Finally, there is an overuse of simple sentences, which could easily be combined to form more complex sentence structures.

Low (Bands 4-5)

This is how detergent is made:

1 Cool down and sulfonate Oleum and Alkene.
2 Add water.
3 Put into thinner/cooler.
4 Remove acid.
5 Mix with phosphate, sodium sulfate, silicate, carboxymethyl cellulose, and fluorescent coloring.
6 Put powder through a pneumatic conveyor belt into the powder storage tank.
7 Add sodium perborate.
8 Mix and sieve powder.
9 Pack detergent.

Comment

This student misunderstood the format of Task 1 writing and presented the ideas in the diagram in bullet points. It is important for IELTS candidates to remember the requirement of writing in complete sentences and in clearly defined paragraphs. By writing in bullet points, this student is unlikely to get satisfactory marks in the 'coherence and cohesion' and 'grammatical range and accuracy' domains because there is an absence of linking words and sentence structure variety.

Peer Evaluation Checklist

Assessment standard		Guiding question
Task achievement	Overview	Did the student indicate what the graph is about?
		Did the student use different wordings or did s/he simply copy the question?
		Did the student summarise the graph in a succinct manner?
	Selecting information	Did the student choose the most important and representative data points to report or report every data point?
		Did the student categorise data and information into groups?
		Did the student report data that represent the extremes in the graph?
	Comparing information	Did the student highlight similar features between data points?
		Did the student highlight contrastive features between data points?
	Format	Did the student write in paragraphs and complete sentences?
		Did the student include a short introductory paragraph (overview), one or two body paragraphs, and an optional concluding paragraph?
	Clarity	Did the student report data by using not only verbs (e.g. increased, decreased) but also adverbs and adjectives to denote the extent of change?
	Relevance	Did the student report data that are presented in the graph or table and not include explanations of the data?
	Accuracy	Did the student include specific numbers to support his/her data description?
	Sufficiency	Did the student report the majority of the data points or information presented in the graph?
Coherence and cohesion	Cohesive devices	Were the cohesive devices used meaningfully and accurately?
		Was there a variety of cohesive devices used?
	Pronouns	Did the student use any pronouns?
		Were the pronouns used accurately?
	Synonyms	Did the student use any synonyms?
	Paragraphing	Did the student connect ideas by organising information thoughtfully and logically within a paragraph?
		Did the student connect ideas by organising information thoughtfully and logically between paragraphs?
Lexical Resource	Variety	Did the student enrich the vocabulary by using four major types of word formation: prefixes, suffixes, compounds, and conversion?
	Difficulty	Did the student use a set of more sophisticated and formal words than we would normally use in our daily life?
	Accuracy	Did the student use collocations accurately?
		Did the students spell the words accurately?
		Did the student use parts of speech accurately?

| Grammatical Range & Accuracy | Structure Variety | Did the student use simple sentences and compound sentences? Did the student use complex sentences? |
| | Sentence Accuracy | Did the student make punctuation errors, such as sentence fragments, run-on sentence and comma splice? Did the student make other error types, such as faulty parallelism, misplaced modifier and subject-verb disagreement? |

12 Task 2

Exemplar Analysis by Question Types

> **In this unit, you will:**
>
> - analyse exemplars of the four most popular Task 2 question types (discuss views, advantages and disadvantages, opinions, problems and solutions) of different bands; and
> - develop a better understanding of the various requirements related to the four domains of Task 2 assessment standards in general.

Do You Remember?

Discuss the following questions with your partner:

1 What kinds of questions are asked in IELTS Writing Task 2?
2 What are some assessment standards related to IELTS Writing Task 2?

   Before you read the analysis of each exemplar, you can attempt to evaluate the quality of each exemplar by using the Peer Evaluation Checklist (Task 2) at the end of this chapter. Please note that these writing samples are authentic and are written by ESL and EFL university students. **Language errors in these samples are only corrected if they impede meaning because these samples intend to showcase a spectrum of writing abilities.** You are advised not to memorise these samples because they are not 'model essays'. In fact, you will benefit a lot more from critically analysing these exemplars using the evaluation checklist and reading the comments at the end of the exemplars.

Discuss Views

T2-42

You should spend about 40 minutes on this task. Write about the following topic:
   Some people advocate that a lingua franca (e.g., English) can facilitate communication among different nations and there is no need to protect the rare languages in the

world. However, others believe that rare languages are a very important component of human culture. Therefore, we have the responsibility to ensure that these languages will not die out.

Discuss both views and give your opinion.

Give reasons for your answer and include any relevant examples from your own knowledge or experience.

Write at least 250 words.

High (Bands 7+)

Some people argue that a *lingua franca* can utterly substitute the rare language in the world because it can foster communication between countries. In my view, we should advocate a *lingua franca* while protecting the rare languages.

On the one hand, a *lingua franca* which has a ubiquitous spread worldwide can surely enhance communication among nations and globalisation. Firstly, it can reduce misunderstanding and discrimination due to language barrier. Without this hindrance, cultures of various areas can easily be shared and understood, and therefore, it can foster understanding between countries and achieve racial harmony. Secondly, a *lingua franca* can enhance globalisation in terms of education, business and tourism. From the educational perspective, a *lingua franca* like English can increase the availability and variety of reference books and research journals, and we can understand the books and journals written by different authors from diverse countries without translation errors. Regarding business development, trading among national enterprises can be enhanced as they can communicate better with their business partners. As far as the development of tourism is concerned, a common language can definitely encourage citizens to broaden their horizons. For example, Asian tourists can travel to Africa without difficulty when they share the same common language.

On the other hand, the rare languages are indispensable for human culture. The world should contain an eclectic mix of traditions; otherwise, it will be monotonic if there is only one language and the same social culture. A rare language lays the groundwork for us to understand our identity. For example, different rare languages contain their own slang terms, and by manipulating them, we can easily evoke resonance and intimacy among the same peer group. Besides, a rare language is a prerequisite to build a unique culture. For instance, when it comes to presenting the legend, music and art of the south Chinese tradition, few art forms can be compared to the Cantonese opera.

In conclusion, both *lingua franca* and rare languages are important to us. (329 words)

Comments

The student presented a clear position throughout the whole essay. There was a clear central topic in each paragraph. She/he supported the main ideas with appropriate examples and explanations in the body paragraphs. And she/he used many cohesive devices (on the one hand, as far as . . .) to organise ideas in a logical way. Meanwhile, she/he used a wide range of less common vocabulary (intimacy, manipulating) and complex sentence structures. She/he had a good command of grammar and punctuation.

Average (Bands 6-7)

Some people argue that common language can be used as a means of communication between different countries. Nevertheless, others say that rare language should be maintained as it is a main factor of our culture. Both views will be discussed in the following essay.

I think rare language should be preserved, not only because it is an important cultural aspect for our societies, but it can also promote a sense of belonging in the society. When one, who speaks rare language, learns the history of their own native language, they can know more about the vicissitude of the rare language. Moreover, people will have some knowledge about the culture of the language they use. Thus, people will be more attached to their societies and will have a sense of belonging to their societies. Therefore, rare language should be maintained.

However, others believe that common language can be used as a means of communication between people from different countries. It is true that common language, such as English, is essential when people from different countries needed to have important business, for example trading and selling. Although it is evident that a *lingua franca* is necessary to facilitate intercultural communication, it is important to maintain the use of rare language and having people continue to use it in order to inherit and pass it to the next generation.

In conclusion, although common language is important for communicating between people from different countries, rare language should be maintained as it can promote a sense of belonging in the society and also can pass the history of the language to the next generation. (269 words)

Comments

The author addressed all parts of the task, although she/he failed to cover all tasks fully. For example, she/he did not provide her/his own view clearly at the beginning, although she/he stated it in the end. The student arranged information and ideas coherently and used cohesive devices (therefore, moreover) effectively. However, the cohesion within and between sentences may sometimes be mechanical. The student tried to use some less common vocabulary but there was a clear repetition of some words (maintain). She/he used a mix of simple and complex sentences but she/he made some errors in terms of punctuation.

Low (Bands 4-5)

With the help of technology different places are more connected and the language used have been united. Lingua franca such as English which are learnt among different countries gradually replace the unpopular language. It is important for people to learn the *lingua franca* as to connect with the world, but this does not mean rare language should be disappeared.

Local language is one of the intangible heritage that have to be protected by the public. The slangs express the culture of the countries; the tone, way of talking, etc. In Hong Kong, Cantonese is used for communication, even so Mandarin is greatly promoted as China is becoming powerful and create different opportunities. Hong Kong government stresses on Putonghua by implementing Putonghua as the medium of teaching Chinese. Less students gain access to Cantonese or even regard Putonghua as their mother tongue. Children get no chance to choose but the public should understand the value of local language. It is easy for a language to extinct when less people are learning and using it.

There are no conflicts or disadvantage of learning more than one dialect or language. Different language are worth to learn and through this experience culture can be exchanged. Therefore, rare language has to be remained and protected by the local people and pass on this kind of culture to the next generation. (225 words)

Comments

The author addressed the task only partially; she/he failed to discuss both views, as required by the task. She/he sometimes used cohesive devices inaccurately, which impeded the delivery of the meaning. She/he used a limited range of vocabulary and sometimes the words were not chosen correctly to express the meaning (unpopular language). The author made frequent grammatical mistakes and punctuation was faulty or missing, which caused certain difficulty for the reader to understand the meaning.

Advantages and Disadvantages

T2-04

You should spend about 40 minutes on this task. Write about the following topic:

Many university students are required to enrol in a number of general education courses. These courses are usually related to the social, cultural, psychological, and spiritual lives of young people.

What are the advantages of general education courses to university students?

Give reasons for your answer and include any relevant examples from your own knowledge or experience.

Write at least 250 words.

High (Bands 7+)

General education courses (GE courses) are normally introduced to college students in the first or the second academic year. Different from other major courses, most educationists believe these modules are distinct in a way that they can cultivate students' knowledge socially, culturally, psychologically and spiritually. GE courses should be compulsory and are crucial for two reasons. Personally, these courses can broaden students' horizons and develop their social consciousness.

To start with, the GE courses play an essential role in expanding university students' intellectual horizons. Through enrolling in the GE courses, students can be bestowed upon a precious opportunity to gain some exposure to knowledge and skills which they cannot gain from attending their major courses. It is undeniable that these individuals can acquire knowledge that they can either apply to their real-life situations or supplement their major subjects. For example, they can employ some practical methods they have learnt in the psychology class to deal with some psychological problems they or their friends have encountered. In addition, courses such as those related to philosophy are effective to develop students' logical and critical thinking, which, as a result, can enable the students to better explore the area they are involved in innovatively and intellectually.

Secondly, enrolling in the GE courses allows students to develop their social consciousness. Since there are a myriad of GE courses that discuss current issues in the society, university students can keep track of the matters. Therefore, their understanding of the society will benefit them enormously when they are hunting for a job. For example, it can be more than vital for candidates who plan to take up a career as teachers to foster a certain level of knowledge pertaining to psychology, which they can borrow to deal with some thorny issues of students' psychology.

To conclude, it is critically important and compulsory for university students to enroll in the GE courses as they can widen their all-round perspectives and being more socially conscious. (327 words)

Comments

The author addressed all parts of the task well and presented a well-developed response to the question with relevant, extended, and supported ideas. She/he used paragraphing sufficiently and appropriately, and employed effective cohesive devices to connect the ideas (therefore, through, different from . . .). She/he used a wide range of vocabulary and skilfully used more academic lexical items (supplement, involve, distinct). A wide range of error-free sentence structures was also used.

Average (Bands 6-7)

I agree that it is important for university students to be introduced to the General Education courses. The reason is that the General Education courses contain different types of information and knowledge which are necessary for students to master. The reasons and explanations are provided below.

First of all, General Education courses can develop students' knowledge, information and content outside their major subjects. Taking the communication skills of the students as an example, they can learn how to be sociable and get along with their peers. This is important as university students need to interact with others effectively. Otherwise, they may not always achieve a smooth communication with others. As a consequence, they may not succeed in performing excellently in their future study, work and life.

Moreover, General Education courses can teach university students how to relax themselves. Nowadays, numerous university students commit suicide because of the ever-increasing pressure and difficulties they are faced with. Usually, they have no idea what to do under such circumstances. In this case, the advantages of the introduction of General Education courses appear. Through gaining knowledge psychologically and spiritually, they can perform better in terms of how to control and adjust their emotions, feelings and pressure. Therefore, they can avoid thinking negatively when they faced with difficulties.

To conclude, it is indeed significant for university students to be exposed to General Education courses so as to develop all-round skills and cope with pressure. (239 words)

Comments

The author addressed all parts of the task, although she/he failed to mention whether GE courses should be regarded as compulsory. The student presented relevant main ideas but the second reason seemed somewhat repetitive and had some overlaps with the first reason.

She/he arranged information and ideas coherently with cohesive devices such as 'moreover' and 'otherwise'. Some further less common vocabulary (circumstance) could be used in the essay. She used a mix of simple and complex sentences.

Low (Bands 4-5)

How can a university student go without studying the general education courses? Or you can't really believe an all-round university student has only studied his or her specialised courses during the four-year studies! No matter what he or she majors in the university, it goes without saying that broadening perspectives in different disciplines has been a common trend in the university!

Studying general education courses has always been the basic criteria of completing an undergraduate degree throughout the universities in the world. General education is one of the branches in the Liberal Education in which it embraces the study of a wide range of courses other than the specialised courses in Year 3 and Year 4. Has it been laying a solid foundation for the undergraduate study, it also paves the way for widening the worldviews in both further studies and the world of work.

Put simply, it doesn't bear any meaning when making the general education courses compulsory. It does matter when students are not taking any initiatives in taking those general education courses because they won't be able to take a glance as soon as they enter Years 3 and 4. (193 words)

Comments

The student responded to the task in only a minimal way and the answer was tangential. The student argued only that general education can widen students' worldviews. Even so, she/he failed to provide the reader with examples and explanations. Most people would not understand the example that the student employed because it was ambiguous. The whole essay was not written in a formal and academic style as there were short forms, questions, and exclamation marks. Moreover, she/he failed to satisfy the word limit of the task requirement. The student used some cohesive devices but not effectively and inadequately. Although some attempts were made to use more complex sentences, their accuracy was in question.

Opinion

T2-11

You should spend about 40 minutes on this task. Write about the following topic:

Nowadays many workers are suffering from joint pains (e.g., neck pain), which they ascribe to sedentary office jobs.

To what extent do you agree or disagree with this opinion?

Give reasons for your answer and include any relevant examples from your own knowledge or experience.

Write at least 250 words.

High (Bands 7+)

Many people claim that occupational diseases are quite a phenomenon nowadays, especially the employees in the office. These white-collar workers suffer from numerous joint pains, which people attribute largely to their sedentary jobs, as they keep the same posture for too long; consequently, they have a minimum chance to exercise. To a large extent, I agree with this statement.

First of all, employees working in offices lack adequate exercises that are enough to balance the pains resulted from sitting for too long. Therefore, not only will people be diagnosed with diabetes when they stay in the office day by day, their muscles will deteriorate when they lack sufficient exercise – a fact that is greatly embodied in the whole-body pain that sedentary office workers suffer. According to research, exercise is a rather essential element of keeping people healthy. If we aspire to stay healthy, it is imperative to exercise at least one hour per day.

Furthermore, white-collar workers are demanded to use computer daily for a long time which causes a serious health problem. To exemplify, in the sedentary office, employees normally have to work in front of the computers and have to keep the same position and stare at the computer for a whole day. According to a study in Canada, using computer for a long time will lead to myriads of problems. Not only radiation but also the sitting posture pose a great hurt to our joints. As a consequence, there is an increasing tendency that white-collar workers resort to massages when they are available.

To conclude, dedicating oneself to a sedentary job has a high likelihood to result in horrible health problems, especially joint pains, since the job lowers the chance of doing exercises and keeps the workers sitting for too long. (294 words)

Comments

The author provided enough background information of the issue mentioned in the question and stated his/her opinion clearly in the introduction. Her/his main ideas were elaborated by giving examples and quoting academic research results. There was a topic sentence at the beginning of each body paragraph. A wide range of effective cohesive devices (as a consequence, to exemplify . . .) were employed to connect the ideas logically. The student enriched the essay by using many less common lexical items (deteriorated, simultaneously). There was a variety of simple and complex sentence structures. She/he only made occasionally grammatical mistakes (Not only radiation but also the sitting posture pose-poses).

Average (Bands 6-7)

To a certain extent, I agree with the statement that a large number of modern workers attribute their joint pains to sedentary jobs. The regular working hours of these victims are from 9:00 – 17:00 or 10:00 – 18:00 and the necessity of utilising technology such as computers limit the opportunity for office workers to move around, which results in the mentioned health problems.

Not having adequate knowledge about proper sitting and not doing sufficient exercises like stretching lead to workers' joint pains, especially neck and back pains. Often, office workers are not taught and they show no motivation to learn how to sit properly in front of computers. Therefore, they usually curve their backs and keep their shoulders tense when trying to concentrate on the screen, whether it be reading or doing assigned responsibilities. Moreover, they do not realise that there is a necessity to stretch their back, limbs, and their whole body to relax their muscles after a long-day work.

For instance, voluminous white-collar workers have to sit all day long to complete their day-to-day tedious workloads using computers. They work from 9:00 to 18:00 and have an hour lunch break only. When they get off work, they would go home complaining the neck and back pains resulted from gazing at the monitor and sitting all day. This is due to the fact that they have never been informed how to sit upright with relaxed shoulders and take small breaks twice to four times a day to stretch arms and back. Had the Human Resources Department instructed the employees how to sit correctly in front of a computer to avoid back pains, they would not have suffered from joint pains. Although this may be seen as a trivial matter, it is essential and important for office workers to gain some knowledge of this aspect.

To conclude, joint pains that modern office workers suffer are brought by their working environment, in which they have little chance to do exercise. Another factor, workers' lack of knowledge in proper sitting, also leads to this problem. (342 words)

Comments

The author addressed all parts of the task, although some parts (knowledge about proper sitting) were more fully covered than others (doing sufficient exercises). She/he arranged information and ideas with a range of cohesive devices (therefore, for instance . . .). She/he attempted to use a range of less common vocabulary (sufficient, adequate, trivial . . .) with some awareness of style and collocation. She/he used a variety of simple and complex sentence structures and there were no serious grammatical mistakes.

Low (Bands 4-5)

To a large extent, I disagree with this opinion. Nowadays, many workers are suffering from joint pains. However, the culprit of suffering from joint pains is the workers' habits, instead of the sedentary office jobs.

First of all, many officer workers are phubbers. Whenever you are hanging out with your friends in the shopping malls, eating in restaurants, or even walking on the streets, you can always see that some people are just focusing on their phones. Phubbers are always paying too much attention on their phone so that their heads are always down, which seriously affect the backbone and the neck. This causes the joint pains. We always see people are still using their phone even eating.

Secondly, we should have a good habit while working in office. For instance, we should keep a distance of 30 cm between our eyes and computer, so that our eyes will not be tired after working a whole day. We should also sit up strict and look for a suitable height of chair which fits us, so that our backbone and neck will not be hurt. What is more, we should take a short break in every hour. We can do some simple exercises like moving our fingers, body, turn around, and relax. We can do the above things to prevent joint pains, like neck pains, backbone pains, and so on.

Some workers may urge that the long working time in office is causing the joint pains. However, keeping a correct pose and having good habit of working in the office is our own responsibility. It hurts if we do not sit up strict or being too close to the computer.

To conclude, I disagree that the sedentary office jobs are the reason why workers suffer from joint pains. A good habit of pose while working and good habit of using our smartphone are important for us to prevent those joint pains problem. (321 words)

Comments

The author only addressed the task in a minimal way. To demonstrate, she/he talked about phubbers, but she failed to make a connection of this phenomenon with the joint pains of office workers. She/he then talked about suggestions to avoid joint pains, which were not required by the task to be addressed. She/he used some cohesive devices to connect her/his ideas. There was an attempt to use some higher-level vocabulary (culprit), but this was minimally adequate for the task. She/he also misused some vocabulary (workers may urge-argue), which caused difficulty in understanding. There was a mix of simple and complex sentences.

Problems and Solutions

T2-45

You should spend about 40 minutes on this task. Write about the following topic:

Nowadays, an increasing number of people are moving from rural areas to urban areas. This urbanisation process has brought about numerous problems. What are some of the problems caused? And what are some possible solutions?

Give reasons for your answer and include any relevant examples from your own knowledge or experience.

Write at least 250 words.

High (Bands 7+)

Urbanisation process has accelerated over the past decades as an increasing number of people are migrating from rural areas and crushing into metropolises. This seemingly unstoppable development not only brings a large amount of labors and resources but also some unavoidable issues into cities.

First of all, traffic conjunction, which is attributed to the fact that people are seeking upward social mobility in urban areas, seems to bother modern citizens tremendously. The unpleasant traffic experience caused by too many people travelling is a reflection of the problem. For instance, there are always long queues in front of the metro doors with people crushing in and out. In addition, workers are normally jammed on the street for a long time before they can reach their workplace. In order to resolve this issue, worldwide city governors have to cater to the needs of numerous citizens' travelling needs by establishing more public transportation and scheduling more metros and buses.

The second but almost equally troublesome issue in cities is housing. It is a natural demand for people to have a place they call home. However, in big cities, the land and houses available are limited and hard to satisfy everyone's demands. With relatively scarce housing resources, the price for estate soars. To demonstrate, the housing price of various world-renowned financial cities is overcharged that owning a decent house is becoming extremely demanding for most ordinary working class. This phenomenon has seriously affected their living qualities and becomes an apparent universal issue. In this case, on the one hand, the local governments are supposed to build enough public houses to satisfy the needs of the grass-root level city dwellers. On the other hand, the central government can also alleviate the problem by enacting certain appealing policies in the rural areas, which can attract people to return to their hometown.

In sum, it is undeniable that urbanisation is a symbol of economic development of a country and has its benefits. Nevertheless, the detrimental outcomes caused by urbanisation process such as traffic conjunction, overwhelmingly high housing price should also be relieved through governments' efforts. (348 words)

Comments

The author sufficiently addressed all parts of the task and presented a sufficient response to the question with relevant and adequate examples and explanations. Contents were well connected through the employment of various effective cohesive devices. The student used a wide range of uncommon lexical items (detrimental, accelerate) skilfully. In addition, a wide range of sentence structures was used. The majority of the sentences were error-free.

Average (Bands 6-7)

City provides a better living quality to people, encouraging many of them migrating to the more affluent areas. When more and more people move to urban areas, urbanisation occurs subsequently, which results in some problems.

The first problem caused is traffic congestion. It is easy to have congestion in some busy roads during peak hours. Consequently, traffic flow will be slow and inefficient. In India, for example, urban size is growing, and the transport problem is also raising since more people are on the road. To solve this issue, the governments could build more bridges and subways to divert the busy traffic in some bottleneck areas, such as the Western Harbour Tunnel being built to alleviate congestion of Cross Harbour Tunnel in Hong Kong. As for the residents in the city, they could take more public transports rather than private cars.

The second problem is pollution. Urbanisation leads to the growth of transports and industries. Both of these activities create tons of pollutants, destroying the environment. Take Hong Kong as an example, vehicles and power plants are the two major air pollution sources. Human activities in the city produce large amount of pollutants that upset the environment and ecosystem. There are various solution to this problem, such as replacing coal and fossil fuels by some renewable and natural energy like solar power, which they would create less pollutants. Riding bike to replace driving is another solution to pollution. It is more eco-friendly because bike does not need fuel to generate.

Urbanisation seems to be the trend globally, the problems coming along are hard to stop. What important is that everyone should cooperate together to solve the problems, creating a better home for everyone. (283 words)

Comments

The student addressed all parts of the task well, and supported the ideas (two problems brought by urbanisation), with ample reasons and solutions. She/he logically organised the ideas with a range of cohesive devices. The author had the awareness to use some higher level lexical items (alleviate, affluent). She/he used a mix of simple and complex sentence structures. However, the student made some errors in grammar (There are various solution) and punctuation (. . . the trend globally, the problems . . .); however, these errors did not affect communication.

Low (Bands 4-5)

Recently, the number of people move from rural areas to urban area is growing, so there are lots of problems of urbanisation. In this essay, I will focus on two main problems and its solution for them.

First of all, socially, this situation called urbanisation can generate that some children are left in home when their parents is moving from rural area, their homes, to the urban area, As we all know, urbanisation need a lot of parents go to the urban area to work but their home is currently in the original place. At the same time, their children will not be brought to the place the parents work. The children, then, will stay at home with not safety environment. It will cause a lot of problems. The Chinese situation is similar. However, there is a way to solve this problem. The government should allow the children that their parents work in urban area to go to this place their parent work to study and stay there. The exact way is the immigration department and different provinces work together to give some certificate for them to stay there, if applied to China, so that the workers who are parents can be working in the same place with their son or daughter. Then, the problem will be solved.

Secondly, environmentally, urbanisation will cause a lot of problems to affect ecology. When there are a lot of cities constructed by the not professionally designed way, the ecology will be affected and even the humankind will be in danger. For example, in India, some animals is freely going out and going inside the city. According to some reports of the government, the citizen in India, from years to years, are reported to be attacked by some dangerous animals like tigers etc. However, there is another solution. The government should send more security guard to protect the general public. It thus solve the problem.

In short, I point out two main problem of urbanisation, which is familial problem for social reason and ecological problem for environmental reason. As coincidence reason, I also point out government's actions as solutions. Not only security guard and issuing certificate but also strong means by the government is important. (371 words)

Comments

The author addressed all parts of the task, but she/he failed to present the readers with a clear understanding of the ideas. She/he presented information with some organisation but there could have been better and more effective cohesive devices to enable a clear progression of the ideas. The author tried to use some high-level vocabulary but was neither minimally adequate nor appropriate (can generate that some children) for the task; there were plenty of errors in singular/plural nouns and subject-verb agreement (main problems and its solution, the citizen in India, some animals is . . .).

Peer Evaluation Checklist

Assessment standard		Guiding question
Task achievement	Content requirements	Did the student state his/her standpoint or thesis statement of his/her essay clearly?
		Did the student present the position in a succinct manner?
		Was there enough scaffolding (e.g., background information) before the position statement is introduced?
		Did the student include an introduction and a conclusion?
		Did the student include at least two body paragraphs?
		Were the body paragraphs organised in a focused and logical manner?
	Content Development	Were the ideas relevant to the topic?
		Were the ideas relevant to the position?
		Were the ideas elaborated by giving examples and/or explanations?
		Are the supports provided effective and adequate?
		Is there a topic sentence at the beginning of a paragraph?
		Is the topic sentence focused and clear?
Coherence and cohesion	Cohesive devices	Were the cohesive devices used meaningfully and accurately?
		Was there a variety of cohesive devices used?
	Pronouns	Did the student use any pronouns?
		Were the pronouns used accurately?
	Synonyms	Did the student use any synonyms?
	Paragraphing	Did the student connect ideas by organising information thoughtfully and logically within a paragraph?
		Did the student connect ideas by organising information thoughtfully and logically between paragraphs?
Lexical Resource	Variety	Did the student enrich the vocabulary by using four major types of word formation: prefixes, suffixes, compounds, and conversion?
	Difficulty	Did the student use a set of more sophisticated and formal words than we would normally use in our daily life?
	Accuracy	Did the student use collocations accurately?
		Did the student spell the words accurately?
		Did the student use parts of speech accurately?
Grammatical Range & Accuracy	Structure Variety	Did the student use simple sentences and compound sentences?
		Did the student use complex sentences?
	Sentence Accuracy	Did the student make punctuation errors, such as sentence fragments, run-on sentence and comma splice?
		Did the student make other error types, such as faulty parallelism, misplaced modifier, and subject-verb disagreement?

13 Question Bank

Theme 1: Economy

T1-O1

You should spend about 20 minutes on this task.

The graph below gives information about the number of academic jobs in some humanities and social sciences disciplines between 2012 and 2014.

Summarise the information by selecting and reporting the main features, and make comparisons where relevant.

Write at least 150 words.

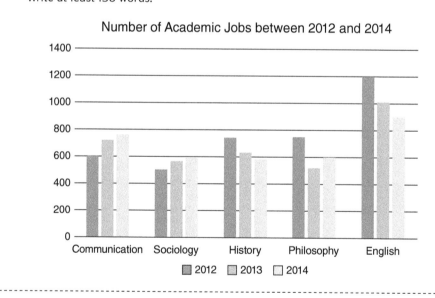

Number of Academic Jobs between 2012 and 2014

T1-02

You should spend about 20 minutes on this task.

The pie chart below gives information about the distribution of sales among products manufactured by an IT product company in 2012.

Summarise the information by selecting and reporting the main features, and make comparisons where relevant.

Write at least 150 words.

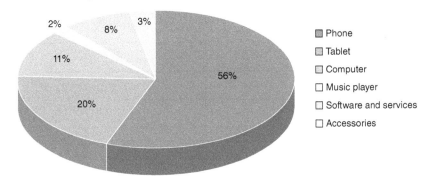

Sales of products of an IT product company

T1-03

You should spend about 20 minutes on this task.

The pie charts below give information about the distribution of sales of e-books in Country A in 2008 and 2018.

Summarise the information by selecting and reporting the main features, and make comparisons where relevant.

Write at least 150 words.

Online sales of e-books in Country A

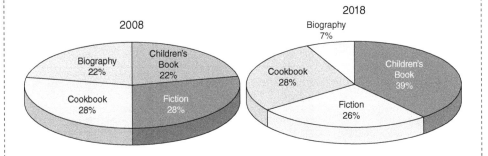

T1-04

You should spend about 20 minutes on this task.

The line graph below gives information about the average tax on salaries paid by residents of two cities between 2004 and 2018.

Summarise the information by selecting and reporting the main features, and make comparisons where relevant.

Write at least 150 words.

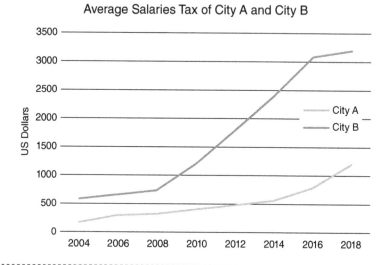

T1-05

You should spend about 20 minutes on this task.

The table below gives information about gross domestic product (GDP) rankings between 2013 and 2014.

Summarise the information by selecting and reporting the main features, and make comparisons where relevant.

Write at least 150 words.

	2013			2014	
Rank	Country	GDP (US$ billion)	Rank	Country	GDP (US$ billion)
1	United States	17,000	1	United States	17,500
2	China	9,000	2	China	10,100
3	Japan	4,900	3	Japan	4,800
4	Germany	3,600	4	Germany	3,700
5	France	2,700	5	United Kingdom	2,800
6	United Kingdom	2,500	6	France	2,750
7	Brazil	2,200	7	Brazil	2,150
8	Russia	2,100	8	Italy	2,100
9	Italy	2,000	9	India	1,950
10	India	1,900	10	Russia	1,930

Theme 2: Age and Gender

T1-06

You should spend about 20 minutes on this task.

The table below gives information about people's attitudes towards gender roles categorised by age.

Summarise the information by selecting and reporting the main features, and make comparisons where relevant.

Write at least 150 words.

A man's duty is to earn money while a woman's duty is to look after her family	18-25	26-35	36-45	46-55	56-65
Agree	5%	13%	10%	6%	12%
Neutral	13%	13%	19%	29%	21%
Disagree	82%	74%	71%	65%	67%

T1-07

You should spend about 20 minutes on this task.

The graph below gives information about the birth rate and death rate in China in every 1,000 people between 1950 and 2015.

Summarise the information by selecting and reporting the main features, and make comparisons where relevant.

Write at least 150 words.

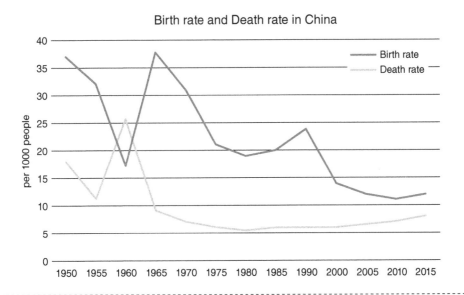

T1-08

You should spend about 20 minutes on this task.

The chart below shows information about suicide methods of middle-aged people in the US by gender in a year.

Summarise the information by selecting and reporting the main features, and make comparisons where relevant.

Write at least 150 words.

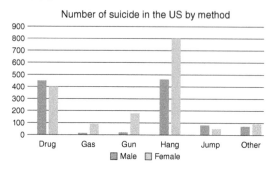

Theme 3: Manufacturing

T1-09

You should spend about 20 minutes on this task.

The diagram below gives information about the process of making detergent.

Summarise the information by selecting and reporting the main features, and make comparisons where relevant.

Write at least 150 words.

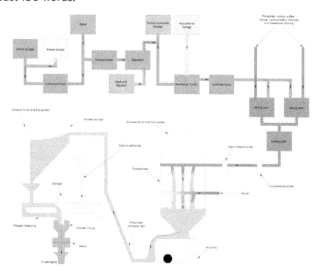

Source: https://commons.wikimedia.org/wiki/File:Soap_and_Detergent_manufacturing_process_03.png

T1-10

You should spend about 20 minutes on this task.

The diagram below gives information about the process of making water drinkable.

Summarise the information by selecting and reporting the main features, and make comparisons where relevant.

Write at least 150 words.

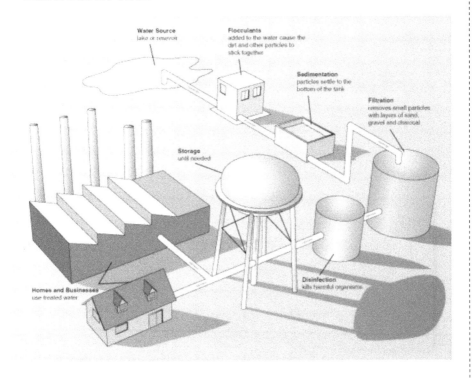

Source: https://commons.wikimedia.org/w/index.php?sort=relevance&search=water+process&title=Special:Search&profile=advanced&fulltext=1&advancedSearch-current=%7B%7D&ns0=1&ns6=1&ns12=1&ns14=1&ns100=1&ns106=1#/media/File:Illustration_of_a_typical_drinking_water_treatment_process.png

T1-11

You should spend about 20 minutes on this task.

The diagram below gives information about the process of manufacturing aircraft components.

Summarise the information by selecting and reporting the main features, and make comparisons where relevant.

Write at least 150 words.

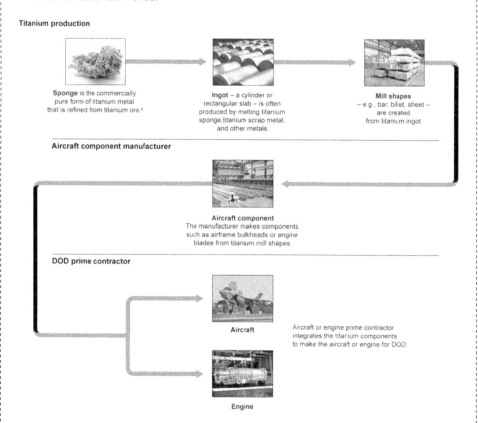

Titanium production

Sponge is the commercially pure form of titanium metal that is refined from titanium ore.ª

Ingot – a cylinder or rectangular slab – is often produced by melting titanium sponge, titanium scrap metal, and other metals.

Mill shapes – e.g., bar, billet, sheet – are created from titanium ingot.

Aircraft component manufacturer

Aircraft component
The manufacturer makes components such as airframe bulkheads or engine blades from titanium mill shapes

DOD prime contractor

Aircraft

Aircraft or engine prime contractor integrates the titanium components to make the aircraft or engine for DOD.

Engine

Source: https://upload.wikimedia.org/wikipedia/commons/a/a7/Figure_2-_DOD_ Titanium_Production_and_Aircraft_Component_Manufacturing_Processes_ %289198094801%29_%282%29.jpg

Theme 4: Education

T1-12

You should spend about 20 minutes on this task.

The bar chart below gives information about different undergraduate courses chosen at three universities in Auckland by gender in 2017.

Summarise the information by selecting and reporting the main features, and make comparisons where relevant.

Write at least 150 words.

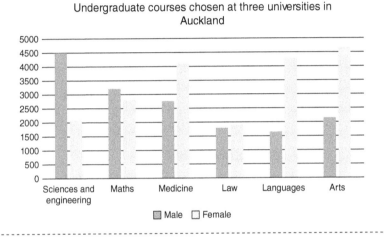

T1-13

You should spend about 20 minutes on this task.

The line graph below gives information about the cumulative median lifetime income by education levels.

Summarise the information by selecting and reporting the main features, and make comparisons where relevant.

Write at least 150 words.

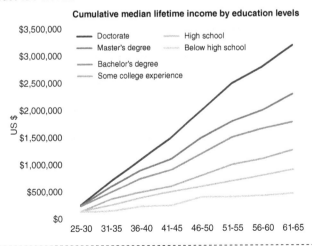

T1-14

You should spend about 20 minutes on this task.

The charts below give information about the survey results about people's views towards studying languages. The first chart shows the reasons for studying an additional language. The second pie chart displays the preferred ways of learning a new language.

Summarise the information by selecting and reporting the main features, and make comparisons where relevant.

Write at least 150 words.

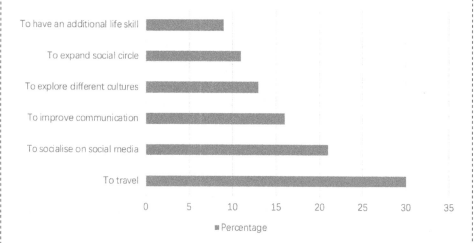

Reasons for learning an additional language

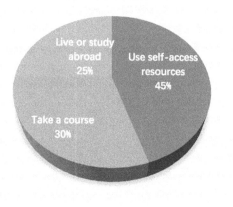

Preferred ways to learn an additional language

Theme 5: Science and Technology

T1-15

You should spend about 20 minutes on this task.

The chart below gives information about the respective sales volume of two kinds of printers from 2006 to 2016.

Summarise the information by selecting and reporting the main features, and make comparisons where relevant.

Write at least 150 words.

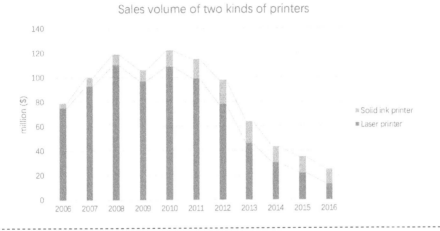

T1-16

You should spend about 20 minutes on this task.

The chart below shows information about a report made by a European newspaper about the internet users in 2010 and the expected numbers in 2025 in six European countries.

Summarise the information by selecting and reporting the main features, and make comparisons where relevant.

Write at least 150 words.

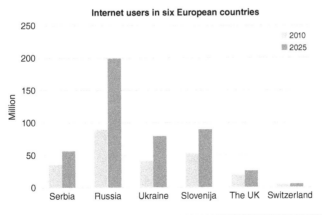

Theme 6: City Development

T1-17

You should spend about 20 minutes on this task.

The diagrams below show floor plans for the first floor of two houses.

Summarise the information by selecting and reporting the main features, and make comparisons where relevant.

Write at least 150 words.

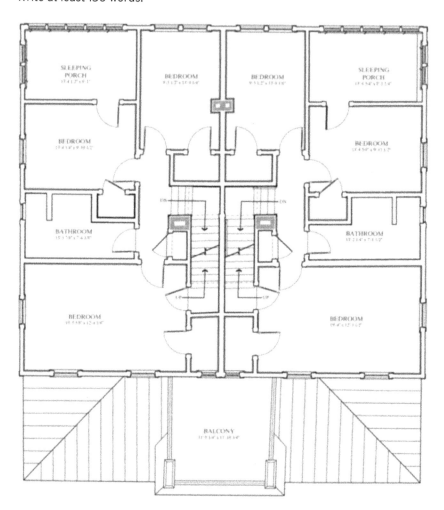

Source: https://commons.wikimedia.org/wiki/File:South_Elevation,_South_Wall_Elevation,_and_Second_Floor_Plan_-_National_Home_for_Disabled_Volunteer_Soldiers,_Mountain_Branch,_Duplex_Quarters,_Lamont_and_Veterans_Way,_HABS_TN-254-N_(sheet_3_of_8).tif

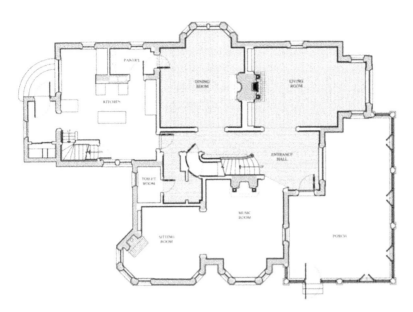

Source: https://commons.wikimedia.org/wiki/File:First_Floor_Plan_-_National_Home_for_Disabled_Volunteer_Soldiers,_Northwestern_Branch,_Governor%27s_Residence,_5000_West_National_Avenue,_Milwaukee,_Milwaukee_County,_WI_HABS_WI-360-C_(sheet_3_of_16).tif

T1-18

You should spend about 20 minutes on this task.

The line graph below shows information about the urbanisation rate of four countries from 1950 to 2010 and with forecasts for the year 2020 and the year 2030.

Summarise the information by selecting and reporting the main features, and make comparisons where relevant.

Write at least 150 words.

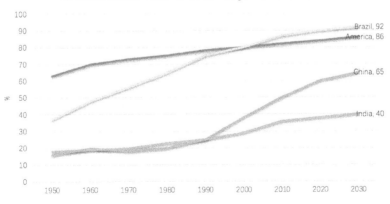

Urbanization rate of four major countries

Theme 7: Environment

T1-19

You should spend about 20 minutes on this task.

The pie charts below display information about the CO_2 emissions in London. The first pie chart shows the CO_2 emissions by different sectors. The second pie chart presents the consumption of different transportation fuels.

Summarise the information by selecting and reporting the main features, and make comparisons where relevant.

Write at least 150 words.

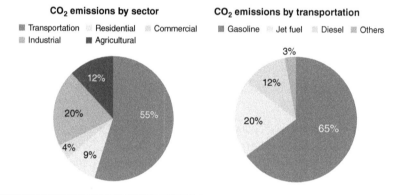

T1-20

You should spend about 20 minutes on this task.

The chart below shows information about the distribution and number of parks in different types of land use from 2015 to 2018.

Summarise the information by selecting and reporting the main features, and make comparisons where relevant.

Write at least 150 words.

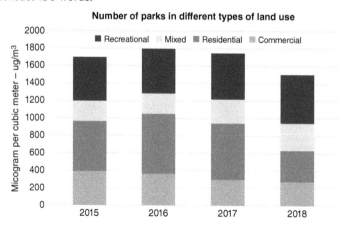

Theme 8: Tourism

T1-21

You should spend about 20 minutes on this task.

The graph below shows information about tourist growth in the last 60 years and the estimates.

Summarise the information by selecting and reporting the main features, and make comparisons where relevant.

Write at least 150 words.

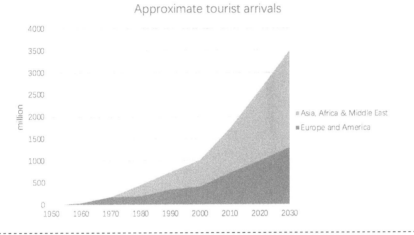

T1-22

You should spend about 20 minutes on this task.

The chart below shows information about the spending of five countries' citizens abroad.

Summarise the information by selecting and reporting the main features, and make comparisons where relevant.

Write at least 150 words.

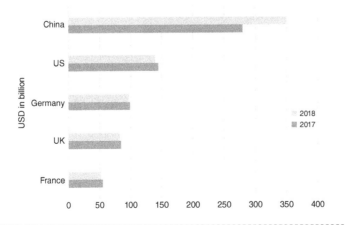

Theme 9: Work

T1-23

You should spend about 20 minutes on this task.

The pie charts below show information about preferred work benefits of employees in Asian and Western societies.

Summarise the information by selecting and reporting the main features, and make comparisons where relevant.

Write at least 150 words.

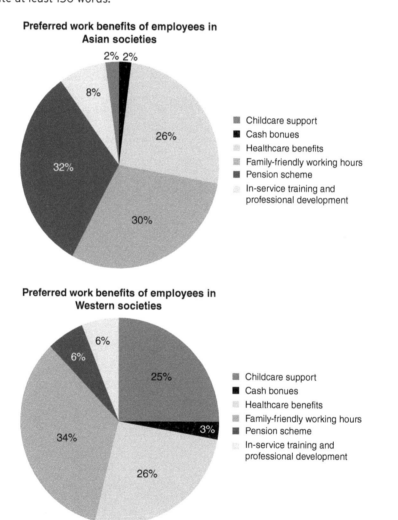

T1-24

You should spend about 20 minutes on this task.

The bar chart below shows the percentages of various types of workplace harassment faced by male and female employees.

Summarise the information by selecting and reporting the main features, and make comparisons where relevant.

Write at least 150 words.

Types of workplace harassment

Theme 10: Socio-cultural Issues

T1-25

You should spend about 20 minutes on this task.

The chart below shows information about the various reasons that people choose not to report spousal violence to the police by gender in a 2016 survey.

Summarise the information by selecting and reporting the main features, and make comparisons where relevant.

Write at least 150 words.

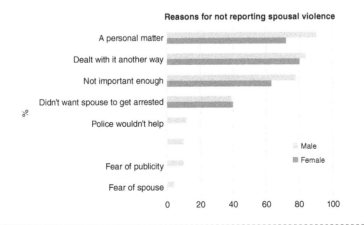

Reasons for not reporting spousal violence

T1-26

You should spend about 20 minutes on this task.

The charts below show information about different types of social welfare benefits between 1995 and 2015.

Summarise the information by selecting and reporting the main features, and make comparisons where relevant.

Write at least 150 words.

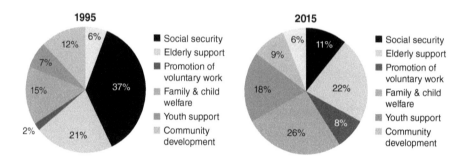

Theme 11: Resources

T1-27

You should spend about 20 minutes on this task.

The line graph below shows information about the number of social problem cases from 2005 to 2012 in a metropolis.

Summarise the information by selecting and reporting the main features, and make comparisons where relevant.

Write at least 150 words.

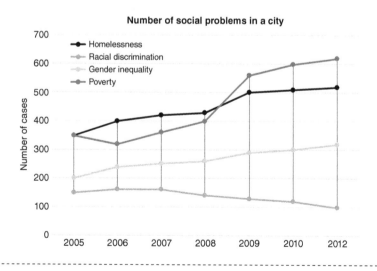

T1-28

You should spend about 20 minutes on this task.

The charts below show information about the energy consumption in the UK in 2017. The first pie chart displays the energy sources. The second pie chart presents different types of renewable energy.

Summarise the information by selecting and reporting the main features, and make comparisons where relevant.

Write at least 150 words.

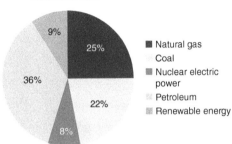

UK energy consumption by source in 2017

- Natural gas
- Coal
- Nuclear electric power
- Petroleum
- Renewable energy

25%, 22%, 8%, 36%, 9%

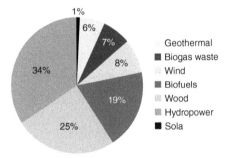

Types of renewable energy

- Geothermal
- Biogas waste
- Wind
- Biofuels
- Wood
- Hydropower
- Sola

1%, 6%, 7%, 8%, 19%, 25%, 34%

Theme 12: Population

T1-29

You should spend about 20 minutes on this task.

The bar chart below shows information about the population distribution in Brazil from 1990 to 2035.

Summarise the information by selecting and reporting the main features, and make comparisons where relevant.

Write at least 150 words.

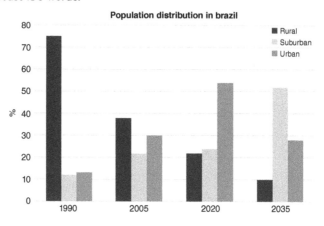

T1-30

You should spend about 20 minutes on this task.

The charts below show information about the estimates of population change in different continents from 1950 to 2050.

Summarise the information by selecting and reporting the main features, and make comparisons where relevant.

Write at least 150 words.

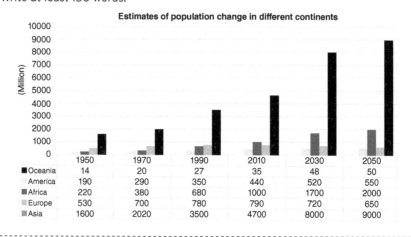

Estimates of population change in different continents

	1950	1970	1990	2010	2030	2050
Oceania	14	20	27	35	48	50
America	190	290	350	440	520	550
Africa	220	380	680	1000	1700	2000
Europe	530	700	780	790	720	650
Asia	1600	2020	3500	4700	8000	9000

Theme 13: Traffic

T1-31

You should spend about 20 minutes on this task.

The charts below give information about road accidents statistics in Mexico in 2017. The first pie chart shows the percentage of traffic accidents of diverse age groups. The second chart displays death by road user category.

Summarise the information by selecting and reporting the main features, and make comparisons where relevant.

Write at least 150 words.

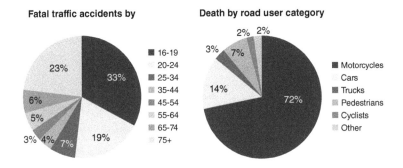

T1-32

You should spend about 20 minutes on this task.

The charts below show information about the number of car parks in four cities in 1970, 1990, and 2010.

Summarise the information by selecting and reporting the main features, and make comparisons where relevant.

Write at least 150 words.

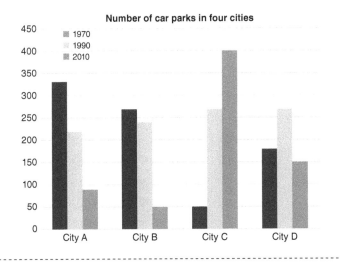

Theme 14: Health

T1-33

You should spend about 20 minutes on this task.

The chart below shows information about the level of public satisfaction with the healthcare system of five countries between 2005 and 2020.

Summarise the information by selecting and reporting the main features, and make comparisons where relevant.

Write at least 150 words.

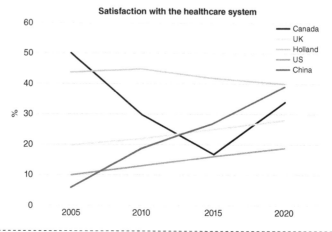

T1-34

You should spend about 20 minutes on this task.

The chart below shows information about a survey result of the most important causes of depression by age in France in 2016.

Summarise the information by selecting and reporting the main features, and make comparisons where relevant.

Write at least 150 words.

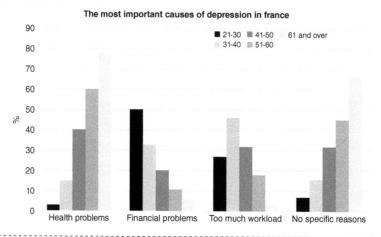

Theme 15: Language

T1-35

You should spend about 20 minutes on this task.

The table below gives information about languages which can be learned through participating in online courses.

Summarise the information by selecting and reporting the main features, and make comparisons where relevant.

Write at least 150 words.

Language	Number of courses on Online Platform A	Number of courses on Online Platform B	Total number of courses
English	92	21	113
Chinese	34	61	95
French	37	12	49
Italian	35	7	42
Korean	21	2	23
French	20	1	21

T1-36

You should spend about 20 minutes on this task.

The chart below shows information about a survey result of the average SAT scores of four kinds of language speakers in 2017.

Summarise the information by selecting and reporting the main features, and make comparisons where relevant.

Write at least 150 words.

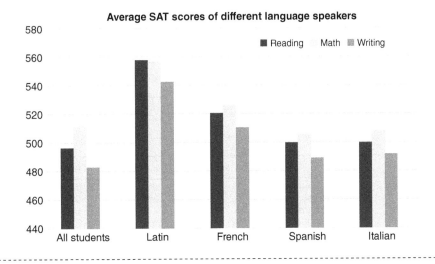

Theme 16: Climate

T1-37

You should spend about 20 minutes on this task.

The line graph below shows information about the personal carbon footprint resulting from three daily activities in 2015 in an Asian country.

Summarise the information by selecting and reporting the main features, and make comparisons where relevant.

Write at least 150 words.

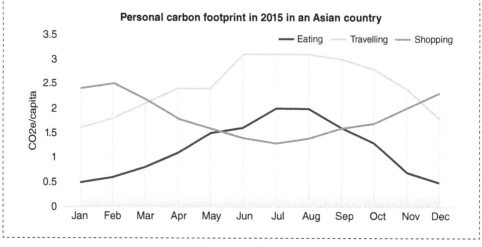

Personal carbon footprint in 2015 in an Asian country

Theme 17: Public's Opinion

T1-38

You should spend about 20 minutes on this task.

The table below shows information about both female and male members' opinions towards the activity variety, facilities, and service quality of a club in a residential area.

Summarise the information by selecting and reporting the main features, and make comparisons where relevant.

Write at least 150 words.

		Very satisfied	Satisfied	Not satisfied
Activity variety	Female members	32%	36%	32%
	Male members	57%	38%	5%
Facilities	Female members	65%	22%	13%
	Male members	64%	26%	10%
Service quality	Female members	71%	24%	5%
	Male members	44%	20%	36%

Theme 18: Sales

T1-39

You should spend about 20 minutes on this task.

The bar chart below shows information about the proportion of sales of three types of electronic products in a store between 2000 and 2025.

Summarise the information by selecting and reporting the main features, and make comparisons where relevant.

Write at least 150 words.

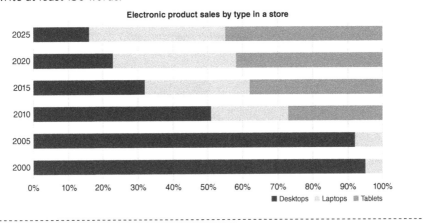

Theme 19: Crime

T1-40

You should spend about 20 minutes on this task.

The chart below displays information about top offences committed by different age groups in 2017.

Summarise the information by selecting and reporting the main features, and make comparisons where relevant.

Write at least 150 words.

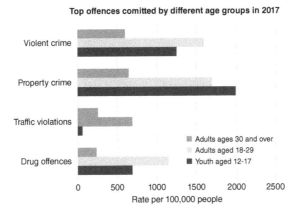

Theme 20: Leisure

T1-41

You should spend about 20 minutes on this task.

The bar chart below shows information about the percentage of preferred video game consoles in 2018.

Summarise the information by selecting and reporting the main features, and make comparisons where relevant.

Write at least 150 words.

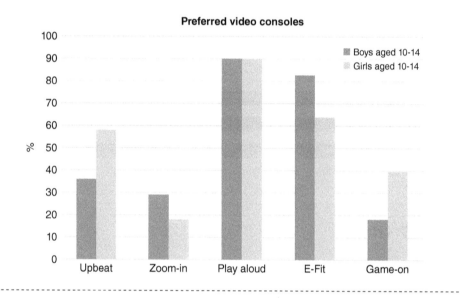

Theme 21: Media

T1-42

You should spend about 20 minutes on this task.

The chart below shows information about magazines read by different age groups in 2014.

Summarise the information by selecting and reporting the main features, and make comparisons where relevant.

Write at least 150 words.

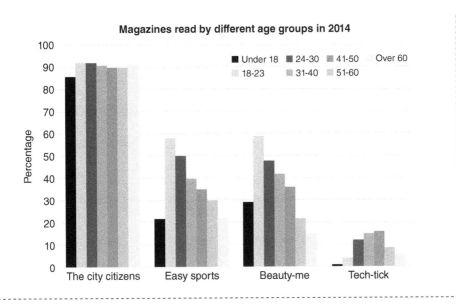

Magazines read by different age groups in 2014

Theme 22: Agriculture

T1-43

You should spend about 20 minutes on this task.

The chart below shows information about the crop yields of three nations in 2016.

Summarise the information by selecting and reporting the main features, and make comparisons where relevant.

Write at least 150 words.

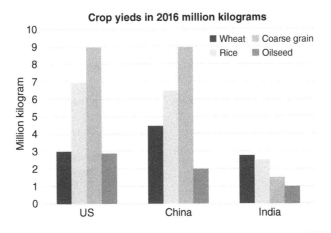

Crop yieds in 2016 million kilograms

Theme 23: Communication

T1-44

You should spend about 20 minutes on this task.

The line graph below shows information about the availability of different types of jobs related to media relations from 2010 to 2015.

Summarise the information by selecting and reporting the main features, and make comparisons where relevant.

Write at least 150 words.

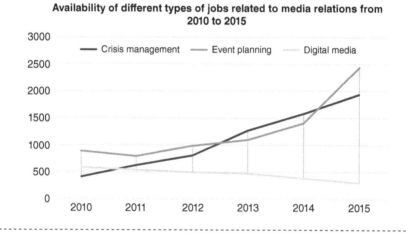

Availability of different types of jobs related to media relations from 2010 to 2015

Theme 24: Food

T1-45

You should spend about 20 minutes on this task.

The charts below show information about the average consumption of food in Korea and Germany in 2016.

Summarise the information by selecting and reporting the main features, and make comparisons where relevant.

Write at least 150 words.

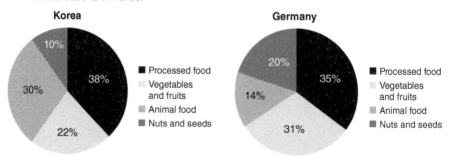

Theme 25: Social Responsibility

T1-46

You should spend about 20 minutes on this task.

The line graph below shows information about the demand, transplant, and donation of organs from 1990 to 2015.

Summarise the information by selecting and reporting the main features, and make comparisons where relevant.

Write at least 150 words.

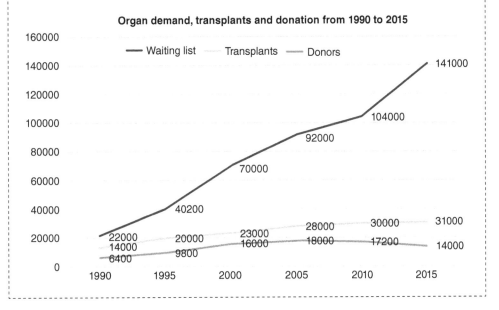

Organ demand, transplants and donation from 1990 to 2015

Theme 26: Airline Business

T1-47

You should spend about 20 minutes on this task.

The chart below shows information about the complaints made by customers about Airline A and Airline B in March 2018.

Summarise the information by selecting and reporting the main features, and make comparisons where relevant.

Write at least 150 words.

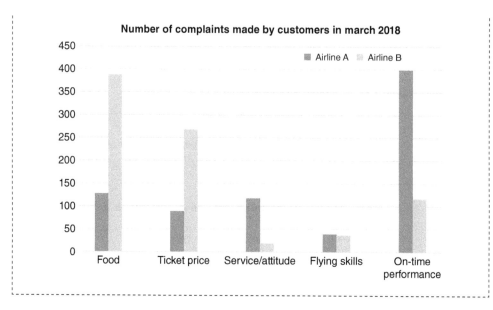

Theme 27: Animals

T1-48

You should spend about 20 minutes on this task.

The chart below shows information about the percentage of endangered animal species by taxonomy in 2014.

Summarise the information by selecting and reporting the main features, and make comparisons where relevant.

Write at least 150 words.

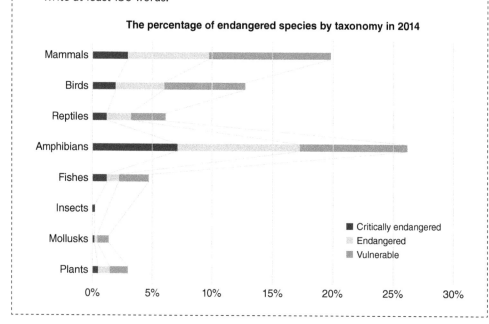

Theme 28: Art

T1-49

You should spend about 20 minutes on this task.

The charts below show information about music preference of teenagers and the middle-aged, respectively.

Summarise the information by selecting and reporting the main features, and make comparisons where relevant.

Write at least 150 words.

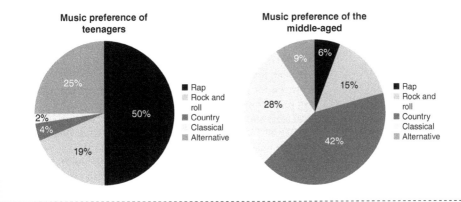

Theme 29: Location

T1-50

You should spend about 20 minutes on this task.

The charts below show information about the regional distribution of Christians from 1915 to 2015.

Summarise the information by selecting and reporting the main features, and make comparisons where relevant.

Write at least 150 words.

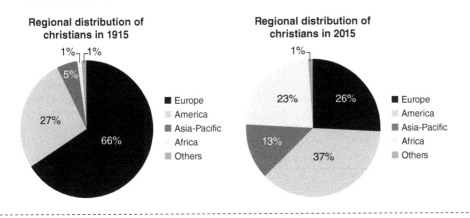

Theme 1: Education

	Question type	*Question*
T2-01	Opinions	You should spend about 40 minutes on this task. Write about the following topic:
		Nowadays, having a higher degree is regarded as a prerequisite for getting a better paid job.
		To what extent do you agree or disagree with this opinion?
		Give reasons for your answer and include any relevant examples from your own knowledge or experience.
		Write at least 250 words.
T2-02	Discuss views	You should spend about 40 minutes on this task. Write about the following topic:
		Advocates of high-stakes standardised tests believe that they provide an objective description of students' abilities; on the contrary, some teachers expressly underscore the many problems that these tests bring to the quality of their teaching.
		Discuss both these views and give your opinion.
		Give reasons for your answer and include any relevant examples from your own knowledge or experience.
		Write at least 250 words.
T2-03	Two-part questions	You should spend about 40 minutes on this task. Write about the following topic:
		Some parents believe in educating their children themselves and homeschool their children. What are the advantages of homeschooling? Should homeschooling become a regular option for parents?
		Give reasons for your answer and include any relevant examples from your own knowledge or experience.
		Write at least 250 words.
T2-04	Advantages and disadvantages	You should spend about 40 minutes on this task. Write about the following topic:
		Many university students are required to enroll in a number of General Education courses. These courses are usually related to the social, cultural, psychological, and spiritual lives of young people.
		What are the advantages of general education courses to university students?
		Give reasons for your answer and include any relevant examples from your own knowledge or experience.
		Write at least 250 words.
T2-05	Problems and solutions	You should spend about 40 minutes on this task. Write about the following topic:
		Distance education enables students to study at their own pace. Nevertheless, it also creates problems including high withdrawal rate and lack of interaction between teachers and students.
		Explain some possible reasons for these problems and suggest some solutions.
		Give reasons for your answer and include any relevant examples from your own knowledge or experience.
		Write at least 250 words.

Theme 2: Work

	Question type	Question
T2-06	Opinions	You should spend about 40 minutes on this task. Write about the following topic: Family friendly measures (e.g., flexible working hours) should be adopted by companies to ensure the work-life balance of their employees. To what extent do you agree or disagree with this opinion? Give reasons for your answer and include any relevant examples from your own knowledge or experience. Write at least 250 words.
T2-07	Discuss views	You should spend about 40 minutes on this task. Write about the following topic: It is not uncommon nowadays for people to work overseas. Working overseas allows people to experience different cultures and extend their social and professional connections. However, some find it hard to adapt due to nostalgia and acculturation. Discuss both these views and give your opinion. Give reasons for your answer and include any relevant examples from your own knowledge or experience. Write at least 250 words.
T2-08	Two-part questions	You should spend about 40 minutes on this task. Write about the following topic: The number of slash workers (people with multiple careers) is on the rise. It is less likely for young people these days to settle on one job for a long time. Why would young people want to be slash workers? What are the social consequences of having more slash workers? Give reasons for your answer and include any relevant examples from your own knowledge or experience. Write at least 250 words.
T2-09	Advantages and disadvantages	You should spend about 40 minutes on this task. Write about the following topic: Due to the rapid technological development, new career options have emerged such as online store owners, and vloggers. People become less willing to work in a workplace. Do you think the advantages of having a 'virtual' career outweigh its disadvantages? Give reasons for your answer and include any relevant examples from your own knowledge or experience. Write at least 250 words.
T2-10	Problems and solutions	You should spend about 40 minutes on this task. Write about the following topic: Given the greater longevity of people these days, some argue that people should retire at a later stage. What are some of the problems if people's retirement is delayed? Give reasons for your answer and include any relevant examples from your own knowledge or experience. Write at least 250 words.

Theme 3: Food and Health

	Question type	Question
T2-11	Opinions	You should spend about 40 minutes on this task. Write about the following topic:
		Nowadays many workers are suffering from joint pains (e.g., neck pain), which they ascribe to their sedentary office jobs.
		To what extent do you agree or disagree with this opinion?
		Give reasons for your answer and include any relevant examples from your own knowledge or experience.
		Write at least 250 words.
T2-12	Discuss views	You should spend about 40 minutes on this task. Write about the following topic:
		It is popular nowadays for people to order takeaway food (e.g., lunch) from their workplace because they are too busy to prepare meals. However, there are still many people who bring home-made food to eat in their workplace because they think DIY food is healthier.
		Discuss both these views.
		Give reasons for your answer and include any relevant examples from your own knowledge or experience.
		Write at least 250 words.
T2-13	Advantages and disadvantages	You should spend about 40 minutes on this task. Write about the following topic:
		In some countries, healthcare expenditure is covered by the government, while in other countries, the cost is undertaken by both the public and the government. Do you think the advantages of 'sharing the cost' outweigh the disadvantages?
		Give reasons for your answer and include any relevant examples from your own knowledge or experience.
		Write at least 250 words.
T2-14	Problems and solutions	You should spend about 40 minutes on this task. Write about the following topic:
		Despite the enhancement of medical care, modern people are still tortured by various physical and psychological problems. What are some of the causes of the above phenomena? What can be done to improve people's health?
		Give reasons for your answer and include any relevant examples from your own knowledge or experience.
		Write at least 250 words.

Theme 4: Socio-cultural and Global Issues

	Question type	Question
T2-15	Opinions	You should spend about 40 minutes on this task. Write about the following topic:
		Investors are more important than teachers in that they usually make more money.
		To what extent do you agree or disagree with this opinion?
		Give reasons for your answer and include any relevant examples from your own knowledge or experience.
		Write at least 250 words.
T2-16	Discuss views	You should spend about 40 minutes on this task. Write about the following topic:
		Some people argue that heredity exerts a greater influence on an individual's development than a person's later experiences.
		Discuss the view and give your opinion.
		Give reasons for your answer and include any relevant examples from your own knowledge or experience.
		Write at least 250 words.
T2-17	Two-part questions	You should spend about 40 minutes on this task. Write about the following topic:
		Some countries donate large sums of money to help other countries in need, while some citizens of these countries are still starving. Why would these countries take the above action? What can be done to help the starving people?
		Give reasons for your answer and include any relevant examples from your own knowledge or experience.
		Write at least 250 words.
T2-18	Advantages and disadvantages	You should spend about 40 minutes on this task. Write about the following topic:
		It is important for travelers to develop adequate understanding of the culture of the destination country. What are some of the advantages of understanding the culture beforehand?
		Give reasons for your answer and include any relevant examples from your own knowledge or experience.
		Write at least 250 words.

Theme 5: Age, Generation and Gender

	Question type	Question
T2-19	Problems and solutions	You should spend about 40 minutes on this task. Write about the following topic:
		It seems that people over forty are difficult to find a satisfactory job. What are the causes? Are there any possible solutions to this problem?
		Give reasons for your answer and include any relevant examples from your own knowledge or experience.
		Write at least 250 words.

T2-20	Discuss views	You should spend about 40 minutes on this task. Write about the following topic:
		When it comes to children's leisure activities, they prefer to stay indoors for computer games rather than go outside for sports. Discuss the view and give your opinion.
		Give reasons for your answer and include any relevant examples from your own knowledge or experience.
		Write at least 250 words.
T2-21	Two-part questions	You should spend about 40 minutes on this task. Write about the following topic:
		Women's status has improved dramatically both in the society and in the family as a result of the development of the society. However, they are still faced with inequalities. What are some of the inequalities? What measures should be adopted to solve the problems?
		Give reasons for your answer and include any relevant examples from your own knowledge or experience.
		Write at least 250 words.

Theme 6: Science, Technology and Innovation

	Question type	Question
T2-22	Opinions	You should spend about 40 minutes on this task. Write about the following topic:
		With the introduction of computers and other electronic devices, people tend to learn by accessing online resources (e.g., e-books, blogs). Therefore, books will not be a necessity in the near future.
		To what extent do you agree or disagree with this opinion?
		Give reasons for your answer and include any relevant examples from your own knowledge or experience.
		Write at least 250 words.
T2-23	Discuss views	You should spend about 40 minutes on this task. Write about the following topic:
		Some people think that the development of science and technology has led to a decrease in privacy (e.g., being monitored of speeches and actions). However, others regard the development of science and technology as positive because they feel more secure.
		Discuss both views and give your opinion.
		Give reasons for your answer and include any relevant examples from your own knowledge or experience.
		Write at least 250 words.
T2-24	Two-part questions	You should spend about 40 minutes on this task. Write about the following topic:
		Nowadays, doing sports is becoming more convenient. In addition to going to sports facilities, people can do virtual sports at home using their game consoles. What are the benefits of doing virtual sports? Will virtual sports replace physical sports one day?
		Give reasons for your answer and include any relevant examples from your own knowledge or experience.
		Write at least 250 words.

Theme 7: Media and Communication

	Question type	Question
T2-25	Opinions	You should spend about 40 minutes on this task. Write about the following topic: Workers who are employed in the area of mass media (e.g., TV programmes and newspaper) are obliged to report the truth as the content they disseminate will largely affect audiences' views. To what extent do you agree or disagree with this opinion? Give reasons for your answer and include any relevant examples from your own knowledge or experience. Write at least 250 words.
T2-26	Discuss views	You should spend about 40 minutes on this task. Write about the following topic: Some customers praise that advertisements introduce to them useful information about certain products. Others, however, reckon that advertisements encourage them to spend money buying products they do not need. Discuss both views and give your opinion. Give reasons for your answer and include any relevant examples from your own knowledge or experience. Write at least 250 words.

Theme 8: Government, Politics and Diplomacy

	Question type	Question
T2-27	Opinions	You should spend about 40 minutes on this task. Write about the following topic: Governments across countries should seek more opportunities to hold more big events (e.g., sports competitions) so as to increase mutual understanding and decrease political tensions. To what extent do you agree or disagree with this opinion? Give reasons for your answer and include any relevant examples from your own knowledge or experience. Write at least 250 words.
T2-28	Discuss views	You should spend about 40 minutes on this task. Write about the following topic: Governments concern more about creating economic benefits for people while they overlook the actions they should take to control pollution resulting from economic development. Discuss the above view and give your opinion. Give reasons for your answer and include any relevant examples from your own knowledge or experience. Write at least 250 words.

Theme 9: Environment

	Question type	Question
T2-29	Two-part questions	You should spend about 40 minutes on this task. Write about the following topic:
		An increasing number of domestic appliances (e.g., air purifiers and water purifiers) are on the market to tackle water pollution and air pollution. Why is this the case? Is this a positive indicator of the development of human beings?
		Give reasons for your answer and include any relevant examples from your own knowledge or experience.
		Write at least 250 words.
T2-30	Advantages and disadvantages	You should spend about 40 minutes on this task. Write about the following topic:
		Some people favor the use of private cars as they bring people much convenience. However, some people think that private cars cause air pollution which is harmful to the environment. Do the advantages of using private cars outweigh the disadvantages?
		Give reasons for your answer and include any relevant examples from your own knowledge or experience.
		Write at least 250 words.

Theme 10: Lifestyle

	Question type	Question
T2-31	Two-part questions	You should spend about 40 minutes on this task. Write about the following topic:
		Some people live in one place all their lives. However, others migrate from cities to cities (and/or countries to countries). Why do some people prefer a sedentary life while others do not? Which kind of lifestyle is better?
		Give reasons for your answer and include any relevant examples from your own knowledge or experience.
		Write at least 250 words.
T2-32	Discuss views	You should spend about 40 minutes on this task. Write about the following topic:
		Some people prefer to choose online shopping because things are cheaper and they will not be limited by time and space. Others, however, still follow the practice of purchasing in brick-and-mortar stores because they think products in the physical stores are more reliable.
		Discuss both views and give your opinion.
		Give reasons for your answer and include any relevant examples from your own knowledge or experience.
		Write at least 250 words.

Theme 11: Traffic

	Question type	Question
T2-33	Opinions	You should spend about 40 minutes on this task. Write about the following topic: Electric cars are becoming more popular nowadays because they are more environmentally friendly. Moreover, electric cars have become an emblem for tech-savvy people. To what extent do you agree or disagree with this opinion? Give reasons for your answer and include any relevant examples from your own knowledge or experience. Write at least 250 words.
T2-34	Two-part questions	You should spend about 40 minutes on this task. Write about the following topic: It seems that traffic congestion is becoming more serious than ever. Some people think that the problem can be solved by raising the petrol price to discourage people from using private cars. Others believe that the government should provide more public transportation to ease the situation. Are the above suggestions feasible in solving traffic jam? What are other possible measures to solve the problem? Give reasons for your answer and include any relevant examples from your own knowledge or experience. Write at least 250 words.

Theme 12: Economy, Money and Trade

	Question type	Question
T2-35	Opinions	You should spend about 40 minutes on this task. Write about the following topic: People who cannot manage their money live a worse life than those who can. To what extent do you agree or disagree with this opinion? Give reasons for your answer and include any relevant examples from your own knowledge or experience. Write at least 250 words.
T2-36	Advantages and disadvantages	You should spend about 40 minutes on this task. Write about the following topic: Some people support the idea that the government should impose high taxes on its citizens to support the construction of public amenities. However, the rest of the group argue that individuals should be given the right to decide how they use their money. Therefore, a minimum amount of tax should be imposed. Discuss both these views and give your opinion. Give reasons for your answer and include any relevant examples from your own knowledge or experience. Write at least 250 words.

Theme 13: Crime, Punishment and Law

	Question type	Question
T2-37	Advantages and disadvantages	You should spend about 40 minutes on this task. Write about the following topic: The public believe that death penalty of severe crimes (e.g., murder) should be strictly enforced to ensure a secure society. Do the advantages of death penalty outweigh its disadvantages? Give reasons for your answer and include any relevant examples from your own knowledge or experience. Write at least 250 words.
T2-38	Opinions	You should spend about 40 minutes on this task. Write about the following topic: These days people have gained an increasing awareness of the downsides of smoking. However, there are still a substantial number of smokers who are addicted to tobacco. Therefore, some people think that smoking should be banned and the government should punish those who smoke. To what extent do you agree or disagree with this opinion? Give reasons for your answer and include any relevant examples from your own knowledge or experience. Write at least 250 words.

Theme 14: Leisure, Sports and Hobbies

	Question type	Question
T2-39	Opinions	You should spend about 40 minutes on this task. Write about the following topic: People who do not have leisure activities apart from work are living a dull and less meaningful life. To what extent do you agree or disagree with this opinion? Give reasons for your answer and include any relevant examples from your own knowledge or experience. Write at least 250 words.
T2-40	Two-part questions	You should spend about 40 minutes on this task. Write about the following topic: In some schools, subjects such as Physical Education and Music are occasionally replaced with examination subjects to better prepare students for examinations. Do you think there is a need to sacrifice these classes for better exam results? What is the importance of art-related and Physical Education classes? Give reasons for your answer and include any relevant examples from your own knowledge or experience. Write at least 250 words.

Theme 15: Language

	Question type	Question
T2-41	Opinions	You should spend about 40 minutes on this task. Write about the following topic: Those who learn a foreign language through attending online courses usually perform less well than those who learn the language in face-to-face settings. To what extent do you agree or disagree with this opinion? Give reasons for your answer and include any relevant examples from your own knowledge or experience. Write at least 250 words.
T2-42	Discuss views	You should spend about 40 minutes on this task. Write about the following topic: Some people advocate that a lingua franca (e.g., English) can facilitate communication among different nations and there is no need to protect the rare languages in the world. However, others believe that rare languages are a very important component of human culture. Therefore, we have the responsibility to ensure that these languages will not die out. Discuss both these views and give your opinion. Give reasons for your answer and include any relevant examples from your own knowledge or experience. Write at least 250 words.

Theme 16: Travelling and Tourism

	Question type	Question
T2-43	Advantages and disadvantages	You should spend about 40 minutes on this task. Write about the following topic: The development of tourism industry has created benefits for many countries (e.g., generate additional revenue). However, expanding tourism industry can also be detrimental, for example, to a country's environment. Do the advantages of developing tourism industry outweigh the disadvantages? Give reasons for your answer and include any relevant examples from your own knowledge or experience. Write at least 250 words.
T2-44	Discuss views	You should spend about 40 minutes on this task. Write about the following topic: Some people think that the purpose of travelling is to explore new cultures and customs whilst others prefer travelling to be a more materialistic experience including shopping. Discuss both these views and give your own opinion. Give reasons for your answer and include any relevant examples from your own knowledge or experience. Write at least 250 words.

Theme 17: Population

	Question type	Question
T2-45	Problems and solutions	You should spend about 40 minutes on this task. Write about the following topic: Nowadays an increasing number of people are moving from rural areas to urban areas. This urbanisation process has brought about numerous problems. What are some of the problems caused? And what are some possible solutions? Give reasons for your answer and include any relevant examples from your own knowledge or experience. Write at least 250 words.

Theme 18: Art and museum

	Question type	Question
T2-46	Discuss views	You should spend about 40 minutes on this task. Write about the following topic: Admission to museums should be charged to encourage the public to better appreciate and cherish the value and beauty of the exhibitions in the museums. However, free admission to museums can provide more chances for the public to know more about the world. Discuss both these views and give your own opinion. Give reasons for your answer and include any relevant examples from your own knowledge or experience. Write at least 250 words.

Theme 19: City development

	Question type	Question
T2-47	Problems and solutions	You should spend about 40 minutes on this task. Write about the following topic: Some people argue that skyscrapers are a symbol of city development. However, others think that skyscrapers can also cause problems. What are some of the problems brought by skyscrapers? What can we do to avoid such problems? Give reasons for your answer and include any relevant examples from your own knowledge or experience. Write at least 250 words.

Theme 20: Climate

	Question type	Question
T2-48	Two-part questions	You should spend about 40 minutes on this task. Write about the following topic: Climate change is damaging our earth in many ways. What are some of the possible reasons of climate change? What are the consequences of climate change? Give reasons for your answer and include any relevant examples from your own knowledge or experience. Write at least 250 words.

Theme 21: Ethics

	Question type	Question
T2-49	Advantages and disadvantages	You should spend about 40 minutes on this task. Write about the following topic: Some students maintain close relationships with their teachers because they regard their teachers as friends. Do the advantages of a close student-teacher relationship outweigh the disadvantages? Give reasons for your answer and include any relevant examples from your own knowledge or experience. Write at least 250 words.

Theme 22: Animals

	Question type	Question
T2-50	Two-part questions	You should spend about 40 minutes on this task. Write about the following topic: Some people choose to raise a dog/cat as their companion. What are some of the advantages of being friends with a dog/cat? What are some of the ways which humans and pets can co-exist harmoniously? Give reasons for your answer and include any relevant examples from your own knowledge or experience. Write at least 250 words.

Part II

Answers to Chapter 3

Task 1: Task Achievement

Check Your Understanding

Read the following statements and determine if they are true or false.

1 I don't have to provide an overview at the beginning of the essay. [True/**False**]
2 I should report both the similarities and differences I observe in the graphs. [True/**False**]
3 I can write every detail I find in the graph(s). [True/**False**]
4 I should highlight the key features in the graph(s). [True/**False**]
5 I should support my description with data from the graph(s). [True/**False**]

Activity 1: Understanding the Assessment Standards of 'Task Achievement'

- Read the concept map which summarises the assessment standards of 'task achievement' of Task 1.
- Discuss with your partner the meanings of these keywords. Note down any differences in your understanding.
- Match these key words with their definitions

Task Requirements

Summarise	Overview	Select
Grouping	Extremes	Compare
Similarities	Differences	

Key word	Definition
Extremes	Report data that represent the extremes in the graph e.g., highest/lowest, oldest/youngest, the most frequent/the least frequent.
Overview	Write a short opening paragraph which tells the reader what the graph or table is about. It is usually done by paraphrasing the writing question. Report the trend noted in the graph or table here.
Grouping	Categorise data and information into groups.
Select	Instead of reporting every data point in the graph or table, choose the most important and representative data points to report.
Summarise	Report key features, data, and information in the graph or table.
Differences	Highlight contrasting features between data points.
Similarities	Highlight similar features between data points.
Compare	Show similarities and differences between data points.

Content Development

Format		Clarity	Relevance
Accuracy		Sufficiency	

Key word	Definition
Relevance	Report data that are presented in the graph or table; it is not necessary to include explanations of the data.
Clarity	Report data by using not only verbs (e.g., increased, decreased) but also adverbs and adjectives to denote the extent of change (e.g., increased drastically, a mild decrease).
Sufficiency	The majority of the data points or information presented in the graph or table are reported in the writing.
Accuracy	Include specific numbers to support your data description.
Format	Write in paragraphs and complete sentences, usually with a short introductory paragraph (overview), one or two body paragraphs, and an optional concluding paragraph.

Do you know?

In IELTS Writing Task 1, even though you are required to report salient features in the graph or table provided, it is not necessary to explain the data. For example, if a graph is showing an increase in global population, you do not need to offer an explanation for that phenomenon.

Activity 2: Writing an Overview

- Read the following question (T1-01) and Exemplars 3.1-3.3.
- Evaluate how well the exemplars are written by referring to the definition of the term 'overview' in Activity 1. If necessary, use these guiding questions to help your evaluation.

    o   Did the student indicate what the graph is about?
    o   Did the student use different wordings or did s/he simply copy the question?
    o   Did the student summarise the graph in a succinct manner?

T1-01

You should spend about 20 minutes on this task.

    The graph below gives information about the number of academic jobs in some humanities and social sciences disciplines between 2012 and 2014.

    Summarise the information by selecting and reporting the main features, and make comparisons where relevant.

    Write at least 150 words.

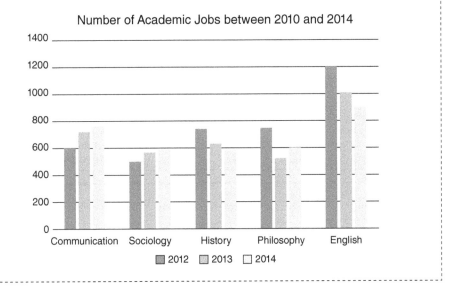

Exemplar 3.1

Referring to the graph, it shows the number of academic jobs in some humanities and social sciences disciplines from 2012 to 2014.

Guiding question	Yes/No	Remark
Did the student indicate what the graph is about?	Yes	The student indicated the topic of the graph and the period concerned.
Did the student use different wordings or did s/he simply copy the question?	Yes. The student used different wordings.	The student started the overview with 'referring to the graph'; replaced 'gives information' with 'shows'; replaced 'between . . . and . . .' with 'from . . . to . . .'.
Did the student summarise the graph in a succinct manner?	No	

Exemplar 3.2

The graph below gives information about the number of academic jobs in some humanities and social sciences disciplines between 2012 and 2014.

Guiding question	Yes/No	Remark
Did the student indicate what the graph is about?	Yes	The student indicated the topic of the graph and the period concerned.
Did the student use different wordings or did s/he simply copy the question?	No	The student simply copied the question.
Did the student summarise the graph in a succinct manner?	No	

Exemplar 3.3

Referring to the graph, it shows the number of academic jobs available in some humanities and social sciences disciplines from 2012 to 2014. Generally speaking, most jobs were available for graduates in the English discipline.

Guiding question	Yes/No	Remark
Did the student indicate what the graph is about?	Yes	The student indicated the topic of the graph and the period concerned.
Did the student use different wordings or did s/he simply copy the question?	Yes. The student used different wordings.	The student started the overview with 'referring to the graph'; replaced 'gives information' with 'shows'; replaced 'between . . . and . . .' with 'from . . . to . . .'
Did the student summarise the graph in a succinct manner?	Yes	'Generally speaking, most jobs were available for graduates in the English discipline.'

Do you know?

It is important to replace the wordings in the question with your own words. In this way, you are giving a good impression to the examiner that you know a wide range of vocabulary.

Activity 3: Selecting Information to Report

- Refer to the same question in Activity 2 (T1-01) and read Exemplars 3.4-3.6.
- Evaluate how well the exemplars are written by referring to the definitions of the terms 'select', 'grouping', and 'extremes' in Activity 1. If necessary, use these guiding questions to help your evaluation.

    o   Did the student choose the most important and representative data points to report?
    o   Did the student categorise data and information into groups?
    o   Did the student report data that represent the extremes in the graph?

Exemplar 3.4

To start with, the number of academic jobs in English declined gradually from 1200 to 900 between 2012 and 2014; yet, the number of English-related jobs was still the highest compared to other disciplines.

Regarding subjects that showed a steady boom in the number of jobs over the three years, there were approximately 200 more academic jobs in the discipline of communication. Furthermore, the number of jobs in sociology escalated slowly between 2012 and 2014.

Guiding question	Yes/No	Remark
Did the student choose the most important and representative data points to report?	Yes	'declined gradually from 1200 to 900 between 2012 and 2014'
Did the student categorise data and information into groups?	Yes	'Regarding subjects that showed a steady boom in the amount of jobs over the three years, ...'
Did the student report data that represent the extremes in the graph?	Yes	'. . . yet English still managed to have the highest number of jobs compared to other disciplines.'

Exemplar 3.5

To start with, the number of academic jobs in English declined gradually from 1200 in 2012 to 1000 in 2013, and from 1000 in 2013 to 900 in 2014; yet the number of English-related jobs was still the highest compared to other disciplines.

On the other hand, communication was one of the two subjects that has shown a steady boom in the number of jobs over 3 years. Furthermore, the number of jobs in sociology escalated slowly between 2012 and 2014.

Guiding question	Yes/No	Remark
Did the student choose the most important and representative data points to report?	No	'. . . the number of academic jobs in English declined gradually from 1200 in 2012 to 1000 in 2013, and from 1000 in 2013 to 900 in 2014'
Did the student categorise data and information into groups?	Yes (though not obvious when compared with paragraph two of Exemplar 3.4)	'. . . communication was one of the two subjects that has shown a steady boom in the amount of jobs over 3 years'
Did the student report data that represent the extremes in the graph?	Yes	'. . . yet English still managed to have the highest number of jobs compared to other disciplines.'

Exemplar 3.6

To start with, the number of academic jobs in English declined gradually from 1200 in 2012 to 1000 in 2013, and from 1000 in 2013 to 900 in 2014.

The number of jobs for communication graduates increased from 600 in 2012 to slightly over 700 in 2013, and to almost 800 in 2014. The number of jobs in the sociology discipline also increased from 500 in 2012 to slightly less than 600 in 2013 and 2014.

Guiding question	Yes/No	Remark
Did the student choose the most important and representative data points to report?	No	'... the number of academic jobs in English declined gradually from 1200 in 2012 to 1000 in 2013, and from 1000 in 2013 to 900 in 2014'
Did the student categorise data and information into groups?	No	The student simply reported the number of academic jobs for each discipline one by one.
Did the student report data that represent the extremes in the graph?	No	The student did not indicate the highest and lowest number of jobs in the graph.

Activity 4: Comparing Data

- Read the following question (T1-02) and Exemplars 3.7-3.9.
- Evaluate how well the exemplars are written by referring to the definitions of the terms 'compare', 'similarities', 'differences' in Activity 1. If necessary, use these guiding questions to help your evaluation.

  o   Did the student highlight similar features between data points?
  o   Did the student highlight contrastive features between data points?

T1-02

You should spend about 20 minutes on this task.

The pie chart below gives information about the distribution of sales among products manufactured by an IT product company in 2012.

Summarise the information by selecting and reporting the main features, and make comparisons where relevant.

Write at least 150 words.

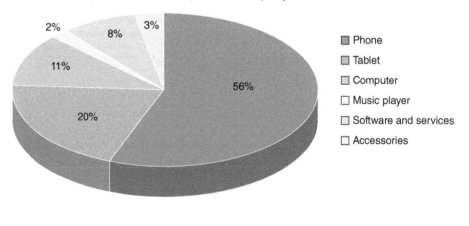

Sales of products of an IT product company

- Phone
- Tablet
- Computer
- Music player
- Software and services
- Accessories

Exemplar 3.7

To begin with, phones occupied the largest distribution of sales among the 6 products in the company, with more than half of the total sales.

Guiding question	Yes/No	Remark
Did the student highlight similar features between data points?	No	No similarities were mentioned.
Did the student highlight contrastive features between data points?	Yes	The student used the superlative 'the largest' to contrast the distribution of phone sales with other sales.

Exemplar 3.8

To begin with, phones occupied the largest distribution of the total sales among the 6 products in the company, with more than half of the total sales. Specifically, the sale of phones was almost 3 times of that of tablets and approximately 5 times more than that of computers. On the other hand, the percentages of sales of music players and accessories were almost identical.

Guiding question	Yes/No	Remark
Did the student highlight similar features between data points?	Yes	'On the other hand, the percentages of sales of music players and accessories were almost identical.'
Did the student highlight contrastive features between data points?	Yes	The student used the superlative 'the largest' to contrast the distribution of phone sales with other sales.

Exemplar 3.9

To begin with, the sale of phones contributed to 56% of the total sales of the company in 2012.

Guiding question	Yes/No	Remark
Did the student highlight similar features between data points?	No	The student only reported the percentage of phone sales with no attempt of comparison.
Did the student highlight contrastive features between data points?	No	The student only reported the percentage of phone sales with no attempt of comparison.

Activity 5: Format

- Read the following question (T1-O3) and read Exemplars 3.10 and 3.11.
- Evaluate how well the exemplars are written by referring to the definitions of the term 'format' in Activity 1. If necessary, use the following guiding questions to help your evaluation.
  - o Did the student write in paragraphs and complete sentences?
  - o Did the student include a short introductory paragraph (overview), one or two body paragraphs, and an optional concluding paragraph?
- Try to reach a consensus regarding the performances of these overviews by rating them as 'appropriate format' or 'inappropriate format'.

T1-03

You should spend about 20 minutes on this task.

The pie charts below give information about the distribution of sales of e-books in Country A in 2008 and 2018.

Summarise the information by selecting and reporting the main features, and make comparisons where relevant.

Write at least 150 words.

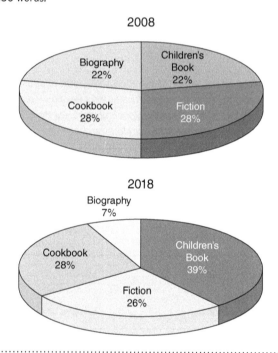

2008

2018

Exemplar 3.10

The pie charts indicate the distribution of online sales for four types of e-books in Country A between 2008 and 2018.

In 2008, all e-book types, including biography, children's book, fiction, and cookbook, occupied more than one-fifth of the sales in Country A. In 2018, children's book dominated the four e-book types with nearly two-fifths of the share. On the other hand, biography had the largest drop in the distribution of sales from one-fifth to less than one-tenth. Besides, the distribution of sales for cookbook remained unchanged at 28%, while fiction showed a slight decline in the distribution of online sales compared to that in 2008.

The e-book sales distributed more evenly in 2008 compared with that in 2018. Moreover, children's book was the only e-book type that demonstrated a greater distribution of sales in this decade.

To conclude, there is a prediction that the distribution of sales for children's book would become bigger and this e-book type would be dominant in the future because children's books are essential for every family. (173 words)

Guiding question	Yes/No	Remark
Did the student write in paragraphs and complete sentences?	**Yes**	
Did the student include a short introductory paragraph (overview), one or two body paragraphs, and an optional concluding paragraph?	**Yes**	**Although the concluding paragraph is irrelevant to the question as it is about the student's prediction, the overall structure of this exemplar is intact.**

Rating: Appropriate format/Inappropriate format

Exemplar 3.11

In 2008, all e-book types, including biography, cookbook, fiction, and children's book, occupied more than one-fifth of the sales in Country A.

In 2018, children's book dominated with nearly two-fifths in the sales distribution.

Sales of biography declined from one-fifth to less than one-tenth.

The distribution of sales for cookbook was 28%; on the other hand, fiction showed a slight decline in the distribution of sales compared to that in 2008.

The e-book sales distributed more evenly in 2008 compared with the situation in 2018.

Children's book was the only e-book type that possessed a greater distribution of online sales in this decade. (103 words)

Guiding question	Yes/No	Remark
Did the student write in paragraphs and complete sentences?	**Not always**	**Paragraphing is done poorly; related ideas are not grouped together to form a paragraph. Some sentence fragments are found.**
Did the student include a short introductory paragraph (overview), one or two body paragraphs, and an optional concluding paragraph?	**No**	**The introductory paragraph (the overview) is missing.**

Rating: Appropriate format/Inappropriate format

Do you know?

The concluding paragraph is optional in Task 1. A summary is optional because the text you are asked to write is already very short.

Activity 6: Clarity, Relevance, Accuracy, and Sufficiency

- Refer to the same question in Activity 5 and read Exemplars 3.12–3.14.
- Evaluate how well the exemplars are written by referring to the definitions of the terms 'clarity', 'relevance', 'accuracy', and 'sufficiency' in Activity 1. If necessary, use the following guiding questions to help your evaluation.

  o Did the student report data by using not only verbs (e.g., increased, decreased) but also adverbs and adjectives to denote the extent of change?
  o Did the student report data that are presented in the graph or table and not include explanations of the data?
  o Did the student include specific numbers to support his/her data description?
  o Did the student report the majority of the data points or information presented in the graph?

Exemplar 3.12

The pie charts indicate the distribution of e-book sales in Country A between 2008 and 2018.

In 2008, all retail sectors, including biography, children's book, fiction, and cookbook, occupied more than one-fifth of the sales in Country A. In 2018, childrens' book dominated the four e-book types. On the other hand, biography dropped in its distribution of sales. Besides, the distribution of sales for cookbook remained unchanged, while fiction showed a decline in the distribution of sales compared to that in 2008.

The sales for e-books distributed more evenly in 2008 compared with that in 2018. Moreover, children's book was the only e-book type that demonstrated a greater distribution of sales in this decade. (114 words)

Guiding question	Yes/No	Remark
Did the student report data by using not only verbs (e.g., increased, decreased) but also adverbs and adjectives to denote the extent of change?	Yes (seldom)	Only one instance of such use is noted: 'The sales for e-books distributed more evenly in 2008 . . .'
Did the student report data that are presented in the graph or table and not include explanations of the data?	Yes	No predictions and personal interpretations of data were included as they are not required by the question.
Did the student include specific numbers to support his/her data description?	No	No percentages from the two pie charts were included.
Did the student report the majority of the data points or information presented in the graph?	Yes	The student reported information related to all four retail sectors as presented in the pie charts.

Exemplar 3.13

The pie charts indicate the distribution of sales for four types of e-books in Country A between 2008 and 2018.

In 2008, all e-book types, including biography, cookbook, fiction, and children's book, occupied more than one-fifth of the sales in Country A. In 2018, children's book dominated the four e-book types with nearly two-fifths of the total share. On the other hand, biography had the most significant drop in the distribution of online sales from one-fifth to less than one-tenth. Besides, the distribution of sales for cookbook remained unchanged at 28%, while fiction showed a slight decline in the distribution of sales compared to that in 2008.

The sales for e-books distributed more evenly in 2008 compared with that in 2018. Moreover, children's book was the only e-book type that demonstrated a greater distribution of sales in this decade. (139 words)

Guiding question	Yes/No	Remark
Did the student report data by using not only verbs (e.g., increased, decreased) but also adverbs and adjectives to denote the extent of change?	Yes	'. . . the most significant drop . . .', 'showed a slight decline', 'distributed more evenly . . .'
Did the student report data that are presented in the graph or table and not include explanations of the data?	Yes	No predictions and personal interpretations of data were included as they are not required by the question.
Did the student include specific numbers to support his/her data description?	Yes	'. . . from one-fifth to less than one-tenth', '. . . remained unchanged at 28%...'
Did the student report the majority of the data points or information presented in the graph?	Yes	The student reported information related to all four e-book types as presented in the pie charts.

Exemplar 3.14

The pie charts indicate the distribution of sales for four types of e-books in Country A between 2008 and 2018.

In 2008, all e-book types, namely cookbook, biography, children's book, and fiction, occupied the sales in Country A evenly. In 2018, children's book dominated the four e-book types. On the other hand, biography dropped in its distribution of online sales. Besides, the distribution of sales for cookbook remained unchanged, while fiction showed a decline in the distribution of sales compared to that in 2008.

Children's book was the only retail sector that demonstrated a greater distribution of sales in this decade. There is a prediction that the distribution of sales for children's book would be enlarged and this e-book type would dominate in the future because children's books are essential for every family. (150 words)

Guiding question	Yes/No	Remark
Did the student report data by using not only verbs (e.g., increased, decreased) but also adverbs and adjectives to denote the extent of change?	**No**	**The student can add adverbs (e.g., slightly, drastically) before verbs (e.g., increase, decrease); alternatively, adjectives (e.g., slight, drastic) can be placed before nouns (e.g., rise, drop) to describe the extent of change.**
Did the student report data that are presented in the graph or table and not include explanations of the data?	**Yes (but included interpretations of data which is not necessary)**	**'There is a prediction that the distribution of sales children's book would become bigger and this e-book type would be dominant in the future because children's books are essential for every family.'**
Did the student include specific numbers to support his/her data description?	**No**	
Did the student report the majority of the data points or information presented in the graph?	**Yes**	**The student reported information related to all four types of e-books as presented in the pie charts**

Activity 7: Peer Evaluation

Based on your understanding of the assessment standards of 'task achievement', complete the evaluation form for Exemplar 3.15 written by a university student.

In the evaluation, complete the 'evaluate' section by assessing (1) whether the element concerned is present in the exemplar (the yes/no questions) and (2) how well the element is presented in the exemplar. Complete the 'suggest' section by writing an improved version of the element concerned. This section can be left blank if the exemplar demonstrates a good quality in a certain aspect.

T1-04

You should spend about 20 minutes on this task.

The line graph below gives information about the average tax on salaries paid by residents of two cities between 2004 and 2018.

Summarise the information by selecting and reporting the main features, and make comparisons where relevant.

Write at least 150 words.

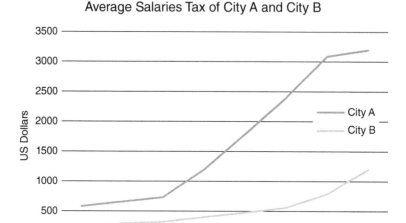

Average Salaries Tax of City A and City B

Exemplar 3.15

The line graph demonstrates the average tax on salaries of City A and City B from 2004 to 2018.

In City A, the average tax on salaries rose steadily between 2004 and 2018 during which the average tax on salaries boomed from $2000 to $12000 approximately. On the other hand, the average tax on salaries in City B had a gradual growth from 2004 to 2008, then swelled rapidly for the next 8 years, followed by another slight increase until 2018, in which the average tax on salaries expanded from $6000 to $32000 approximately.

Apparently, the average tax on salaries in City B was higher. However, the percentage of increase in City A was larger than that in City B. Particularly, the average tax on salaries in City A and City B in 2018 was 6 times and 5 times the average tax on salaries back in 2004 respectively.

To conclude, both City A and City B had experienced boosts in their average tax on salaries between 2004 and 2018. In the future, it is predicted the average tax on salaries of both cities would climb, provided that they have been escalating over the past 14 years. (187 words)

Assessment standard	Guiding question	Evaluate	Suggest
Overview	Did the student indicate what the graph is about?	*e.g The student includes information related to graph type (line graph), the topic of the graph (average tax on salaries in two cities), and the period of time concerned (from 2004 to 2018).*	N/A
	Did the student use different wordings or did s/he simply copy the question?	*e.g., Yes, the student used the verb 'demonstrates' instead of 'gives information about'. The student replaced the prepositions 'between ... and ...' with 'from ... to ...'.*	*The verb 'demonstrates' was not used appropriately here because of the wrong collocation between 'graph' and 'demonstrates'. The student can consider using 'shows' or 'reports'.*
	Did the student summarise the graph in a succinct manner?	**No, the student did not summarise the information presented in the graph succinctly.**	**The student could add a sentence at the end of paragraph 1: 'In general, a rise in average tax on salaries of the two cities was evident in the specified period.'**
Selecting information	Did the student choose the most important and representative data points to report or report every data point?	**Yes, the student selected the most important and representative data points to report. He/she described the average tax on salaries in 2004 and 2018.**	
	Did the student categorise data and information into groups?	**Yes, the student categorised the increase of average tax on salaries in City B into three periods: 2004–2008 (gradual growth), 2009–2016 (rapid growth), and 2017–2018 (slight increase).**	
	Did the student report data that represent the extremes in the graph?	**Yes, the student described the lowest average tax on salaries in 2004 and the highest average tax on salaries in 2018 for both cities.**	
Comparing information	Did the student highlight similar features between data points?	**Not found in the body paragraphs but in the concluding paragraph: 'both City A and City B has experienced boost in their average tax on salaries between 2004 and 2018'.**	**The student could add a sentence or two highlighting the similarities between the average tax on salaries in Cities A and B in the body paragraphs e.g., 'The average tax on salaries of City A and City B experienced a steady growth from 2004 to 2008./The average tax on salaries of City A experienced a steady growth from 2004 to 2008; a similar increase was noted in City B in the same period.'**
	Did the student highlight contrastive features between data points?	**Yes, e.g., in paragraph 2, 'apparently, the average tax on salaries in City B was higher', '... the percentage of increase in City A was larger than that in City B'.**	

Format	Did the student write in paragraphs and complete sentences?	**Yes**	
	Did the student include a short introductory paragraph (overview), one or two body paragraphs, and an optional concluding paragraph?	**Yes. However, the concluding paragraph is not appropriate because students are not expected to predict the future or interpret the data.**	**Remove the last sentence in the concluding paragraph.**
Clarity	Did the student report data by using not only verbs (e.g., increased, decreased) but also adverbs and adjectives to denote the extent of change?	**Yes e.g., in paragraph 2 'rose steadily', 'approximately', 'a gradual growth', 'another slight increase', 'swelled rapidly'.**	
Relevance	Did the student report data that are presented in the graph or table and not include explanations of the data?	**The student reported data which are presented in the graph, but she added a prediction at the end of the concluding paragraph, which is not necessary.**	**Remove the last sentence in the concluding paragraph.**
Accuracy	Did the student include specific numbers to support his/her data description?	Yes, especially in paragraph 2.	
Sufficiency	Did the student report the majority of the data points or information presented in the graph?	Yes, the student reported data related to the two cities between 2004 and 2018.	

Activity 8: Writing Practice

Based on your understanding of 'task achievement', write an overview for the following student's work.

T1-12

You should spend about 20 minutes on this task.

The bar chart below gives information about different undergraduate courses chosen at three universities in Auckland by gender in 2017.

Summarise the information by selecting and reporting the main features, and make comparisons where relevant.

Write at least 150 words.

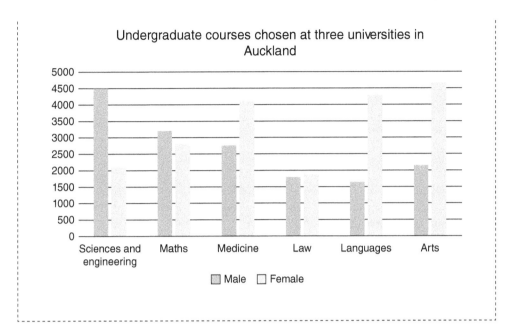

The bar chart illustrates the male and female students' choice between six undergraduate courses provided by three universities in Auckland in 2017. Overall, most female students chose arts while the majority of male students chose Science and Engineering.

The most significant difference between male and female students' choice was shown in two courses - sciences and engineering and arts. On the other hand, the number of male and female students who chose law was almost the same.

Arts was chosen by approximately 2,000 male students and 4,500 female students in 2017. In other words, the number of female students who chose arts is around double of that of male students. Similarly, about 6,500 students chose sciences and engineering in 2017, including 4,500 male students and around 2,000 female students. Both the number of male and female students who chose law in 2017 was about 2,000.

Do you know?

Provide a summary of the chart by rephrasing the question. You may refer to Activity 2 if you find it difficult to complete this task.

Answers to Chapter 4

Task 1: Coherence and Cohesion

Check Your Understanding

Read the following statements and determine if they are true or false:

1 It is a good idea to use as many connections as I can. [True/**False**]
2 Using only basic and repetitive connectives may lead to an unsatisfactory score in the domain 'coherence and cohesion'. [True/**False**]
3 I can use some other words that have similar meanings (i.e., synonyms). [True/**False**]
4 I should divide my essay into paragraphs. [True/**False**]

Activity 1: Understanding the Assessment Standards of 'Coherence and Cohesion'

What is meant to be 'coherent' and 'cohesive' in writing? What techniques do you usually adopt to achieve the above?

- Read the concept map which summarises the assessment standards of 'coherence and cohesion' of Task 1.
- Discuss with your partner the meanings of these keywords. Note down any differences in your understanding.
- Match these key words with their definitions.

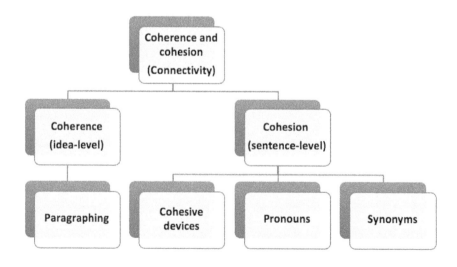

Coherence	Cohesion	Paragraphing
Cohesive devices	Pronouns	Synonyms

Key word	Definition
Paragraphing	Ways a writer employ to organise information thoughtfully and logically into paragraphs
Synonyms	Words which have similar meanings
Pronouns	Words which function as nouns or noun phrases mentioned in the previous sentences
Cohesive devices	Linking words used to connect ideas and sentences logically and meaningfully
Coherence	Connection of ideas at the idea level
Cohesion	Connection of ideas at the sentence level

Activity 2: Achieving Coherence through Paragraphing

- Read the following question (T1-05) and Exemplars 4.1–4.3.
- Evaluate how well the exemplars are written by referring to the definitions of the terms 'coherence' and 'paragraphing' in Activity 1. If necessary, use these guiding questions to help your evaluation:

  o Did the students connect ideas by organising information thoughtfully and logically within a paragraph?
  o Did the students connect ideas by organising information thoughtfully and logically between paragraphs?

T1-05

You should spend about 20 minutes on this task.

The table below gives information about the gross domestic product (GDP) rankings between 2013 and 2014.

Summarise the information by selecting and reporting the main features, and make comparisons where relevant.

Write at least 150 words.

2013			2014		
Rank	Country	GDP (US$ billion)	Rank	Country	GDP (US$ billion)
1	United States	17,000	1	United States	17,500
2	China	9,000	2	China	10,100
3	Japan	4,900	3	Japan	4,800
4	Germany	3,600	4	Germany	3,700
5	France	2,700	5	United Kingdom	2,800
6	United Kingdom	2,500	6	France	2,750
7	Brazil	2,200	7	Brazil	2,150
8	Russia	2,100	8	Italy	2,100
9	Italy	2,000	9	India	1,950
10	India	1,900	10	Russia	1,930

Exemplar 4.1

In 2013, the US had the highest GDP -17000 billion US dollars. China was second place while Japan and Germany ranked the third and forth by having a GDP of 9000, 4900 and 3600 billion respectively. They are followed by France, the UK and Brazil where GDP reached 2700, 2500 and 2200 billion. Russia ranked the eighth and Italy and India were in the ninth and the tenth place.

Although GDP in Japan dropped from 4900 to 4800 billion in 2014, the top 4 in GDP ranking of the year remained unchanged. They were the US where GDP grew from 17000 to 17500, China where it raised from 9000 to 10100 and Germany where it increased from 3600 to 3700 billion. GDP in both the UK and France raised in 2014; however, their ranking switched to the fifth and the sixth with 2800 and 2750 billion US dollars respectively. Brazil remained in the seventh place, followed by Italy, India and Russia.

Guiding question	Yes/No	Evidence
Did the students connect ideas by organising information thoughtfully and logically within a paragraph?	Yes	Although not explicitly stated by a topic sentence (e.g., the three columns on the left of the table show the GDP of the 10 countries in 2013), the ideas in the two paragraphs are coherent, i.e., the first paragraph is about GDP in 2013 and the second paragraph is about GDP in 2014.
Did the students connect ideas by organising information thoughtfully and logically between paragraphs?	Yes	Although not explicitly stated by a topic sentence (e.g., comparing the countries' GDP between 2013 and 2014, a number of fluctuations could be noted), ideas between the two paragraphs are connected. For example, in the second paragraph, the writer mentions the changes between 2013 and 2014, after reporting the GDP in 2013.

Exemplar 4.2

The highest increase in GDP from 2013 to 2014 was China. It had increased US$1100 billion. Although China had increased the most GDP from 2013 to 2014, United States was still the top of the GDP ranking in 2013 and 2014. It was US$17000 billion in 2013 and US$17500 billion in 2014. It had increased US$500 billion.

The countries of the top four GDP ranking also remained unchanged. However, France and Russia fell in the GDP ranking from 2013 to 2014. Although France's GDP increased, its ranking decreased because the rise of United Kingdom was higher.

Guiding question	Yes/No	Evidence
Did the students connect ideas by organising information thoughtfully and logically within a paragraph?	Yes & No	While the ideas in the first paragraph are connected (i.e., reporting the increase of GDP), the ideas in the second paragraph are not. It is unclear whether the writer wants to focus on countries where GDP remained unchanged or those where their GDP ranking decreased.
Did the students connect ideas by organising information thoughtfully and logically between paragraphs?	No	No logical connection is drawn by the writer between the two paragraphs. A suggestion for the writer is that in the first paragraph, s/he can focus on countries where GDP/GDP ranking changed; in the second paragraph, s/he can focus on countries where GDP/GDP ranking remained unchanged.

Exemplar 4.3

In 2014, alterations in the GDP in some countries were noted, when compared to the situation in 2013. The United States still had the highest GDP, which was US$17500 billion; however, Russia had the lowest GDP, which was US$1930 billion. The GDP of India became the second lowest in 2014. China was the second highest country with GDP increasing from US$9000 billion to US$10100 billion. Also, Japan ranked third with the GDP decreasing from US$4900 billion to US$4800 billion.

While most of the countries' GDP increased or remained the same from 2013 to 2014, GDP of Japan, Brazil, Italy did not. The GDP of Japan decreased US$100 billion; the GDP of Brazil and Italy decreased US50 billion. In general, the ranking of these countries with GDP did not fluctuate too much from 2013 to 2014.

Guiding question	Yes/No	Evidence
Did the students connect ideas by organising information thoughtfully and logically within a paragraph?	**Yes**	**The first paragraph is about changes noted between 2013 and 2014. The second paragraph is about exceptional cases.**
Did the students connect ideas by organising information thoughtfully and logically between paragraphs?	**Yes**	**The two paragraphs are connected with a transitional sentence: 'While most of the countries' GDP increased or stayed the same from 2013 to 2014 GDP of Japan, Brazil, Italy did not'.**

Activity 3: Achieving Cohesion through using Cohesive Devices

- Read the following question (T1-06) and Exemplars 4.4-4.5.
- Evaluate how well the exemplars are written by referring to the definitions of the terms 'cohesion' and 'cohesive devices' in Activity 1. If necessary, use these guiding questions to help your evaluation:

    o   What cohesive devices did the students use in the paragraphs?
    o   Were the cohesive devices used meaningfully and accurately?
    o   Were there a variety of cohesive devices used?

T1-06

You should spend about 20 minutes on this task.

The table below gives information about people's attitudes towards gender roles categorised by age.

Summarise the information by selecting and reporting the main features, and make comparisons where relevant.

Write at least 150 words.

'A man's duty is to earn money while a woman's duty is to look after her family.'

	18-25	26-35	36-45	46-55	56-65
Agree	5%	13%	10%	6%	12%
Neutral	13%	13%	19%	29%	21%
Disagree	82%	74%	71%	65%	67%

Exemplar 4.4

It is seen that relatively younger interviewees felt negative about the stated gender roles. The 18-25 age group had the highest percentage against the statement. In contrast, less supporters were found among people who are between 45 and 55 than the 18-25 group regarding the statement 'A man's duty is to earn money while a woman's duty is to look after her family.'

On the contrary, three age groups, 26-35, 36-45 and 56-65, are recorded with more than one-tenth of support on the attitudes towards gender role. Around one third of the people aged 45-55 interviewed responded neutrally towards the statement. Only 13 per cent of the respondents under 35 held a neutral view towards the gender role description.

Guiding question	Yes/No	Response
What cohesive devices did the students use in the paragraphs?		'In contrast', 'On the contrary'
Were the cohesive devices used meaningfully and accurately?	Yes	The two cohesive devices were used to show different/opposing ideas.
Was there a variety of cohesive devices used?	No	The only type of cohesive devices used in this exemplar is showing differences.

Exemplar 4.5

As for the positive responses, no more than 6% of the interviewees of two age groups, 18-25 and 46-55, agreed with the statement. On the other hand, around one out of ten of the interviewees of the other age groups agreed with it.

Finally, for the neutral stance, 13% of the interviewees of age groups 18-25 and 26-35 voted for it. Moreover, one out of five of the 36-45 and 56-65 age groups held a neutral stance. The age group which voted the most in the neutral stance is 46-55, with almost 30%.

Guiding question	Yes/No	Response
What cohesive devices did the students use in the paragraphs?		'As for . . ', 'On the other hand', 'Finally', 'Moreover'
Were the cohesive devices used meaningfully and accurately?	Yes	'As for . . .' = use to show aspects of ideas 'On the other hand' = use to show contrast 'Finally' = use to show sequence of ideas 'Moreover' = use to add new ideas
Was there a variety of cohesive devices used?	Yes	refer to the above remark

---

Learn online

You can find out more about cohesive devices at this website: https://www.smart-words.org/linking-words/

Activity 4: Achieving Cohesion through using Pronouns

- Read the following question (T1-07) and Exemplar 4.6.
- Evaluate how well the exemplars are written by referring to the definitions of the terms 'cohesion' and 'pronouns' in Activity 1. If necessary, use these guiding questions to help your evaluation:

  o   What pronouns did the students use in the paragraphs?
  o   What did the pronouns refer to?
  o   Were the pronouns used accurately?

T1-07

You should spend about 20 minutes on this task.

The graph below gives information about birth rate and death rate in China in every 1000 people between 1950 and 2015.

Summarise the information by selecting and reporting the main features, and make comparisons where relevant.

Write at least 150 words.

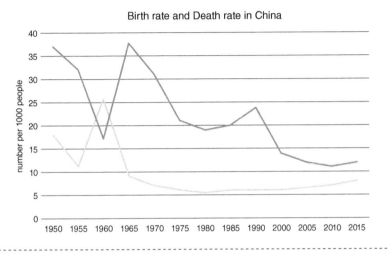

Birth rate and Death rate in China

Exemplar 4.6

The birth rate in China per 1000 people stood at around 37% in 1950 and dramatically decreased to approximately 17% in 1960, after which it experienced a sharp rise, peaking at about 38% in 1965. Then, the birth rate in China per 1000 people fell again considerably to about 12% in 2015, with a fluctuation between 1975 and 1995.

The death rate in China in every 1000 people was about 17% in 1950. It increased by around 5% in the next five years. After that, it went up significantly and overtook the birth rate, reaching its peak at about 26% in 1960. But it started to decline again to about 9% in 1965, and then remained stable and was lower than the birth rate per 1000 people in China in the next 50 years, finally reaching at 8% in 2015.

Guiding question	Response
What pronouns did the students use in the paragraph?	'it' (subject pronoun) (para 1), 'it' (subject pronoun) (para 2), 'its' (possessive adjective) (para 3)
What did the pronoun refer to?	'it' (subject pronoun) (para 1) = birth rate in China 'it' (subject pronoun) (para 2) = death rate in China 'its' (possessive adjective) (para 3) = death rate in China
Were the pronouns used accurately?	Yes

Do you know?

In English, pronouns are used to avoid repetitions. At the same time, anaphoric pronouns (i.e., pronouns which refer to the preceding sentence) are used to strengthen linkage between sentences.

Activity 5: Achieving Cohesion through using Synonyms

- Read the following question (T1-08) and Exemplars 4.7-4.8.
- Evaluate how well the exemplars are written by referring to the definitions of the terms 'cohesion' and 'synonyms' in Activity 1 and respond to the guiding questions under each exemplar.

T1-08

You should spend about 20 minutes on this task.

The chart below shows information about suicide methods of middle-aged people in the US by gender in a year.

Summarise the information by selecting and reporting the main features, and make comparisons where relevant.

Write at least 150 words.

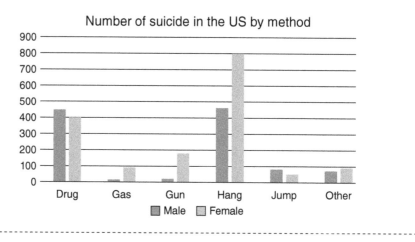

Number of suicide in the US by method

Exemplar 4.7

Two main suicide methods in the US are drug abuse and hanging. Referring to the chart, there is 1 person who dies by hanging and taking drugs every day in the US.

Guiding question	Response
Did the student use any synonyms?	**Yes. The writer used 'taking drugs' to replace 'drug abuse'.**
Which words could be replaced by synonyms? What synonyms do you suggest the students use?	**'US' could be replaced by 'United States of America' 'hanging' could be replaced by 'being sent to the gallows'**

Exemplar 4.8

From the above chart, it shows some statistics of middle-aged people's suicide methods in the United States. It is displayed by gender. Firstly, we can observe that the most common suicide method for both male and female is by hanging. There are 450 males and 900 females committing suicide by hanging respectively. At the same time, taking drug is also another most common suicide way for males. There are also 450 males taking drugs to commit suicide.

Guiding question	Response
Did the student use any synonyms?	Yes. The word 'statistics' is used to replace the word 'information' in the question.
Which words could be replaced by synonyms? What synonyms do you suggest the students use?	'US' could be replaced by 'United States of America' 'hanging' could be replaced by 'being sent to the gallows' 'commit suicide' could be replaced by 'attempt self-murder'

Learn online

wordandphrase.info is a great resource for you to find synonyms which match the sense of the word you want to use. Alternatively, Collins has a decent thesaurus (https://www.collinsdictionary.com/dictionary/english-thesaurus) with synonyms, antonyms (words with opposite meanings), and real-life examples from search engines.

Activity 6: Peer Evaluation

Based on your understanding of the assessment standards of 'coherence and cohesion', complete the evaluation form for Exemplars 4.9–4.10.

In the evaluation, complete the 'evaluate' section by assessing (1) whether the element concerned is present in the exemplar (the yes/no questions) and (2) how well the element is presented in the exemplar. Complete the 'suggest' section by writing an improved version of the element concerned. This section can be left blank if the exemplar demonstrates a good quality in an aspect.

T1-09

You should spend about 20 minutes on this task.

The diagram below gives information about the process of making detergent.

Summarise the information by selecting and reporting the main features, and make comparisons where relevant.

Write at least 150 words.

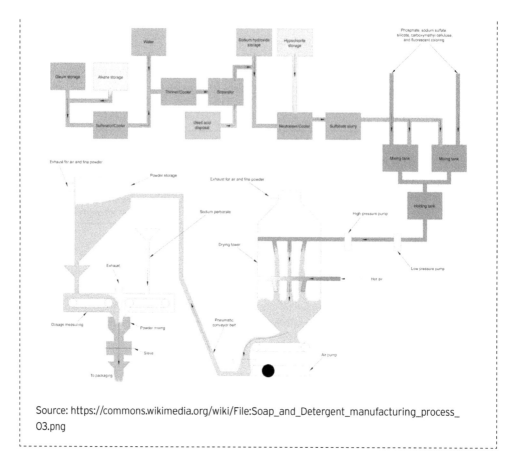

Source: https://commons.wikimedia.org/wiki/File:Soap_and_Detergent_manufacturing_process_03.png

Exemplar 4.9

The diagram demonstrates the process of making detergent.

The process contains three major stages. In the first stage, Oleum and Alkene are cooled down and sulfonated by adding water. Next, the processed materials are processed first in the thinner or cooler and then the separator to produce sodium hydroxide and remove used acid. Then, the stored sodium hydroxide is added into the neutralizer or cooler together with hypochlorite to produce sulfonate slurry. When it comes to the second phase, the sulfonate slurry is mixed with phosphate, sodium sulfate, silicate, carboxymethyl cellulose, and fluorescent colouring. Then, the mixed chemicals in the holding bank are pumped into the drying tower where they interact with the hot air. After the drying process, the powder is air pumped via a pneumatic conveyor belt into the powder storage tank. In the final stage, sodium perborate is added to the powder for mixing. Having been sieved, the detergent is ready for packaging. (156 words)

Assessment standard	Guiding question	Yes/No	Evaluate	Suggest
Paragraphing	Did the students connect ideas by organising information thoughtfully and logically within a paragraph?	**Yes**	**The student followed the diagram to describe the process of making detergent from the beginning to the end.**	**N/A**
	Did the students connect ideas by organising information thoughtfully and logically between paragraphs?	**Yes**	**The student began with an overview telling the reader what the subsequent paragraph is about, i.e., the process of detergent making.**	**It would be better if the second paragraph could be further divided.**
Cohesive devices	Were the cohesive devices used meaningfully and accurately?	**Yes**	**The cohesive devices used, e.g., 'first of all', 'next' were used effectively to show the sequence or steps of making chewing gum.**	**N/A**
	Was there a variety of cohesive devices used?	**Yes**	**Although there was variety in the cohesive devices used, more advanced or formal cohesive devices to show sequence can be used, e.g., instead of using 'then' twice, the student could consider using the word 'subsequently'.**	
Pronouns	Did the student use any pronouns?	**No**	**Pronouns were not used.**	**Pronouns could be used to replace some nouns/noun phrases mentioned in the previous sentence to avoid repetition, e.g., instead of repeating 'the sulfonate slurry is mixed with . . .', the student could replace 'the sulfonate slurry' with 'it' because it is mentioned before.**
	Were the pronouns used accurately?	**N/A**	**N/A**	**N/A**
Synonyms	Did the student use any synonyms?	**Some attempts**	**'demonstrates' to replace 'gives information' in the question** Although there were some attempts to use synonyms, most of the words provided in the diagram were copied.	**'sieve' = strain** **'package' = wrap**

T1-12

You should spend about 20 minutes on this task.

The bar chart below gives information about different undergraduate courses chosen at three universities in Auckland by gender in 2017.

Summarise the information by selecting and reporting the main features, and make comparisons where relevant.

Write at least 150 words.

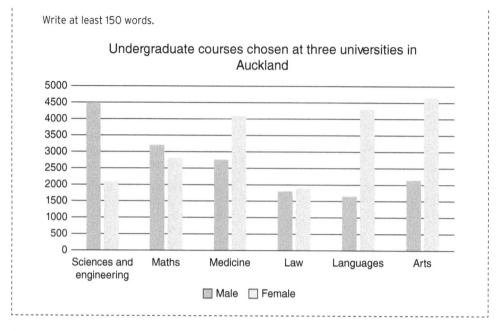

Undergraduate courses chosen at three universities in Auckland

Exemplar 4.10

The result of the bar chart reveals the proportion of male and female undergraduates and their choice of undergraduate courses. For the proportion of male and female undergraduates, there were more female undergraduates than male in the three universities in Auckland. According to the bar chart, there were around 19000 female undergraduates while there were only around 13000 male undergraduates, which reveals that more females receive tertiary education than males. For the choice of undergraduate courses, female undergraduates were found to choose courses related to Languages, Arts and Medicine. For the Arts course, there were 4600 females in the course while 2100 males took the same course, which was less than half of the female population. Male undergraduates tended to choose courses related to logic like Sciences and engineering and Maths. There were 4500 males who took Science and engineering when there were only 2100 females taking the course. The result reveals that female undergraduates tended to study Language-related courses while males tended to take Science-related courses. (167 words)

Assessment standard	Guiding question	Yes/ No	Evaluate	Suggest
Paragraphing	Did the students connect ideas by organising information thoughtfully and logically within a paragraph?	Yes	**The student used expressions like 'for . . .' to indicate the start of a new idea.**	**N/A**
	Did the students connect ideas by organising information thoughtfully and logically between paragraphs?	No	**Ideas were not o rganised logically and progressively between paragraphs.**	**It is suggested that the information be organised into three paragraphs: (1) an overview stating the general picture of the chart, (2) a paragraph on courses which were taken mostly by female students, and (3) a paragraph on courses which were taken mostly by male students.**

Cohesive devices	Were the cohesive devices used meaningfully and accurately?	Yes	e.g., 'according to . . .' to show reference, 'for . . .' to indicate a new idea.	N/A
	Was there a variety of cohesive devices used?	Yes	Two types of cohesive devices were used. See the comment above.	Other types of cohesive devices could be used: contrasting = while, whereas, conversely comparing = similarly, in a similar vein, likewise giving examples = for example, for instance, this is illustrated by . . . giving results = therefore, as a result, consequently
Pronouns	Did the student use any pronouns?	Yes	'It' (line 4) = the phenomenon of having more female students	'For the Arts course, there were 4600 females studied that course while 2100 males took the course, . . .' could be rewritten using a pronoun as 'For the Arts course, it was attended by 4600 females and 2100 males.'
	Were the pronouns used accurately?	Yes	N/A	N/A
Synonyms	Did the student use any synonyms?	Yes	e.g., 'choose courses' is replaced with 'take the course'. Some words were used repeatedly, e.g., 'tended to'.	tended to ⇨ xx preferred to . . . language, Arts ⇨ humanities subjects/courses universities ⇨ higher education institutions proportion ⇨ distribution

Activity 7: Writing Practice

Based on your understanding of 'coherence and cohesion', evaluate an example of paragraphs of T1-16.

T1-16

You should spend about 20 minutes on this task.

The chart below shows information about a report made by a European newspaper about the internet users in 2010 and the expected numbers in 2025 in six European countries.

Summarise the information by selecting and reporting the main features, and make comparisons where relevant.

Write at least 150 words.

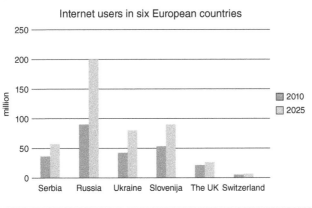

Internet users in six European countries

The bar graph illustrates the data of internet users and the expected numbers in six European countries in 2010 and 2025 respectively from an Asian newspaper.

As can be perceived from the chart, the highest numbers of internet users in 2010 and 2025 are noted in Russia, while Swiss netizens remain the lowest in number in both years. Even so, the expected internet users in 2025 are higher than those in 2010 in all six European countries.

Guiding question	Response
Did the student use any synonyms?	**"bar graph"/"chart", "internet users"/"netizens"**
Were there some well-written cohesive devices?	**"while", "even so"**
Did the student use any pronouns?	**No**

Write one to two paragraphs by describing the graph of T1-48 by using the good features in the above example.

T1-48:

You should spend about 20 minutes on this task.

The chart below shows information about the percentage of endangered animal species by taxonomy in 2014.

Summarise the information by selecting and reporting the main features, and make comparisons where relevant.

Write at least 150 words.

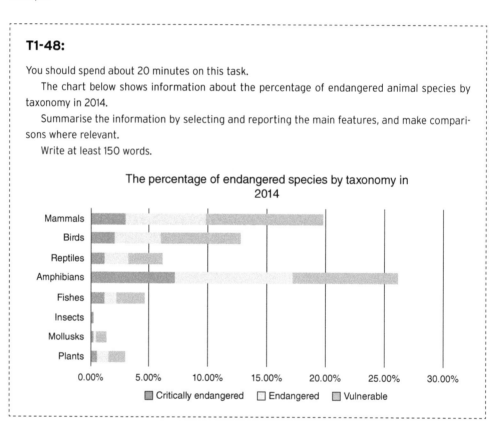

The chart outlines the serious levels including critically endangered, endangered and vulnerable of various endangered animals in 2014.

As can be perceived from the chart, amphibians are noted as the most endangered animal type and they are also the most critically endangered species compared to other animals; on the contrary, insects were ranked as the least endangered kind.

Answers to Chapter 5

Task1: Lexical Resource

Check Your Understanding

Discuss these questions with a partner:

1 What techniques have you used to achieve a better score in the lexical resource domain?
2 Is it preferrable to overuse less common academic vocabulary? Why?
3 What are some ways to enrich your vocabulary?

Activity 1: Understanding the Assessment Standards of Lexical Resource

- Read the concept map which summarises the assessment standards of lexical resource.
- Discuss with your partner the meanings of these keywords. Note down any differences in your understanding.

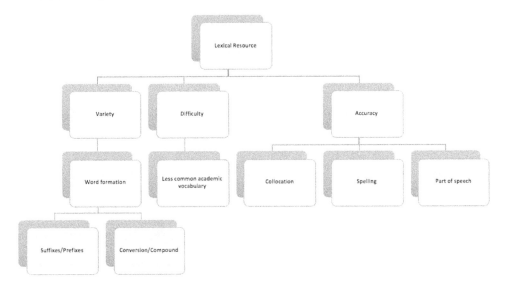

The term lexical resource' is used in the IELTS writing assessment standards to denote vocabulary. Three aspects of use of vocabulary are considered by IELTS writing examiners, which include: (1) variety of vocabulary; (2) difficulty of vocabulary; and (3) accuracy of vocabulary.

Aspect 1: Variety of Vocabulary

Variety of vocabulary is achieved through word formation. There are four major types of word formation: **prefixes**, **suffixes**, **compounds**, and **conversion**.

Learning online

The following websites can help you learn more about prefixes, suffixes, and compounds.

http://www.prefixsuffix.com/
https://www.enchantedlearning.com/grammar/compoundwords/
https://www.spellingcity.com/compound-words.html

Write down the type of word formation next to the corresponding definition and example.

Type of word formation	Definition	Example
Compounds	It connects two or more base words to form a new word.	foremost
Prefixes	It is a group of letters that are placed before the root of a word. It usually changes the meaning of the word, but not the part of speech of the word.	in-disputably
Conversion	It is the change of a word from one part of speech to another.	process (n.) ⇨ process (v.)
Suffixes	It is a group of letters that are placed at the end of the root of a word. It usually changes the part of speech of the word, but not the meaning of the word.	second-ly

---

Aspect 2: Difficulty of Vocabulary

Writing in an academic context requires the use of a set of more sophisticated and formal words than we would normally use in our daily life.

Learn online

For examples of commonly used academic vocabulary, you can refer to Dr. Averil Coxhead's Academic Word List (https://www.victoria.ac.nz/lals/resources/academicwordlist).

Complete the following table.

Word in a less academic style	*Word in a more academic style*
The process of making white wine is growing and harvesting grapes, pressing grapes to extract juice . . .	The process of making white wine **involves** growing and harvesting grapes, pressing grapes to extract juice . . .
Since grapes are important to making white wine, growing grapes in good soil is . . .	Since grapes are **essential/crucial** to making white wine, growing grapes in good soil is . . .
For it is key to start with the clear juice, the particles need to form sediment at the bottom of the tanks, also called settling, as the next step.	For it is key to start with the clear juice, the particles need to form sediment at the bottom of the tanks, also **referred to as/known as/termed settling,** as the next step.
Afterwards, it should go through racking process to remove the clear wine from the sediment.	Afterwards, it should **undergo** racking process to remove the clear wine from the sediment.

Aspect 3: Accuracy of Vocabulary

Three types of vocabulary accuracy are mentioned in the IELTS writing assessment standards, including (1) collocation, (2) spelling, and (3) part of speech.

Write down the type of vocabulary accuracy next to the corresponding definition and example.

Type of vocabulary accuracy	Definition	Example
Part of speech	The accurate use of word forms in sentences e.g. noun, verb, adjective, adverb.	(✗) Thirdly, the harvested grapes are pressed to extraction (n.) the pulp of juice and skins also known as the must.
		(✔)Thirdly, the harvested grapes are pressed to extract (v.) the pulp of juice and skins also known as the must.
Spelling	The accurate alphabetical formation of words.	(✗) For it is key to start with the clear juice, the particles need to form sentiment at the bottom of the tanks, also called settling, as the next step.
		(✔) For it is key to start with the clear juice, the particles need to form sediment at the bottom of the tanks, also called settling, as the next step.
Collocation	The accurate combination of words.	(✗) After this step, Malolactic conversion process should begin when it is oaked, so as for convert malic acid . . .
		(✔) After this step, Malolactic conversion process should begin when it is oaked, so as to convert malic acid . . .

Activity 2: Using a Variety of Vocabulary

- Read the following question (T1-14) and read Exemplars 5.1-5.3.
- Evaluate how well the exemplars are written in terms of using a variety of vocabulary by referring to the definitions and examples of the related terms in Activity 1. If necessary, use the following guiding questions to help your evaluation:

  o   Did the student form new words through the use of prefixes?
  o   Did the student form new words through the use of suffixes?
  o   Did the student form new words through the use of conversion?
  o   Did the student form new words through the use of compounding?

T1-14

You should spend about 20 minutes on this task.

The charts below give information about the survey results about people's views towards studying languages. The first chart shows the reasons for studying an additional language. The second pie chart displays the preferred ways of learning a new language.

Summarise the information by selecting and reporting the main features, and make comparisons where relevant.

Write at least 150 words.

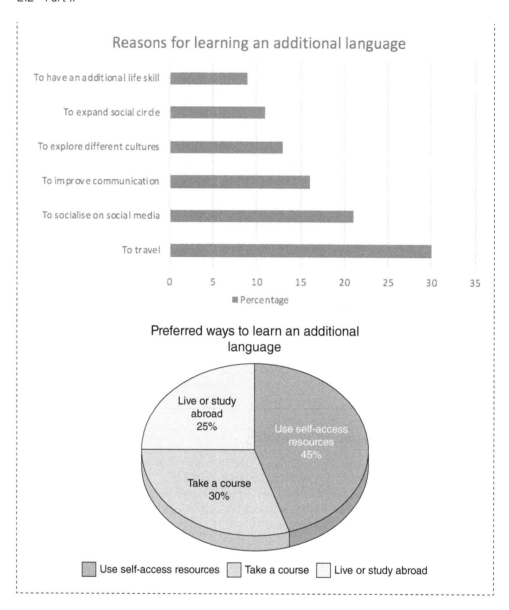

Exemplar 5.1

As shown by the survey results, the main reason for learning an additional language is due to people's interest in travelling and there are around thirty percent of interviewees who agree with it. To socialise on social media is the second important reason for people to have further study. About one of five people agree with it. Improving communication is the third crucial reason for them to learn a new language as reflected by the chart. On the other hand, around half of the interviewees agree that people should use self-access resources to learn an additional language. The second way to learn another language is to register for a formal course and thirty percent of people agree with it. However, the least effective way to learn a new language is to live or study overseas as only twenty five percent of people agree with it. The percentages of taking a course and go overseas are quite similar but there is no doubt that using online resources remains the most effective means to acquire a new language. (176 words)

Guiding question	Yes/No	Example/Suggestion
Did the student form new words through the use of prefixes?	**No**	**The word crucial can be replaced by indispens- able which is formed by adding a prefix in in front of the adjective dispensable.**
Did the student form new words through the use of suffixes?	**Yes**	**interviewees**
Did the student form new words through the use of conversion?	**No**	**the verb study used in the paragraph can be used as a noun as well**
Did the student form new words through the use of compounding?	**Yes**	**overseas**

Exemplar 5.2

The graphs illustrate interviewees' opinions on the reasons for learning a new language and preferred ways to do so.

To begin with, in the first chart, it is obvious that most interviewees (30% of the interviewees) think that their own interest to travel is the main reason for learning a new language. 'To have an additional life skill' and 'to explore different cultures' can also be classified as individual reasons, and they are chosen by almost 9% and 13% of interviewees respectively. It seems that more than half of interviewees make decision towards learning an additional language based on their personal factors, and it may be the reason why most people (45% of the interviewees) think that people should make good use of online self-access resources to do so.

Following this, 'to expand social circle', 'to improve communication', and 'to socalise on social media' are chosen by almost 11%, 16% and 21% of interviewees respectively, and they can be grouped as social reasons. Most social reasons have higher ranking than those individual reasons, and it can explain why 30% of interviewees think that they should socialise with other students in a formal language course.

To conclude, more people have the incentive to learn an additional language because of individual reasons rather than social reasons. Also, they mostly think that the most effective way to learn a new language is to get hold of online resources. (235 words)

Guiding question	Yes/No	Example/Suggestion
Did the student form new words through the use of prefixes?	**No**	**the word ir-respective can be used e.g. irrespec- tive of age, most interviewees agreed that . . .**
Did the student form new words through the use of suffixes?	**Yes**	**interviewees, respectively**
Did the student form new words through the use of conversion?	**No**	**the noun interest (para 2) can be used as a verb**
Did the student form new words through the use of compounding?	**No**	**the compound word therefore can be used to re- place and it may be the reason of (para 2).**

Exemplar 5.3

The bar chart illustrates the proportion of six reasons (to have an additional life skill, to expand social circle, to explore different cultures, to improve communication, to socialise on social media, and to travel) why people want to learn an additional language.

Overall, the most significant percentage of why people want to learn a new language was their desire to travel, which accounted for 30%. To network on social media platforms is the second main purpose, making up more than 20%. On the other hand, the percentage of people who learn a foreign language to gain an additional life skill was in stark contrast with those who want to travel and socialise. It was the least important reason for learning a new language and it was less than half of the percentages of the two most popular reasons.

On the other hand, the other pie chart illustrates the proportion of three methods (use self-access resources, take a course, live or study abroad) to learn a foreign language. It shows that 45% of the respondents think that the person who is going to learn a new language should learn it independently through online self-access resources. (194 words)

Guiding question	Yes/No	Example/Suggestion
Did the student form new words through the use of prefixes?	**No**	**illustrates can be replaced by il-luminates on**
Did the student form new words through the use of suffixes?	**Yes**	**additional**
Did the student form new words through the use of conversion?	**No**	**contrast (para 3) can be used as a verb**
Did the student form new words through the use of compounding?	**Yes**	**network**

Activity 3: Using Academic Vocabulary

- Read the following question (T1-15) and read Exemplar 5.4.
- Evaluate how well the exemplars are written in terms of using academic vocabulary by referring to the definitions and examples of the related terms in Activity 1. If necessary, use the following guiding question to help your evaluation:

  o   Did the student use a set of more sophisticated and formal words than we would normally use in our daily life?

T1-15

You should spend about 20 minutes on this task.

The chart below gives information about the respective sales volume of two kinds of printers from 2006 to 2016.

Summarise the information by selecting and reporting the main features, and make comparisons where relevant.

Write at least 150 words.

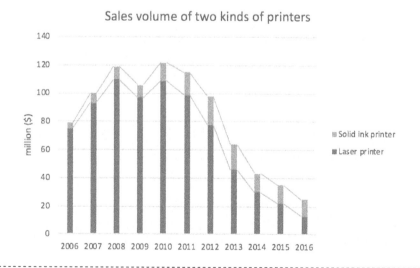

Sales volume of two kinds of printers

Exemplar 5.4

The bar chart illustrates the sales volume of two different kinds of printers, namely, solid ink printers and laser printers. Generally, the trend of these two kinds of printers increased in the first three or four years and then decreased gradually.

For the solid ink printer, its sales rose for 40 million from 2006 to 2008, and dropped in 2009. After peaking at around 120 million the following year, it turned to a steady decline until 2012, followed by a significant decrease in 2013. In the period of 2014 to 2016, the sales volume dropped continuously. On the other hand, the sales volume of laser printers shared a similar trend with solid ink printers. The main difference is that they peaked in different years.

To sum up, the graph shows the trend of the sales volume of two kinds of printers, and it is likely that the trend of the sales volume of these two printer types would decline in the future. (162 words)

Categorise the following words into word/expression in a less academic style and word/expression in a more academic style by putting a tick (✓) in the appropriate boxes. Suggest a more formal and sophisticated word for the latter.

Word/expression	Word/expression in a less academic style	Word/expression in a more academic style	Suggestion (if any)
illustrates		✓	
For . . .	✓		**In terms of . . ./Regarding . . .**
rose	✓		**escalated/surged/ soared**
drops	✓		**plummet/dwindle**
shows	✓		**demonstrate/ explicate/elucidate**

Activity 4: Using Accurate Vocabulary

- Read the following question (T1-17) and read Exemplar 5.5.
- Evaluate how well the exemplars are written in terms of using accurate vocabulary by referring to the definitions and examples of the related terms in Activity 1. If necessary, use the following guiding questions to help your evaluation:

  o   Did the student use collocations accurately?
  o   Did the student spell words accurately?
  o   Did the student use parts of speech accurately?

T1-17

You should spend about 20 minutes on this task.

The diagrams below show floor plans for the first floor of two houses.

Summarise the information by selecting and reporting the main features, and make comparisons where relevant.

Write at least 150 words.

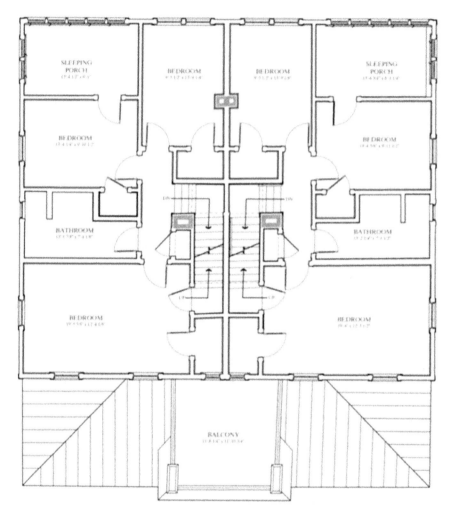

Source: https://commons.wikimedia.org/wiki/File:South_Elevation,_South_Wall_Elevation,_and_
Second_Floor_Plan_-_National_Home_for_Disabled_Volunteer_Soldiers,_Mountain_Branch,_
Duplex_Quarters,_Lamont_and_Veterans_Way,_HABS_TN-254-N_(sheet_3_of_8).tif

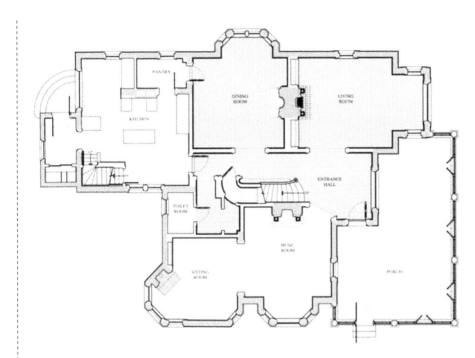

Source: https://commons.wikimedia.org/wiki/File:First_Floor_Plan_-_National_Home_for_Disabled_Volunteer_Soldiers,_Northwestern_Branch,_Governor%27s_Residence,_5000_West_National_Avenue,_Milwaukee,_Milwaukee_County,_WI_HABS_WI-360-C_(sheet_3_of_16).tif

Exemplar 5.5

There are both similarities and differences from the designs of the two floor plans of the two houses.

One of the major different in the two floor plans is that the first floor plan has five bedrooms while the second one does not have any. While both floor plans include bathrooms, the first one has more bathrooms than the second one. Addition, there are more diverse room types in the first floor of the second floor plan namely kitchen, pantry, living room, dining room, music room, and sitting room. In the other hand, the first floor of the first floor plan mainly comprises bedrooms.

As far as similarities are concerned, both floor plans contain an outdoor or semi-outdoor arena. In the first floor plan, it is the baconly whereas a pouch can be find in the second floor plan.

Correct the lexical errors you find in the following exemplars. Focus on collocation, spelling, and part of speech. Write 'NA' if there are no such errors.

Type of error	Error	Correction
Collocation	both similarities and differences from, in the first floor, In the other hand	both similarities and differences between, on the first floor, on the other hand
Spelling	baconly, arena, pouch	balcony, area, porch
Part of speech	Addition, different, can be find	Additionally, differences, can be found

Activity 5: Peer Evaluation

Based on your understanding of the assessment standards of lexical resource, complete the evaluation form for Exemplar 5.6 written by a university student.

In the evaluation, identify problematic aspects of vocabulary use in relation to (1) **variety**, (2) **difficulty**, and (3) **accuracy** by responding to the guiding questions.

T1-18

You should spend about 20 minutes on this task.

The line graph below shows information about the urbanisation rate of four countries from 1950 to 2010 and with forecasts for the year 2020 and the year 2030.

Summarise the information by selecting and reporting the main features, and make comparisons where relevant.

Write at least 150 words.

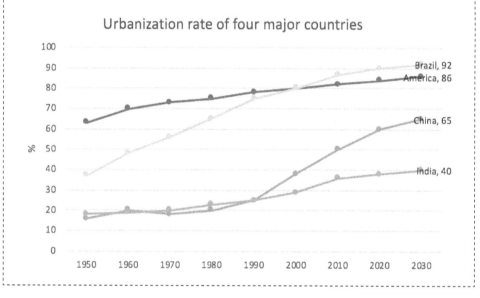

Exemplar 5.6

The line graph shows the urbanization rate of four countries, including America, China, India and Brazil from 1950 to 2030.

From 1950 to 2010, the rate of the country urbanization in America and India followed the same trend. In 1950, the figures were 63% and 18% respectively, rising to 82% and 36% respectively. Thereafter, their urbanization rates are forecast to steady rise to 84% and 38% until 2020, after which it is expected to increase to 86% and 40% respectively in 2030.

Although China's urbanization rate is similar to that of India and shares the same endpoint of 25% from 1950 to 1990, it went up dramatically to 50% in 2010. This increase is forecast to continue until 2030 with an estimated rate of 65%.

The situation in Brazil differs considerably, with a rapid increase of urbanization rate between 1950 (37%) and 1990 (75%), followed by a marked rise until 2010 (87%). This rise is projected to continue until 2030, when the urbanization rate of Brazil is expected to reach 92%.

The overall trend is a rise in the urbanization rate of four major countries between 1950 and 2030.

Question for paragraph 1:

Q1.   What is a more formal and academic word to replace 'shows'?

_____

Questions for paragraph 2:

Q1.   The word respectively has been used a few times. Can you suggest a synonymous expression for the word?

correspondingly

Q2.   The parts of speech of steady rise are wrong. How will you correct them?

steadily rose

Questions for paragraph 3:

Q1.   What is a more formal and academic word to replace although?

despite/in spite of ⇨ Despite/In spite of the fact that . . .

Q2.   What is a more formal and academic word to replace went up?

escalated, surged, soared

Q3.   Use the conversion technique to rewrite the sentence: *This increase is forecast to continue until 2030 with an estimated rate of 65 per cent* by changing the part of speech of 'forecast' from a verb to a noun.

The forecast was that the increase would continue until 2030 with an estimated rate of 65 per cent.

Questions for paragraph 4:

Q1.   What is the collocation problem with the phrase with a rapid increase of the urbanisation rate . . .?

with a rapid increase in the urbanisation rate . . .

Q2.   The word rise has been used a few times. Can you suggest a synonymous expression for the word?

hike, upsurge, upswing, growth, ascent

Activity 6: Writing Practice

Based on your understanding of lexical resource, rewrite the words in italics which are too simple. Replace the simple words with more sophisticated vocabulary. Remember that word changes may result in changes in sentence structures as well. So, modify the sentences if necessary.

T1-24

You should spend about 20 minutes on this task.

The bar chart below shows the percentages of various types of workplace harassment faced by male and female employees.

Summarise the information by selecting and reporting the main features, and make comparisons where relevant.

Write at least 150 words.

This bar chart *shows* the different types of workplace harassment *affecting* employees. For the two gender groups, they *have* similar experience in hostile behaviour and verbal abuse. But for the *other* types of workplace harassment, they hold different opinions. More female employees report being *sexually harassed*.

Answer:

This bar chart reveals the different types of workplace harassment distressing employees. For the two gender groups, they recount similar experience in hostile behaviour and verbal abuse. But for the remaining types of workplace harassment, they hold different opinions. More female employees report *falling victim to sexual harassment.*

Answers to Chapter 6
Task 1: Grammatical Range and Accuracy

Check Your Understanding

Discuss the following questions in pairs:

1 Are we required to use many complex sentences when attempting IELTS writing?
2 Is accuracy of the sentence patterns used in my writing as important as their variety?

Activity 1: Understanding the Assessment Standards of 'Grammatical Range and Accuracy'

- Read the concept map which summarises the assessment standards of 'grammatical range and accuracy'.
- Discuss with your partner the meanings of these keywords. Note down any differences in your understanding.

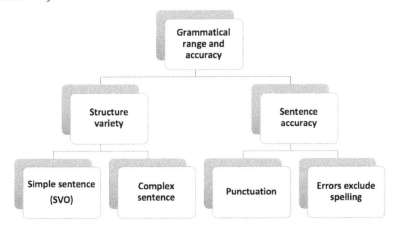

In the grammar domain of IELTS writing descriptors, the major focus is on sentences. Candidates are required to write with a variety of accurate sentence structures. As shown from the concept map, this domain is divided into two aspects: (1) structure variety; and (2) sentence accuracy.

Learn online

You can know more about different types of sentences by visiting this website: https://www.english-grammar-revolution.com/sentence-structure.html.

In the following, definitions and examples of structure variety will be given. The example sentences are taken from student exemplars on the following writing topic:

T1-19

You should spend about 20 minutes on this task.

The pie charts below display information about the CO_2 emissions in London. The first pie chart shows the CO_2 emissions by different sectors. The second pie chart presents the consumption of different transportation fuels.

Summarise the information by selecting and reporting the main features, and make comparisons where relevant.

Write at least 150 words.

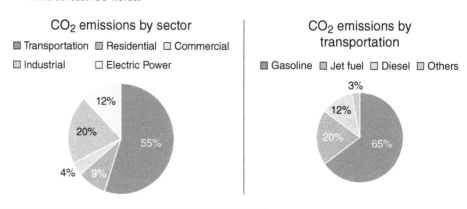

Structure Variety

According to the official IELTS writing descriptors, candidates are expected to 'use a mix of simple and complex sentence forms' at Band 6. For higher achievers, in addition to writing both simple and complex sentence patterns, candidates should be able to demonstrate their ability to 'use a variety of complex structures' (Band 7).

a) *Simple sentences (SVO)*

A simple sentence contains one 'independent clause'. An 'independent clause' has a subject (S) (a noun or noun phrase which the rest of the clause is predicated), a verb (V) (a word to describe an action or state), and sometimes an object (O) (a noun or noun phrase influenced by an active transitive verb); alternatively, an 'independent clause' can contain a subject (S) and a predicate (P) (a part of a clause which contains a verb and gives information about the subject). They are called 'independent' because these two can stand alone in terms of meaning and syntax.

e.g. *The pie charts illustrate the breakdown of CO_2 emissions in London.*

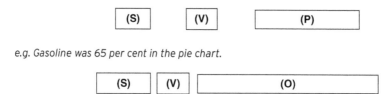

e.g. *Gasoline was 65 per cent in the pie chart.*

An associated concept of simple sentences is 'compound sentences'. A compound sentence comprises at least two independent clauses (simple sentences) and no dependent clauses (which means clauses which are incomplete in terms of meaning and syntax, and thus, cannot stand alone). These two independent clauses are joined together by a 'coordinating conjunction' such as 'and', 'or', 'but'.

e.g. *The pie charts show the CO_2 emissions by sectors* and *by transportations.*

e.g. *Residential use only consumed 9 per cent of CO_2 emissions* but *it used 20 per cent of jet fuel.*

Note that from the two examples above, the compound sentences could be separated into two independent clauses. However, for the sake of avoiding repetition and enhancing cohesion, writers usually choose to combine the two clauses by a coordinating conjunction.

Compound sentence	Independent clause
The pie charts show the CO_2 emissions by sectors **and** by transportations.	The pie charts show the CO_2 emissions by sectors. The pie charts show the CO_2 emissions by transportations.

Compound sentence	Independent clause
Residential use only consumed 9 per cent of CO2 emissions **but** *it* used 20 per cent of jet fuel.	Residential use only consumed 9 per cent of CO_2 emissions. But, it used 20 per cent of jet fuel.

b) *Complex sentences*

A complex sentence includes an independent clause and at least one dependent clause. A 'dependent clause' (also known as 'subordinate clause') refers to a clause which cannot stand alone regarding its meaning and syntax.

There are three major types of dependent clause:

- Adjective clauses (clauses which function as adjectives by using **relative pronouns** (e.g., which, when, who, where, that), also known as relative clause)

Independent clause	Dependent clause
Electric power consumed 12 per cent of total CO_2 emissions	which was larger than that for residential use.

- Adverbial clauses (clauses which function as adverbs by using **subordinating conjunctions**, e.g., because, although, so)

Independent clause	Dependent clause
Gasoline was the main contributor of CO_2 emissions	because of heavy transportation.

- Participle clauses (a type of adverbial clause which can be used when the participle and the verb of the main clause share the same subject)

Dependent clause	Independent clause
Contributing the most to CO_2 emission,	gasoline was regarded as the major cause of air pollution and global warming.

Sentence Accuracy

The second aspect of 'grammatical range and accuracy' is related to sentence accuracy, which is further broken down into two sub-categories: (1) punctuation errors; and (2) other error types.

a) *Punctuation errors*

o   Comma splice: The misuse of a comma instead of a coordinating conjunction to form a compound sentence.

e.g. *According to the diagram, the highest emission in Boston of dinitrous oxide was 100 ug/m³, and for the other kind of pollutant, sulphur dioxide, did not exceed 50 ug/m3.* (incorrect)

e.g. According to the diagram, the highest emission in Boston of dinitrous oxide was 100 ug/m³. As for the other kind of pollutant, sulphur dioxide, it did not exceed 50 ug/m3. (correct)

o　Run-on sentence: A compound sentence which has not been correctly punctuated.

e.g. Overall, Beijing and Mexico emitted more sulphur dioxide than the other 2 cities on the other hand Boston and Mexico emitted more dinitrous dioxide than the other 2 cities. (incorrect)

e.g. Overall, Beijing and Mexico emitted more sulphur dioxide than the other 2 cities; on the other hand, Boston and Mexico emitted more dinitrous dioxide than the other 2 cities. (correct)

o　Sentence fragments: This error occurs when a sentence is treated as an independent clause when it is not.

e.g. For the emission of sulphur dioxide. Beijing and Mexico showed a considerable difference. (incorrect)

e.g. For the emission of sulphur dioxide, Beijing and Mexico showed a considerable difference. (correct)

Learn online

You can know more about how different punctuations are used by visiting this website: https://www.thepunctuationguide.com/.

---

b)　*Other error types*

According to the IELTS official writing rubric, it mentions 'errors' without clearly defining it. Below is a non-exhaustive list of common sentence-level errors.

- Faulty parallelism: A parallel sentence becomes faulty when one or more than one part of the sentence is not presented to be identical with the rest in terms of grammatical structure.

    e.g. The differences in the minimum and maximum Sulphur dioxide were 105 and it was 120 respectively. (incorrect because of unidentical parts)

    e.g. The differences in the minimum and maximum Sulphur dioxide were 105 and 120 respectively. (correct because of identical parts)

- Subject-verb disagreement: This happens when the verb of a sentence or clause does not agree with the subject in terms of singularity/plurality.

    *e.g. The chart **show** the fluctuations in the emissions of two pollutants in four cities, namely, Boston, Calcutta, Beijing and Mexico in 2015.* (incorrect)

    *e.g. e.g. The chart **shows** the fluctuations in the emissions of two pollutants in four cities, namely, Boston, Calcutta, Beijing and Mexico in 2015.* (correct)

- Misplaced modifiers: A 'modifier' is a word or phrase that modifies another word or phrase. A modifier is misplaced if it is used to modify the wrong word or phrase.

    e.g. Despite discharging fewer pollutants than developing cities, the chart shows that developed cities like Boston still had high emission level. (incorrect because the participle ('discharging') and the verb ('shows') do not share the same subject i.e. while the chart 'shows', the chart does not 'discharge')

    e.g. Despite discharging fewer pollutants than developing cities, developed cities like Boston still had high emission level. (correct because the participle ('discharging') and the verb ('had') share the same subject)

Learn online

You can learn more about how to avoid different sentence-level errors by reading this online document: Resource: https://www.uts.edu.au/sites/default/files/sentence.pdf.

Activity 2: Structure Variety

- Read the following question (T1-21) and read Exemplars 6.1-6.3.
- Evaluate how well the exemplars are written in terms of using a variety of sentence structures by referring to the definitions and examples of the related terms in Activity 1.

T1-21

You should spend about 20 minutes on this task.

The graph below shows information about tourist growth in the last 60 years and the estimates.

Summarise the information by selecting and reporting the main features, and make comparisons where relevant.

Write at least 150 words.

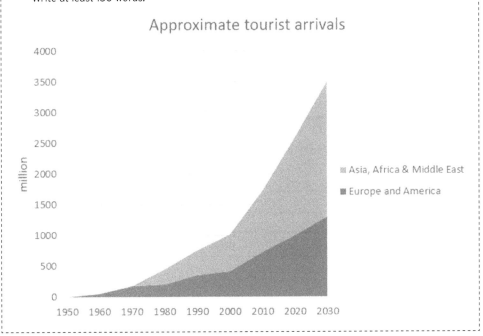

Exemplar 6.1

(1) The graph shows an obvious growing tendency of approximate tourist arrivals. Overall, the number of tourists from Europe and America appeared to be less than those from Asia, Africa and Middle East in the whole process.

In detail, the number of approximate tourist arrivals is increasing. The graph can be divided into three parts according to growth rates. (2) In the first part of the graph, from 1950 to 1970, it can be found that the approximate number of tourists was low, with a slight growth throughout these years. The second part of the graph is the period 1970 to 2000. (3) During this time, the number of tourists who visited Asia, Africa and Middle east started to grow swiftly. In 2000, (4) it witnessed a turning point of the escalation. (5) The number of tourists is predicted to increase dramatically from 2000 to 2030, and reaches 3500 million in 2030. (152 words)

Categorise the underlined sentences into three types: (1) simple sentences; (2) compound sentences; and (3) complex sentences.

Sentence pattern	Sentence number
Simple sentence	(1), (4)
Compound sentence	(5)
Complex sentence	(2), (3)

Exemplar 6.2

(1) The graph demonstrates the statistics of the approximate tourists' arrivals in the last sixty years and the estimation of growth between 2020 and 2030. (2) It includes the arrivals from Europe and America and the arrivals from Asia, Africa and the Middle East.

(3) The figure reveals that there was a gradual increase from zero to 500 million of European and American visitors. (4) From 2000 onwards, there was a relatively rapid rise from 2000 to 2010. (5) Regarding this trend, therefore, it is reasonable to estimate that there will be continuous add-ons from 2020 to 2030.

(6) Compared with the tourists from Europe and America, there was a relatively huge number of visitors from Asia, Africa and the Middle East. (7) During the period 1970 to 2000, the number of tourists had been experiencing a stable gain from 250 million to 1000 million, which was a fourfold increase. (8) From 2000 until the foreseeable future, the number could surge to 3500 million by 2030.

(9) Both arrivals had been increasing from 1950 to 2010 and could be increasing in the twenty years to come. (186 words)

Categorise the underlined sentences into three types: (1) simple sentences; (2) compound sentences; and (3) complex sentences.

Sentence pattern	Sentence number
Simple sentence	/
Compound sentence	(1), (2), (9)
Complex sentence	(3), (4), (5), (6), (7), (8)

Exemplar 6.3

The graph unfolds the number of approximate tourist arrivals in Asia, Africa and Middle East area, and Europe and America Area separately. It is clear that ascending patterns were shown in numbers of tourist arrivals in these regions.

(1) The tourist industry started blooming in 1950 for both areas. The number of tourists travelling increased from 0 to approximately 250 million for both areas in 1970. Starting from 1970, the travel industry of Asia, Africa and Middle East countries flourished. (2) It showed a significant increase. It reached 1000 million in 2000.

The trend kept on increasing rapidly. (3) The number of tourists visit Asia, Africa and Middle East countries reached 2000 million in the following 15 years. It is predicted that, it will reach 3500 million people in 2030. Meanwhile, the number of tourists visiting Europe and America will grow steadily by 200 per cent from 500 millions (in 2000) to 1000 millions (in 2030).

To sum up, (4) we can say that the tourism industry shows positive progress all around the world. Asia, Africa and Middle East are relatively more popular destinations than Europe and America. (186 words)

Sentence number	Instruction	Rewritten sentence
1	Combine the two sentences into a compound sentence using the coordinating conjunction 'and'	**The tourist industry started booming in 1950 for both areas and the amount of tourists travelling increased from 0 to approximately 250 million for both areas in 1970.**
2	Combine the two sentences into a complex sentence using the subordinating conjunction 'which'	**It showed a significant increase, which reached 1,000 million in 2000.**
3	Correct this complex sentence (relative clause)	**The number of tourists who visited Asian, African, and Middle Eastern countries reached 2,000 million in the following 15 years.**
4	Combine the two sentences into a complex sentence by using the subordinating conjunction 'although'	**Although the tourism industry shows positive progress all around the world, Asia, Africa, and the Middle East are relatively more popular destinations than Europe and America.**

Activity 3: Sentence Accuracy

- Read the following question (T1-23) and read Exemplars 6.4-6.5.
- Evaluate how well the exemplars are written in terms of using a variety of sentence structures accurately by referring to the definitions and examples of the related terms in Activity 1.

T1-23:

You should spend about 20 minutes on this task.

The pie charts below show information about preferred work benefits of employees in Asian and Western societies.

Summarise the information by selecting and reporting the main features, and make comparisons where relevant.

Write at least 150 words.

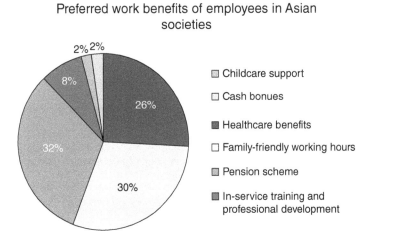

Preferred work benefits of employees in Asian societies

- 26%
- 30%
- 32%
- 8%
- 2%
- 2%

- Childcare support
- Cash bonues
- Healthcare benefits
- Family-friendly working hours
- Pension scheme
- In-service training and professional development

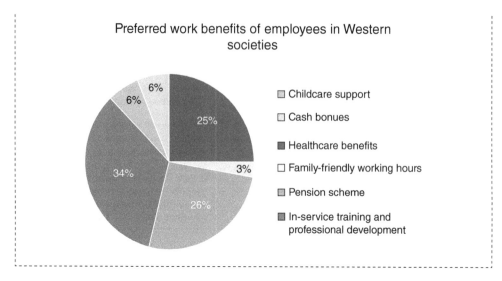

Preferred work benefits of employees in Western societies

- Childcare support
- Cash bonues
- Healthcare benefits
- Family-friendly working hours
- Pension scheme
- In-service training and professional development

Exemplar 6.4

(1) For the pie chart of preferred work benefits of Asian employees, it reveal that 32% of the employ-ees preferred childcare support, which was the highest percentage. There were only 2% who opted for cash bonuses, which was the lowest percentage. (2) On the other hand, as for the preference of western employees, it shows that family-friendly work hours was the most popular option, there were nearly one-third of employees voting for it.

(3) Comparing the two pie charts. Having a flexible working hours appeared to appeal to both Asian and western employees . (4) Moreover the charts display that among various benefits, the percentages of Asian and western workers who preferred intangible benefits were quite high, both with more than 50%. (5) Being at 32%, the charts show that more Asian workers preferred pension scheme than their western counterpart.

(6) Overall, the two pie chats illustrate and discusses the preferences of Asian and western employees towards work benefits. (159 words)

Match sentences (1) to (6) with the six types of errors described at the outset of the chapter. These error types include: comma splice, run-on sentence, sentence fragment, faulty parallelism, subject-verb disagreement, and misplaced modifiers. Rewrite a grammatically correct sentence for each.

Sentence number	Error type	Rewritten sentence
1	Subject-verb disagreement	For the pie chart of preferred work benefits of Asian employees, it reveals 32 per cent of the employees preferred childcare support, which was the highest percentage.
2	Comma splice	On the other hand, as for the preference of Western employees, it shows that family friendly work hours was the most popular option. Nearly one-third of employees voted for it.
w	Sentence fragment	Comparing the two pie charts, having flexible working hours appeared to appeal to both Asian and Western employees.
4	Run-on sentence	Moreover, the charts display that . . .
5	Misplaced modifier	Being at 32 per cent, more Asian workers preferred a pension scheme than their Western counterparts.
6	Faulty parallelism	Overall, the two pie chats illustrate and discuss . . .

Exemplar 6.5

Asian employees mainly preferred monetary benefits. (1) As the information shows. There were 34% of the Asian employees who preferred monetary benefits, which had a higher percentage than western employees as the latter only had 9% also less than half of the workers who worked in Asian communities opted for healthcare benefits, childcare support, and professional development opportunities, which shows that they did not value non-monetary reward as much .

(2) The most popular benefit option of Asian workers is pension scheme, which had more than 30%, it proves that these employees tend to look for long-term security, especially after they have retired.

(3) The most popular benefit choice of western employees is having flexible and family-friendliness working hours, which was 34%. It had a higher percentage than those who work in Asian.

(4) Being at approximately 30%, the charts show that family-friendly working hours was a popular option among Asian and western employees. (5) It show that striking a balance between work and life is important to both groups. (166 words)

Sentence number	Error type	Rewritten sentence
1	**Sentence fragment, run-on sentence**	As the information shows, there were 34 per cent of the Asian employees who preferred monetary benefits, which had a higher percentage than Western employees as the latter only had 9 per cent; also, fewer than half . . .
2	**Comma splice**	The most popular benefit option of Asian workers is a pension scheme, which had more than 30 per cent. It proves that . . .
3	**Faulty parallelism**	The most popular benefit choice of Western employees is having flexible and family friendly working hours
4	**Misplaced modifier**	Being at approximately 30 per cent, family friendly working hours was a popular option among . . .
5	**Subject-verb disagreement**	It shows that striking a balance between work and life is important to both groups.

Activity 4: Peer Evaluation

Based on your understanding of the assessment standards of 'grammatical range and accuracy', complete the evaluation form for Exemplar 6.6 written by a university student.

In the evaluation, identify problematic aspects of sentence use in relation to (1) **variety** and (2) **accuracy** by responding to the guiding questions.

T1-28

You should spend about 20 minutes on this task.

The charts below show information about the energy consumption in the UK in 2017. The first pie chart displays the energy sources. The second pie chart presents different types of renewable energy.

Summarise the information by selecting and reporting the main features, and make comparisons where relevant.

Write at least 150 words.

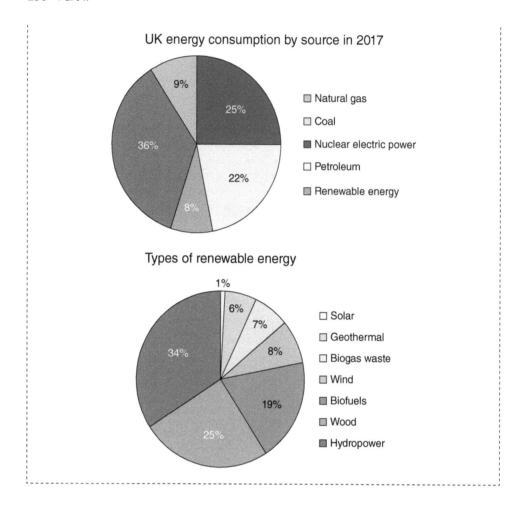

UK energy consumption by source in 2017

- Natural gas
- Coal
- Nuclear electric power
- Petroleum
- Renewable energy

Types of renewable energy

- Solar
- Geothermal
- Biogas waste
- Wind
- Biofuels
- Wood
- Hydropower

Exemplar 6.6

(1) The pie charts above illustrate the different sources of UK energy consumption in 2017 and displays the different types of renewable energy, one of the sources that only occupies a relatively small proportion.

(2) In 2017, petroleum as an available resource was the main drive of energy in the United Kingdom. Making up 36% of the total consumption. Natural gas was the second most-used resource, covering 25% while Coal ranked the third, with only 3% less. Renewable energy and nuclear electric power only accounted for 9% and 8% respectively.

(3) As one of the least commonly used energy sources, the charts show that renewable energy is divided into 7 types. (4) The main body consists of three resources: the most popular type of renewable energy was Hydropower (34%), second was Wood (25%), in the third place was Biofuels (19%). Wind resource, Biogas waste and Geothermal accounted for 8%, 7%, and 6% of the total renewable energy consumption respectively while Solar only occupied 1% of renewable energy consumption.

In summary, (5) renewable energy still do not play an important role in energy consumption. (6) Although there are different resources making up renewable energy it is still important to continuously develop resources other than Hydropower. (204 words)

Q1. Identify the types of error of sentences (1) to (6) and correct those errors.

Sentence number	Error type	Rewritten sentence
1	Faulty parallelism	The pie charts above illustrate . . . and display . . .
2	Sentence fragment	In 2017, petroleum as an available resource was the main drive of energy in the United Kingdom, making up 36 per cent of the total consumption.
3	Misplaced modifier	As one of the least commonly used energy sources, renewable energy is divided into seven types.
4	Comma splices	The main body consists of three resources: the most popular type of renewable energy was hydropower (34 per cent); second was wood (25 per cent); in third place was biofuels (19 per cent).
5	Subject-verb disagreement	renewable energy still does not play an important role in energy consumption
6	Run-on sentence	Although there are different resources making up renewable energy, it is still important to continuously develop resources other than hydropower.

Q2. Give one example of compound sentence used in the exemplar.

Wind resource, Biogas waste and Geothermal accounted for 8 per cent, 7 per cent, and 6 per cent of the total renewable energy consumption respectively . . .

Q3. Give one example of complex sentences used in the exemplar.

Natural gas was the second most-used resource, covering 25 per cent . . . (participle clause)

Activity 5: Writing Practice

Based on your understanding of 'grammatical range and accuracy', try to identify the grammatical errors and punctuation errors of T1-30. Rewrite the paragraph using some complex sentences.

T1-30:

You should spend about 20 minutes on this task.

The charts below show information about the estimates of population change in different continents from 1950 to 2050 according to an official report.

Summarise the information by selecting and reporting the main features, and make comparisons where relevant.

Write at least 150 words.

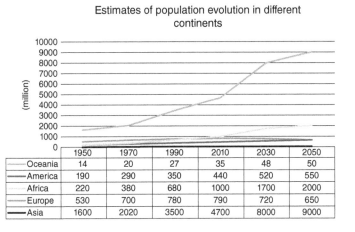

Estimates of population evolution in different continents

	1950	1970	1990	2010	2030	2050
Oceania	14	20	27	35	48	50
America	190	290	350	440	520	550
Africa	220	380	680	1000	1700	2000
Europe	530	700	780	790	720	650
Asia	1600	2020	3500	4700	8000	9000

About the change of population in different continents. From 1990 to 2050 the population of Asia and Africa increased in a rather fast speed, but more people will bear in Asia and the population of Asia will far exceed the others up to nine billion, and Africa's population will only up to 2000 million. In addition, the population of other continents don't have too big change.

Answer:

Regarding the change of population in different continents from 1990 to 2050, the population of Asia and Africa is expected to experience a rather fast increase, which can be ascribed to the fact that more people will be born in Asia and Africa, reaching up to nine billion and 2,000 million respectively. Among the five continents, Asia will witness the most rapid surge in population. In addition, there is only a slight change in population of other continents, ranging only within 1,000 million.

Answers to Chapter 7
Task 2: Task Achievement

Check Your Understanding

Discuss the following question with a partner:

> Are there any differences and similarities between Task 1 'task achievement' and Task 2 'task achievement'? How?

Activity 1: Understanding the Assessment Standards of 'Task Achievement'

- Read the concept map which summarises the assessment standards of 'task achievement' of Task 2.
- Discuss with your partner the meanings of these keywords. Note down any differences in your understanding.

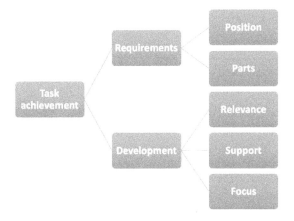

Content Requirements

There are two keywords under the 'requirements' aspect of this domain: (1) position; and (2) parts. Write down the two keywords next to the corresponding definitions.

Keyword	Definition
Position	The writer's standpoint or thesis statement, usually placed in the introductory paragraph
Parts	The essential components of a Task 2 essay, usually comprises an introduction, two body paragraphs, and a conclusion

Content Development

Three keywords are identified from the official IELTS writing descriptors which help explicate the expectations for candidates to develop their ideas. These keywords include (1) relevance, (2) support, and (3) focus. Write down the keywords next to the corresponding definitions.

Keyword	Definition
Support	Explanations, examples, reasons given by the writer to elaborate on or substantiate his/her points
Focus	A clearly defined topic for each paragraph, usually demonstrated by a clear topic sentence at the beginning of each body paragraph
Relevance	Ideas discussed in the essay are related to the question and the standpoint

---

Do you know?

'Task achievement' of Task 1 is a little bit different from 'task achievement' of Task 2 because the nature of the writing task is different. In Task 1, you are asked to report data from a graph; thus, you will be assessed based on your ability to summarise and compare data. In Task 2, on the other hand, you are asked to write a short essay on a given topic. Accordingly, your work will be evaluated with reference to the quality of your arguments and how you elaborate and/or support your arguments.

To understand more about these keywords, let's read two writing exemplars (Exemplars 7.1-7.2) written by university students to see what they (should not) look like in action.

T2-09

You should spend about 40 minutes on this task. Write about the following topic:

Due to the rapid technological development, new career options have emerged such as online store owners, and vloggers. People are becoming less willing to work in an office. Do you think the advantages of having a 'virtual' career outweigh its disadvantages?

Give reasons for your answer and include any relevant examples from your own knowledge or experience.

Write at least 250 words.

Exemplar 7.1	*Remarks*
Recently, there has been a popular trend of being vloggers or online store owners because of the rapid development of the Internet and modernisation of lifestyle. Moreover, many people start to consider the aforesaid 'virtual' roles as their full-time jobs and stop working in a physical workplace. Undoubtedly, there must be advantages and disadvantages of having a virtual career. Yet, it is my belief that the advantages outweigh its disadvantages.	Parts: Introduction *Standpoint/thesis statement*
To begin with, pursuing a virtual career, namely running an online store, brings flexible working schedule to the owners which enables them to design their personal timetable every day, including day-offs. Moreover, people like vloggers can kill two birds with one stone. In particular, they can videotape their daily matters while enjoying their time, such as, shopping and eating. Furthermore, the number of people who are obsessed with the Internet world continue to surge due to technological advancement which provides a major opportunity for those who have a virtual career to be well-known. In addition, these virtual jobs are not paid monthly; therefore, the 'workers' have the ability to earn a lot more by being slash workers.	Parts: Body 1 *A clear topic sentence focusing on advantages*
On the other hand, opponents to having a virtual career contend that it is risky to have a profession that relies solely on Internet communication. Specifically, while most of the 'workers' invest all of their time and money in order to be successful and popular, there is no guarantee that they would succeed; from what is reported on the news and social media, countless people have failed during the journey of becoming 'online celebrities'.	Parts: Body 2 *A clear topic sentence focusing on disadvantages* *Support through explanation* *Support through providing examples*
To conclude, every coin has two sides. Admittedly, while it is not necessary that being a youtuber or vloggers will bring you fame and glory eventually, I personally consider taking risk as a key to success and it will be worthwhile, especially to teenagers.	Parts: A concluding paragraph

Exemplar 7.2	*Remarks*
For example, Ricky Wong, is a businessman in Hong Kong; after his failure of getting a free TV license, he changed to open a TV channel and open an online store, he succeeded in attracting young people to buy his products and make a great profit. I think being a successful man do not need to follow the traditional track, but learn how to be innovative. I will take this as a good example.	Irrelevant example because the topic is about virtual career, but the example given is a successful businessman in Hong Kong

> **Do you know?**
>
> Unlike Task 1, there must be a concluding paragraph for IELTS Writing Task 2.

Activity 2: Writing a Position

- Read the following questions (T2-02 and T2-04) and read Exemplars 7.3-7.4.
- Evaluate how well the exemplars are written by referring to the definitions and examples of the related terms in Activity 1. If necessary, use the following guiding questions to help your evaluation:
  - o   Did the student state his/her standpoint or thesis statement of his/her essay clearly?
  - o   Did the student present the position in a succinct manner?
  - o   Was there enough scaffolding (e.g., background information) before the position statement is introduced?

T2-02

You should spend about 40 minutes on this task. Write about the following topic:

Advocates of high-stakes standardised tests believe that they provide an objective description of students' abilities; on the contrary, some teachers expressly underscore the many problems that these tests bring to the quality of their teaching.

Discuss both these views and give your opinion.

Give reasons for your answer and include any relevant examples from your own knowledge or experience.

Write at least 250 words.

Exemplar 7.3

Supporters of high-stakes standardized tests believe that they provide an objective description of students' abilities while some teachers concern about the quality of their teaching because of these standardized tests.

Guiding question	Yes/No	Explanation
Did the student state his/her standpoint or thesis statement of his/her essay clearly?	Yes	The student addressed the fact that there are two viewpoints on this issue. However, s/he could introduce her own opinion at the end, as requested by the question.
Did the student present the position in a succinct manner?	Yes	N/A
Was there enough scaffolding (e.g., background information) before the position statement is introduced?	No	One sentence could be added at the beginning of the paragraph to mention that high-stakes standardised tests are becoming more popular these days to establish the fact that this topic is worth discussing.

T2-04

You should spend about 40 minutes on this task. Write about the following topic:

Many university students are required to enrol in a number of general education courses. These courses are usually related to the social, cultural, psychological, and spiritual lives of young people.

What are the advantages of general education courses to university students?

Give reasons for your answer and include any relevant examples from your own knowledge or experience.

Write at least 250 words.

Exemplar 7.4

It is important for university students to take general education courses and I agree that it should be a compulsory course for the students. It is because general education courses disseminate different types of information and knowledge which students should learn. For example, social, cultural, psychological and spiritual knowledge. The above knowledge and information are good for student development. I will give reasons and explain my standpoint in this article.

Guiding question	Yes/No	Explanation
Did the student state his/her standpoint or thesis statement of his/her essay clearly?	Yes	The student addressed both parts of the question: (1) how important general education courses are and (2) whether general education courses should be made compulsory.
Did the student present the position in a succinct manner?	Yes	The standpoint is presented in one clear sentence.
Was there enough scaffolding (e.g., background information) before the position statement is introduced?	No	The student should start the paragraph with background information but not his/her position.

Activity 3: Writing a Four-part Essay

- Read the following question (T2-03) and Exemplar 7.5.
- Evaluate how well the exemplar is written by referring to the definitions and examples of the related terms in Activity 1. If necessary, use the following guiding questions to help your evaluation:

  o   Did the student include an introduction?
  o   Did the student include at least two body paragraphs?
  o   Were the body paragraphs organised in a focused and logical manner?
  o   Did the student include a conclusion?
  o   Do you think the essay is too long? How can it be shortened?

T2-03

You should spend about 40 minutes on this task. Write about the following topic:

Some parents believe in educating their children themselves and homeschool their children. What are the advantages of homeschooling? Should homeschooling become a regular option for parents?

Give reasons for your answer and include any relevant examples from your own knowledge or experience.

Write at least 250 words.

Exemplar 7.5

Homeschooling has become an increasingly hot topic among parents. Parents might have seen failures in their children at standard schools, or might have seen talents in their children which could not be developed in schools, and start to wonder if homeschooling is their right option.

While it is still widely recognized as an unlawful act for parents to deprive their children from the right to receive formal education, more and more parents realize that there are exceptional situations which can be accepted by government authorities as legitimate cases for homeschooling.

However, there are both advantages and disadvantages arisen from the homeschooling practice which we shall discuss below.

One size doesn't fit all. If we appreciate that each student is a special individual, how can we not question if the standard curriculum is suitable for all children? Even in a class of 40, there are students who are good at mathematics and students who are good at music. Standard curriculum is designed for 'average' children. For example, when 80% of the students in Grade 3 are ready to learn how to do the multiplication 3 x 3, the standard curriculum neglects the need of those who can do 1+1 only, and those who are doing 33 x 33 at the same age. Schools teach these standard curriculums to build our children like a gear in the mechanism of the society, like a clerk, an accountant, a doctor. It is not flexible enough to fit every student's need.

Homeschooling can be advantageous to students who have individual strength that cannot be developed at school, and those with special education needs whose needs cannot be addressed at school as well. Moreover, during homeschooling, parents can develop their relationship with their children and build a harmonious family.

On the other hand, parents have to be very careful if they adopt homeschooling. Currently, there are insufficient supports and lack of resources for parents to homeschool their children. If the parents have not received sufficient education themselves, it is questionable how the effect of their homeschooling would be. Also, there is no standard assessment for the parents to understand the developmental levels of their children. Parents could not provide the best teaching to their children based on the results.

It is also important for parents to understand that schools are not only a place to develop their children's academic abilities, but also a place to teach children social skills, ethical values, physical strength, in order to ensure students' whole person development. Children who receive education at home lack the chance to socialize with fellow classmates and are deprived of the chance to develop social skills. Someday, when they are back to school or when they go to work, they will have a hard time cooperating with others if they did not develop their social skills at an early stage.

Homeschooling can be advantageous to some students, but there are lots of things that parents have to be careful of. If parents decide to take this route, they must be well advised of all the advantages and disadvantages of homeschooling, and make the right choice for their children. (521 words)

Guiding question	Yes/No	Explanation
Did the student include an introduction?	**Yes**	**N/A**
Did the student include at least two body paragraphs?	**Yes**	**N/A**
Were the body paragraphs organised in a focused and logical manner?	**No**	**Topic sentences are missing in most of the body paragraphs. Sometimes, the main idea of the paragraph is only revealed at the end of the paragraph (e.g., in para 4)**
Did the student include a conclusion?	**Yes**	**N/A**
Do you think the essay is too long? How can it be shortened?	**Yes**	**Paras 1–3 can be combined and shortened into one introductory paragraph.** **Para 4 can be deleted because it is about the limitations of traditional schooling but not related to adv. and disadv. of homeschooling.**

Activity 4: Writing with Relevant Ideas

- Read the following question (T2-05) and Exemplars 7.6-7.8.
- Evaluate how well the exemplars are written by referring to the definitions and examples of the related terms in Activity 1. If necessary, use the following guiding questions to help your evaluation:

  o   Were the ideas relevant to the topic?
  o   Were the ideas relevant to the position?

T2-05

You should spend about 40 minutes on this task. Write about the following topic:

Distance education enables students to study at their own pace. Nevertheless, it also creates problems including high withdrawal rate and lack of interaction between teachers and students. Explain some possible reasons for these problems and suggest some solutions.

Give reasons for your answer and include any relevant examples from your own knowledge or experience.

Write at least 250 words.

Exemplar 7.6

Distance education allows students to study wherever they want. However, it also creates problems including high withdrawal rate and lack of interaction between teachers and students. I reckon that inadequate monitoring and time-consuming student-teacher communication between are the causes of the above problems.

First and foremost, inadequate monitoring brought by distance education will cause high withdrawal rate. By adopting distance education, teachers and students are no longer sitting in the same classroom in class - students are required to watch pre-recorded video lessons instead. In view of the phenomenon that most parents need to work in daytime, there will not be any authorities to supervise students in classes. As a result, this may contribute to a high withdrawal rate. Offering a tutor for every student is clearly unaffordable. Therefore, assigning after-lesson quizzes to students is a way to solve the problem. If all students are required to take a test regarding teaching content after each lesson, they will be more willing to attend online lessons with a view to get a pass. The pupils will attend and concentrate in online classes.

Guiding question	Yes/No	Explanation
Were the ideas relevant to the topic?	Yes	The question asks about causes of the problem of high withdrawal rate and solutions; the student provides one reason here, i.e., inadequate monitoring and a relevant solution.
Were the ideas relevant to the position?	Yes	In the introduction, the student mentions inadequate monitoring as a cause. Then, s/he discusses this cause in the subsequent paragraph.

Exemplar 7.7

Distance education is advantageous because students can study at their own pace. They can choose the time and the place to study. Technology is an important element in distance education. Online education is the focus of distance education.

...

Moreover, distance education causes the lack of interactions between teachers and students. As distance education is not face-to-face study, students do not have time to communicate with teachers. They only need to finish the task and learn by themselves. When they do not have much time to interact with teachers, their relationships are not close. It makes students feel alienated because their teachers do not know them. It is difficult to help them to make an efficient teaching plan. Students cannot get the efficient way to learn too.

Guiding question	Yes/No	Explanation
Were the ideas relevant to the topic?	**No**	**The position (thesis statement) is irrelevant to the question.**
Were the ideas relevant to the position?	**No**	**The thesis statement in the introduction is about the advantages of distance education, but the subsequent paragraph is about the disadvantages.**

Exemplar 7.8

As technology develops, many students learn by themselves in distance education. However, students who study in front of the computer lack interactions with teachers and it causes high withdrawal rate. In this article, I will provide some reasons and solutions to solve these problems.

The main reason is that students lack supervision in distance education. It is good that students can dominate their own study and learn flexibly. However, it requires students to have high self-regulated skill, which is challenging for some students. For example, students may play with their phones during the class. Also, it is hard for teachers to assess students' real performance because students can search for answers online. The solution is that parents can be the supervisors to supervise their children's learning to ensure the effectiveness of distance education.

Guiding question	Yes/No	Explanation
Were the ideas relevant to the topic?	**Partly relevant**	**While the topic sentence of the second paragraph is relevant to the topic, some of the content is not, e.g., playing phones, hard for teachers to assess students' performance, parents as supervisors.**
Were the ideas relevant to the position?	**No**	**The position mentioned in the introduction is about interactions, but the subsequent paragraph is about supervision.**

Activity 5: Writing with Support

- Read the following question (T2-06) and Exemplars 7.8-7.9.
- Evaluate how well the exemplars are written by referring to the definitions and examples of the related terms in Activity 1. If necessary, use the following guiding questions to help your evaluation:

  o   How are the ideas elaborated (e.g., giving examples, explanations)?
  o   Are the supports provided effective and adequate? Why/why not?
  o   If your answer is 'no' for Q2, how can the support be strengthened?

T2-06

You should spend about 40 minutes on this task. Write about the following topic:

Family friendly measures (e.g., flexible working hours) should be adopted by companies to ensure the work-life balance of their employees.

To what extent do you agree or disagree with this opinion?

Give reasons for your answer and include any relevant examples from your own knowledge or experience.

Write at least 250 words.

Exemplar 7.8

First and foremost, some caring initiatives commonly implemented by companies, namely the change of working environment from office to home, could bring a range of benefits to employees which ultimately lead to the rise of productivity. Parents could make use of the extra time to be with their children which undoubtedly strengthen their relationship and help relieve pressure from work. Meanwhile, staff could concentrate on their projects in a less crowded environment. While the mental wellbeing of staff is becoming positive, companies which offer similar flexible measures would definitely enjoy relatively higher productivity than those without family caring policies.

Q1. How are the ideas elaborated (e.g., giving examples, explanations)?

Explanation ('parents could make use of extra time …')

Q2. Are the supports provided effective and adequate? Why/why not?

No, because no examples are given to illustrate 'a range of benefits'.

Q3. If your answer is 'no' for Q2, how can the support be strengthened?

Give some examples to illustrate 'a range of benefits' e.g., family relationship, personal health, concentration, etc.

Exemplar 7.9

Without doubt, long working hours have been a major source of discontent for almost all the employees. The reason for insisting on pushing them to beat their brains out and work until the last moment of the day is to ensure a high level of productivity of the company. Surprisingly, the weekly working hours in Germany are 30 hours while those in Hong Kong are 50 hours. However, the former leads to greater productivity than the latter. This demonstrates that working quality should be the key to a company's high productivity instead of long working hours. Therefore, companies should take good care of their employees by implementing measures like flexible working hours, instead of simply prolonging their employees' working hours.

Q1. How are the ideas elaborated (e.g., giving examples, explanations)?

Giving an example ('… the weekly working hours in Germany …')

Q2. Are the supports provided effective and adequate? Why/why not?

No, because no explanations are provided regarding why shorter working hours may increase productivity.

Q3. If your answer is 'no' for Q2, how can the support be strengthened?

Explain why shorter working hours may increase productivity.

Activity 6: Writing with a Clear Focus

- Read the following question (T2-07) and Exemplars 7.10-7.11.
- Evaluate how well the exemplars are written by referring to the definitions and examples of the related terms in Activity 1. If necessary, use the following guiding questions to help your evaluation:

  o   What is the topic sentence of the paragraph?
  o   Is the topic sentence focused and clear?

T2-07

You should spend about 40 minutes on this task. Write about the following topic:

It is not uncommon nowadays for people to work overseas. Working overseas allows people to experience different cultures and extend their social and professional connections. However, some find it hard to adapt due to nostalgia and acculturation.

Discuss both these views and give your opinion.

Give reasons for your answer and include any relevant examples from your own knowledge or experience.

Write at least 250 words.

Exemplar 7.10

However, working overseas is a double-edged sword, which could lead to pros and cons, because people from different countries have distinctive cultures. For example, westerners and Chinese treat their co-workers differently. As a result, foreign people may feel awkward when interacting with local people. At the end, it may result in positive or negative effects. For instance, I used to work in Beijing for my internship. I was an administrator assistant in a corporation. Because of the language barrier, it caused me to miss Hong Kong. Luckily, the local people were pleasant enough to take care of every colleague, and I convinced myself to adapt to the new environment in order to learn new working skills. Hence, no matter what people earn by working overseas, having an open mind is the key.

Q1. What is the topic sentence of the paragraph?

'However, working overseas is a double-edged sword, which could lead to pros and cons, because people from different countries have distinctive cultures.'

Q2. Is the topic sentence focused and clear?

No, because the topic sentence simply states the fact that people from different countries have different cultures; however, it does not argue whether it is a pro or con.

Exemplar 7.11

On one side of the argument, oversea working experience enables people to have cultural explorations. People who work abroad might face the challenges of new languages, customs and lifestyles. All of these cultural aspects provide them with valuable cultural experiences in both professional and personal life in other countries. Apart from the cultural experience, working abroad facilitates people's expansion of their social and professional connections. They can meet and work with local people and people from all walks of life in their workplace, which allows them to establish friendships and partnerships. Therefore, working abroad provides chances to enrich people's cultural experiences and helps the formation of international relationships in their professional lives.

Q1. What is the topic sentence of the paragraph?

'On the one side of the argument, overseas working experience enables people to have cultural explorations.'

Q2. Is the topic sentence focused and clear?

Yes, because it focuses on one pro – cultural explorations. However, some ideas in the paragraph do not support this focus e.g., the student mentioned about 'the challenges of new languages, customs and lifestyles', which should be put under a con paragraph.

Activity 7: Peer Evaluation

Based on your understanding of the assessment standards of 'task achievement', provide feedback to Exemplar 7.12 written by a university student. The guiding questions at the end of each paragraph focus on the different facets of the 'task achievement' domain we discussed in this chapter.

T2-12

You should spend about 40 minutes on this task. Write about the following topic:

   It is popular nowadays for people to order takeaway food (e.g., lunch) from their workplace because they are too busy to prepare meals. However, there are still many people who bring home-made food to eat in their workplace because they think DIY food is healthier.

   Discuss both these views.

   Give reasons for your answer and include any relevant examples from your own knowledge or experience.

   Write at least 250 words.

Exemplar 7.12

Nowadays, it is common for people to order takeaway food (e.g. lunch) from their workplace because they are too busy to prepare meals. Yet, there are numerous people who bring homemade food to eat at workplace as they consider DIY food is healthier. In this essay, both advantages and disadvantages of the two methods will be discussed.

Questions for paragraph 1:

Q1.   What is the position given by the writer?

   'In this essay, both advantages and disadvantages of two methods will be discussed' (thesis statement).

Q2.   Is the position given in a concise manner?

   Yes.

Q3.   Is the position scaffolded by background information?

   Yes, the background information is related to how some people prepare their own meals while others do not.

Q4.   Is the position relevant to the question?

   Yes, because the question asks the writer to discuss both views, i.e., why some people prepare their own meals while others do not.

   To begin with, ordering takeaway is undoubtedly convenient for people as it only takes a short time for people to decide what they want to have for lunch and pay for it. The whole process does not take more than 3 minutes; so this way helps to save time, which is vitally important in a hectic and fast-paced society. However, the food is believed to be less healthy as lots of sugar, salt, oil and seasoning would be added into most of the dishes.

Questions for paragraph 2:

Q1.   What is the topic sentence?

   'To begin with, ordering takeaway is undoubtedly convenient for people as it only takes a short time for people to decide what they want to have for lunch and pay for it.'

Q2. Is the topic sentence focused and clear?

Yes, because the topic sentence focuses on one advantage, i.e., convenience.

Q3. How does the writer provide support to his/her topic sentence?

Explanation: 'The whole process does not take more than 3 minutes; so this way helps to save time, which is vitally important in a hectic and fast-paced society.'

Q4. Is the support in the paragraph adequate and relevant to the topic sentence? If not, give suggestions.

No. The last sentence is not related to pro of buying takeaway food. This last part should be put in a paragraph which focuses on the con of buying takeaway food.

On the other hand, making homemade food means that the person can design the most suitable recipe for oneself. For example, if a person is allergic to specific kinds of ingredients or food, he is able to avoid it when he cooks his lunch. Moreover, cooking at home saves money. Furthermore, making DIY food can ensure the hygiene of the food. However, people will have less time to take a rest as they need extra time to prepare a meal every day at night.

Questions for paragraph 3:

Q1. What is the topic sentence?

'On the other hand, making homemade food means that the person can design the most suitable recipe for oneself.'

Q2. Is the topic sentence focused and clear?

Yes, because it focuses on one advantage of preparing homemade food, i.e., a personalised recipe.

Q3. How does the writer provide support to his/her topic sentence?

Example: 'For example, if the person is allergic to specific kinds of ingredients or food, he is able to avoid it when he cooks his lunch'.

Q4. Is the support in the paragraph adequate and relevant to the topic sentence? If not, give suggestions.

No, the writer is trying to incorporate too many ideas in a single paragraph. In total, three main ideas were mentioned: (1) personalised recipe; (2) save money; and (3) hygiene. I suggest the student focus on one or two and provide explanations and examples.

To sum up, ordering takeaway or bringing home-made food has its merits and drawbacks. What matters is that the person has extra time and knows his food preference.

Questions for paragraph 4:

Q1. How many parts are there in this exemplar? What are the parts?

Four parts – Introduction, body paragraph 1, body paragraph 2, conclusion

Activity 7: Exercise

Based on your understanding of 'task achievement', evaluate the essay of T2-10 using the guiding questions in the form. Try to imitate the exemplar when responding to T2-29.

T2-10

You should spend about 40 minutes on this task. Write about the following topic:

Given the greater longevity of people these days, some argue that people should retire at a later stage. What are some of the problems if people's retirement is delayed?

Give reasons for your answer and include any relevant examples from your own knowledge or experience.

Write at least 250 words.

People have a longer life expectancy nowadays so some may suggest retirement can be delayed, since they believe the old citizens can still enjoy a meaningful life. However, others think the retirement age should not be delayed as it may pose a threat to social mobility and to the long-term development of a company.

On the one hand, delaying retirement age may affect social mobility because it obstructs the younger generation to enhance their social status and financial capability. As the older generation starts their career earlier than the younger, the former is much more experienced and sophisticated. Thus, it is conceivable that the older generation usually is at a higher position in workplace. When they decide to retire, those who are younger and capable enough would be promoted. However, if the society encourages people to retire at a later stage, there would be insufficient vacancies to raise the social status of the younger generation. Despite the numerous attempts of the younger generation, they may still fail to improve their social status.

On the other hand, postponing the retirement age can be detrimental to the development of an institution. To demonstrate, as people begin to age, they are destined to experience slower metabolism, which exerts an undesirable influence on both their body and mind. As a consequence, they tend to act slowly in their job position, having a negative effect on their working efficiency and quality. In addition, the elderly people are also inclined to show less commitment to their career. This is attributed to the fact that the older generation face less challenges and difficulties in their work. Therefore, they are likely to focus more on their family and leisure life, which may lead to their under-performed results.

The later people retire, the lower the social mobility and the worse the institution develops. This probably is the concern of both the young generation and the decision-makers of those corporations. (320 words)

Guiding question	Yes/No	Explanation
Did the student state the standpoint clearly?	**Yes**	**Standpoint is given in the last paragraph.**
Did the student include at least two body paragraphs?	**Yes**	**Para. 2 and 3 are the body paragraphs.**
Was there a topic sentence in each body paragraph?	**Yes**	**The first sentences of para. 2 and 3 are topic sentences.**
Were the ideas relevant to the topic?	**Yes**	**The main ideas are related to the negative impact of delayed retirement.**
Were the ideas elaborated by giving sufficient and appropriate examples and explanations?	**Yes**	**Explanations are provided in the two body paragraphs.**

T2-29

You should spend about 40 minutes on this task. Write about the following topic:

An increasing number of domestic appliances (e.g., air purifiers and water purifiers) are on the market to tackle water pollution and air pollution. Why is this the case? Is this a positive indicator of the development of human beings? Give reasons for your answer and include any relevant examples from your own knowledge or experience. Write at least 250 words.

Tip

If you don't remember the requirements of 'task achievement' of Task 2, you can refer to Activity 1 in this chapter before writing.

Answers to Chapter 8

Task 2: Coherence and Cohesion

Check Your Understanding

According to what you have learnt in Chapter 4, choose the elements that are essential to 'coherence and cohesion' from the following choices:

A. Paragraphs
B. Collocation
C. Punctuation
D. Pronouns
E. Various sentence structures
F. Cohesive devices
G. Synonyms
H. Supporting ideas

Activity 1: Understanding the Assessment Standards of 'Coherence and Cohesion'

Since the assessment standards of this domain in Task 2 are identical to those in Task 1, refer to Activity 1 in Chapter 4 for definitions of keywords of the assessment standards.

Activity 2: Achieving Coherence through Paragraphing

- Read the following question (T2-13) and Exemplars 8.1-8.3.
- Evaluate how well the exemplars are written by referring to the definitions of the terms 'coherence' and 'paragraphing'. If necessary, use these guiding questions to help your evaluation.

  o Did the students connect ideas by organising information thoughtfully and logically within a paragraph?
  o Did the students connect ideas by organising information thoughtfully and logically between paragraphs?

Do you know?

When writing a body paragraph, it is important to bear in mind that there is a 'subject' and a 'controlling idea' in each paragraph. A 'subject' can be 'national health care insurance' and a 'controlling idea' can be an advantage of having a national health insurance (e.g., improve the health of residents).

T2-13

You should spend about 40 minutes on this task. Write about the following topic:

   In some countries, healthcare expenditure is covered by the government, while in other countries, the cost is undertaken by both the public and the government. Do you think the advantages of 'sharing the cost' outweigh the disadvantages?

   Give reasons for your answer and include any relevant examples from your own knowledge or experience.

   Write at least 250 words.

Exemplar 8.1

So important is social productivity that it is reflected in the gross domestic product (GDP) of a country. A sound health care system does not only improve the wellbeing of its citizens, but also boosts the country's productivity, and, by the same token, its economy. Therefore, the government should not be penny-pinching on medical care from a bird's eye view.

Furthermore, tackling inequality is one of the major goals for most of the governments in the world. Having paid taxes, citizens are excepted to receive basic public services – health care, to name but a few. From the perspective of citizen rights, it is the government's responsibility that no one be turned a blind eye to by medical practitioners because of a lack of money.

Guiding question	Yes/No	Evidence
Did the students connect ideas by organising information thoughtfully and logically within a paragraph?	**Yes**	**1st para: about how a good health care system can increase productivity** **2nd para: about citizen rights**
Did the students connect ideas by organising information thoughtfully and logically between paragraphs?	**No**	**The two ideas in the two paragraphs do not seem to connect. The student can begin the second paragraph with 'In addition to increasing social productivity, it is the citizens' right to enjoy quality healthcare benefits'.**

Exemplar 8.2

First and foremost, 'sharing the cost' reduces financial burden of the government. Even the government pays for the medical cost, it does not mean that there is nothing to do with citizens financially. There is no magic money tree. Looking at the UK, the financial issue of NHS has been discussed for decades. To cover the rising amount of health care expenditure, the so-called 'solutions' carried out by the government are either cutting the budget of another area or increasing tax rates, sometimes both. On façade, people do not need to pay a penny for the services they received. They may even pay more than they expect at the end of the day. 'Sharing the cost reduces the financial burden of both the government and the citizens, to a certain extent.

In addition to solving financial problems, the fact that the public share the medical cost can somehow increase the quality of health care services. 'Sharing the cost' means that more money can be spent on national health services and more money means a better quality of services. Take nurses as an example, the inadequate number of nurses working in public hospitals is not a new topic to Hong Kongers. Nurses have always suffered from heavy workload and stressful working environment. If more financial resources for professional employment are available, public hospitals are able to employ more nurses to provide a better service for patients. Therefore, it is not difficult to find that sharing of cost by the public can contribute to higher service quality in return.

Guiding question	Yes/No	Evidence
Did the students connect ideas by organising information thoughtfully and logically within a paragraph?	Yes	1st para: about reducing the government's financial burden 2nd para: about healthcare services of higher quality
Did the students connect ideas by organising information thoughtfully and logically between paragraphs?	Yes	The two paragraphs are joint with the phrase 'as well as solving financial problems'. A more appropriate phrase to connect the two paragraphs can be: 'apart from solving financial problems'.

Exemplar 8.3

To begin with, fresh graduates couldn't afford to pay the medical cost annually, not to mention that many are unemployed or are still paying the student loan. If Hong Kong is planning to propose the 'sharing cost' plan, many students and fresh graduates, especially for those who suffer financially, will surely struggle to pay an extra cost for social welfare. Being a year-three undergraduate, I have to work hard to repay my own school fee. After completing the four-year program, the government loan will start rolling like a snowball, with the interest rate gradually increasing over years; I am therefore determined to put an end to it as quickly as I can. However, once implementing the new medical policy, every student on loan like me is given no choice but to delay the government loan payment. This could be bad news for us all, not to mention that fresh graduates could hardly earn a promising income when they first embark on a new career. Hence, being a soon-to-be fresh graduate carrying heavy loans, I urge the authority to consider whether 'sharing the cost' is applicable to all of their people or not.

In addition, the notion of 'sharing cost' is mostly distributed to the elderly care or those with serious illness; healthy individuals are likely to be excluded from getting the welfare. Unlike medical insurance, the expenditure on health care protection mainly concerns those with very urgent medical needs, but do not necessarily guarantee every taxpayer's access to the service. Helping others in need should be a voluntary act out of sincerity, but not a kind of responsibility enforced by the authority. I wouldn't want to feel unwanted to help those in dire emergencies, but it could feel like a burden with big responsibility to 'share the cost' with strangers. Doing kind acts is everyone's moral responsibility, but they should never come from obeying the commands of the authority.

Guiding question	Yes/No	Evidence
Did the students connect ideas by organising information thoughtfully and logically within a paragraph?	Yes	1st para: students cannot afford medical cost 2nd para: the issue of unfairness
Did the students connect ideas by organising information thoughtfully and logically between paragraphs?	No	the two paragraphs are not connected in terms of ideas. The 2nd paragraph is not built upon the first one.

Activity 3: Achieving Cohesion through using Cohesive Devices

- Read the following question (T2-14) and Exemplars 8.4–8.6.
- Evaluate how well the exemplars are written by referring to the definitions of the terms 'cohesion' and 'cohesive devices'. If necessary, use these guiding questions to help your evaluation.

    o   What cohesive devices did the students use in the paragraphs?
    o   Were the cohesive devices used meaningfully and accurately?
    o   Was there a variety of cohesive devices used?

T2-14

You should spend about 40 minutes on this task. Write about the following topic:

Despite the enhancement of medical care, modern people are still tortured by various physical and psychological problems. What are some of the causes of the above phenomena? What can be done to improve people's health?

Give reasons for your answer and include any relevant examples from your own knowledge or experience.

Write at least 250 words.

Exemplar 8.4

Secondly, lack of leisure time also affects the physical health and mental health of people. For the working population, most of them need to work more than ten hours a day because there is no law or regulation to regulate the working hours. Long working hours result in the lack of leisure time. People suffer from great pressure from their jobs but they do not have time to relax or do exercise. Thus, the physical and psychological problems exist. To solve the problem, the government need to have regulations on working hours. If people have more leisure time, they may have less pressure.

Guiding question	Yes/No	Response
What cohesive devices did the students use in the paragraphs?		'secondly', 'for . . .', 'thus', 'to solve the problem'
Were the cohesive devices used meaningfully and accurately?	Yes	'secondly' to show sequence of ideas
Was there a variety of cohesive devices used?	Yes	'for . . .' to show aspect 'thus' to show result 'to solve the problem' to present solution

Exemplar 8.5

First, citizens could not deal with the high medical expenses. Along with the improvement of medical care, the cost of existing medical technology may be reduced. However, the cost of new or more effective treatment would be. Although the government has set up some welfare policies, such as providing public medical service and medical subsidies to the elderly, the expenditure on medical treatment is still high. So, many patients, especially those who suffer from serious illness, such as cancer, are still tortured by the sickness.

Guiding question	Yes/No	Response
What cohesive devices did the students use in the paragraphs?		'first', 'along with . . .', 'however', 'although', 'such as', 'so'
Were the cohesive devices used meaningfully and accurately?	Yes	'first' to show sequence of ideas
Was there a variety of cohesive devices used?	Yes	'along with . . .' to show parallel ideas 'however' and 'although' to show contrast 'such as' to give examples 'so' to show result

Exemplar 8.6

Undoubtedly, more sports facilities would enhance the public's motivation to exercise. Even more and more people like to work out at fitness clubs, it is still too expensive for the low-income people to afford this kind of sport facility. Therefore, if the government provides more open areas for recreation, it would definitely give the public a great chance to do exercises and stay healthy without spending too much money on joining a fitness club. According to the news reports, a person could lose about 5 kg in three weeks if he exercises for 30 minutes a day regularly. Some health problems could be avoided like high blood pressure. Also, doing exercises could make us happy and relaxed. We could stay away from depression.

Guiding question	Yes/No	Response
What cohesive devices did the students use in the paragraphs?		'even', 'therefore', 'according to', 'also'
Were the cohesive devices used meaningfully and accurately?	Yes	'even' to show contrast 'therefore' to show result
Was there a variety of cohesive devices used?	Yes	'according to' to show reference 'also' to show addition of ideas

Learn online

If you want to learn more about different cohesive devices (e.g., connectives, conjunctions, transitional phrases), visit this website: https://www.smart-words.org/linking-words/.

Activity 4: Achieving Cohesion through using Pronouns

- Read the following question (T2-15) and Exemplars 8.7–8.8.
- Evaluate how well the exemplars are written by referring to the definitions of the terms 'cohesion' and 'pronouns'. If necessary, use these guiding questions to help your evaluation.

  o   What pronouns did the students use in the paragraphs?
  o   What did the pronouns refer to?
  o   Were the pronouns used accurately?

T2-15

You should spend about 40 minutes on this task. Write about the following topic:

Investors are more important than teachers in that they usually make more money.

To what extent do you agree or disagree with this opinion?

Give reasons for your answer and include any relevant examples from your own knowledge or experience.

Write at least 250 words.

Exemplar 8.7

Though investors might make more money than teachers, there are many factors in determining the importance of a job, such as the contributions and impacts on the society. Teachers are important as they *make tremendous contribution to the society - educating new generations continuously. Although knowledge is intangible, it is long-lasting. Comparatively, earning money is temporary, as we exchange money for the product or service we want. For the contributions teachers made to the society, it could be seen that a lot of successful people are well-educated, such as professors in the university. These people are continually nurturing the young generations before they enter the society. People learn, use their knowledge and teach. These people are needed in a healthy and progressive society. Hence, teachers are very important in the society.*

Guiding question	Response
What pronouns did the students use in the paragraph?	'they' (line 3), 'it' (line 4), 'we' (lines 5 & 6), 'it' (line 7), 'they' (line 9)
What did the pronouns refer to?	'they' (line 3): teachers 'it' (line 4): knowledge 'we' (lines 5 & 6): people 'it' (line 7): dummy pronoun 'they' (line 9): young generations 'their' (line 9): people
Were the pronouns used accurately?	Yes, but the two 'we' should be replaced with 'people when 'people' is mentioned the first time

Exemplar 8.8

From the economic perspective, investors improve our quality of life. Through different investments and technological advancements, investors make our life much easier and more convenient. As for the teachers, they may have indirect contribution to the economy. As mentioned, teachers help to build up the ability of investors in dealing with different problems including human management, technological innovation etc. The investors may not be successful without receiving education.

Guiding question	Response
What pronouns did the students use in the paragraph?	'our' (lines 1 & 2), 'they' (line 3)
What did the pronouns refer to?	'our': people 'they': teachers
Were the pronouns used accurately?	Yes

Activity 5: Achieving Cohesion through using Synonyms

- Read the following question (T2-17) and Exemplars 8.8–8.10.
- Evaluate how well the exemplars are written by referring to the definitions of the terms 'cohesion' and 'synonyms' and responding to the guiding questions under each exemplar.

T2-17

You should spend about 40 minutes on this task. Write about the following topic:

Some countries donate large sums of money to help other countries in need, while some citizens of these countries are still starving. Why would these countries take the above action? What can be done to help the starving people?

Give reasons for your answer and include any relevant examples from your own knowledge or experience.

Write at least 250 words.

Exemplar 8.9

I think the main reason for some countries to donate money to other countries is that they want to get a bigger influence in the world. They give other countries resources to build schools and rails. And their names may be the name of the school or the station. This is one of the ways for them to be popular in the world. Their countries will be praised by other countries, and their power in the world may be bigger, since they show that they have enough resources and they are willing to help others. It is a way for them to make friends with other countries and they may have a bigger influence in the world; on the contrary, helping their local people may not get this effect. Therefore, they neglect their citizens' needs.

Guiding question	Response
Did the student use any synonyms?	Yes e.g., 'donate money' = 'give . . . resources', 'get a bigger influence' = 'be popular' = 'their power in the world may be bigger'
Which words could be replaced by synonyms? What synonyms do you suggest the students use?	'countries', 'get a bigger influence' 'countries' = nations/communities 'get a bigger influence' = exert more potent influence/impact on . . .

Exemplar 8.10

Unfortunately, the wealth gap is enlarging in lots of places in the world, including these countries. To help the starving people, there are mainly two approaches. In order to solve the problem from the root, the government should embrace equity in the society. For example, ensuring a better access to tertiary education. On the other hand, the government can provide subsidies or allowances to people living below the poverty line.

Guiding question	Response
Did the student use any synonyms? Which words could be replaced by synonyms? What synonyms do you suggest the students use?	No 'the government', 'people' 'the government' = authorities 'people' = individuals

Exemplar 8.11

Some countries donate a large amount of money to help the suffering countries. The former are usually developed countries while the latter are less developed countries. Food products in poor countries are usually exported to other countries for profit, even if people in the poor country are in need of food. More developed countries benefit from the export of these food products, but the countries that produce the food may experience food scarcity and higher food prices with no proper interventions from the corrupted government. As a result, most developed countries, which put emphasis on human rights and morality, would help the poor countries.

Guiding question	Response
Did the student use any synonyms?	'less developed countries' = 'poor countries' = 'suffering countries'
Which words could be replaced by synonyms? What synonyms do you suggest the students use?	'export', 'food' 'export' = 'ship'/ 'sell overseas', 'food' = 'nourishment'

Activity 6: Peer Evaluation

Based on your understanding of the assessment standards of 'coherence and cohesion', complete the evaluation form for Exemplar 8.11.

In the evaluation, complete the 'evaluate' section by assessing (1) whether the element concerned is present in the exemplar (the yes/no question) and (2) how well the element is presented in the exemplar. Complete the 'suggest' section by writing an improved version of the element concerned. The 'suggest' section can be left blank if the exemplar demonstrates a good quality in an aspect.

T2-18

You should spend about 40 minutes on this task. Write about the following topic:

It is important for travellers to develop adequate understanding of the culture of the destination country. What are some of the advantages of understanding the culture beforehand?

Give reasons for your answer and include any relevant examples from your own knowledge or experience.

Write at least 250 words.

Exemplar 8.12

There are many different cultural differences that travelers can be aware of when traveling to different nations. Cultures can sometimes vary drastically from one's own. So, it is advised that travelers research the local conventions and try to understand the culture of the area prior to departure.

Having a basic idea of the region's culture can help travelers to form a deeper understanding of the local people and can prevent them from offending anyone. Sometimes, traditions are deeply rooted within a culture. People take things very seriously that outsiders aren't typically aware of or understand. For example, in America, the 'OK' gesture is a kind of standard communication for daily use; however, in Japan, it means 'money'; in Brazil, it's akin to extending the middle finger in the U.S. People in China may think that touching children's head would be normal behavior, which, in Myanmar, is regarded to be a very disrespectful behavior. Without knowing the actual meaning of such cross-cultural gesture in different countries, it will not only cause misunderstanding but also conflicts. If travelers get well-prepared and search for the cultural differences beforehand, they will avoid causing faux-pas and embarrassing situations.

Another advantage for having some fundamental grasp of local cultures is that it's a great way to open doors and gain access to experiences that other travelers may not get to enjoy. Imagine, there are two travelers visiting the Arc de Triomphe now. One of them knows its history and local people's view about it, the other does not. It is easy to foresee that the former will have a better understanding of the architecture and immerse successfully into the environment; the latter one will probably view it as a building and quickly take a photo to have it 'instagramed'. Knowing the cultural and historical background of a country and its architectures will give travelers more colorful and memorable experiences.

To conclude, developing the understanding of the culture of the traveling destination will bring benefits to travelers as they are able to avoid offences and gain more fruitful experiences. (339 words)

Assessment standard	Guiding question	Yes/No	Evaluate	Suggest
Paragraphing	Did the students connect ideas by organising information thoughtfully and logically within a paragraph?	Yes	**1st body paragraph: about being able to avoid offending local people + relevant examples** **2nd body paragraph: about being able to enjoy the travelling experience more + a relevant example**	N/A
	Did the students connect ideas by organising information thoughtfully and logically between paragraphs?	Yes	**The second body paragraph is connected with the first body paragraph by the words 'another advantage …'.**	**The linkage between the two body paragraphs can be strengthened by using the following sentence in the outset of the second body paragraph: 'Developing a better understanding of foreign cultures not only lowers the likelihood of offending the locals, it also enables travellers to enjoy the cultural experience to the fullest.'**
Cohesive devices	Were the cohesive devices used meaningfully and accurately?	Yes	**'for example', 'for instance' to give examples** **'to conclude' to show concluding thoughts**	**Other forms of cohesive devices could be used to show contrast, comparison, reason, consequence, addition of ideas etc.**
	Was there a variety of cohesive devices used?	No	**Only two types of cohesive devices were used.**	
Pronouns	Did the student use any pronouns?	Yes	**'you' = travellers (para 2, line 2), 'it' = the ok gesture (para 2, line 6), 'they' = travellers (para 2 line 12), 'it' = understanding of foreign culture (para 3, line 2), 'them' = two travellers (para 3, line 4), 'former & latter' = two travellers (para 3, lines 5–6), 'it' = Arc de Triomphe (para 3, line 7), 'they' = travellers (para 4, line 2)**	N/A
	Were the pronouns used accurately?	Partly	**inconsistent use of pronouns for 'travellers'** **inaccurate use of 'former' and 'latter'**	**use 'they' (but not 'you') to refer to travellers.** **should write 'the former' and 'the latter' but not 'the former one' and 'the latter one'.**
Synonyms	Did the student use any synonyms?	Yes	**'nations' (para 1) = 'destinations' (para 4), 'cultures' (para 1) = 'traditions' (para 2), 'faux pas' (para 2) = 'embarrassing situation' (para 2), 'architecture' (para 3) = 'buildings' (para 3)**	**the words 'culture' and 'travellers' can be replaced with 'custom' and 'tourists' respectively.**

Activity 7: Writing Practice

Based on your understanding of 'coherence and cohesion', try to use the italicised cohesive devices of the response to T2-23 to finish writing two body paragraphs of T2-28.

T2-23

You should spend about 40 minutes on this task. Write about the following topic:

Some people think that the development of science and technology has led to a decrease in privacy (e.g., being monitored of speeches and actions). However, others regard the development of science and technology as positive because they feel more secure. Discuss both views and give your opinion.

Give reasons for your answer and include any relevant examples from your own knowledge or experience.

Write at least 250 words.

Regarding the advantages, the development of science and technology enables us to feel more secure. One of the examples is the use of iPhones. *In the past*, we used to use the four-digit passcode to prevent others from using our phone. However, it is not a very reliable method of security. *Nowadays*, we can use fingerprints as passwords instead of the four-digit passcode. Since we all have our unique fingerprints, it will be more difficult for others to get the important information from our phones. *Hence*, it is more secure for us.

In terms of disadvantages, it has led to a decrease in privacy. *According to* some news reports, with the use of some software and IT skills, *not only* the words that we typed, *but also* the activities that we did on our electronic devices can be easily monitored by some professionals. *To exemplify*, when we look for some hotel information on computers, some social media like Facebook can show us some recommended hotels *because* they can 'read' what we have read before. *Therefore*, it is true that our privacy becomes vulnerable with such scientific and technological development.

T2-28

You should spend about 40 minutes on this task. Write about the following topic:

Governments are more concerned about creating economic benefits for people while they overlook the actions they should take to control pollution resulting from economic development.

Discuss the above view and give your opinion.

Give reasons for your answer and include any relevant examples from your own knowledge or experience.

Write at least 250 words.

Answers to Chapter 9

Task 2: Lexical Resource

Check Your Understanding

In Activity 1 in Chapter 5, three important aspects of the 'lexical resource' domain were defined and discussed, which are (1) variety of vocabulary, (2) difficulty of vocabulary, and (3) accuracy of vocabulary.

Check your understanding of these three aspects of the 'lexical resource' domain by indicating whether the following statements are 'True' or 'False':

1   There are four major types of word formation, which are prefixes, suffixes, compounds, and conversion. [True/**False**]
2   We are required to use formal and sophisticated vocabulary to express our ideas. [True/**False**]
3   Accuracy of vocabulary is assessed with reference to collocation use, spelling and parts of speech. [True/**False**]

Activity 1: Understanding the Assessment Standards of 'Lexical Resource'

Since the assessment standards of this domain in Task 2 are identical to those in Task 1, refer to Activity 1 in Chapter 5 for definitions of keywords of the assessment standards.

Activity 2: Using a Variety of Vocabulary

*   Read the following question (T2-05) and read Exemplars 9.1–9.3.
*   Evaluate how well the exemplars are written in terms of using a variety of vocabulary by referring to the definitions and examples of the related terms. If necessary, use the following guiding questions to help your evaluation:

    o   Did the student form new words through the use of prefixes?
    o   Did the student form new words through the use of suffixes?
    o   Did the student form new words through the use of conversion?
    o   Did the student form new words through the use of compounds?

T2-05

You should spend about 40 minutes on this task. Write about the following topic:

Distance education enables students to study at their own pace. Nevertheless, it also creates problems including high withdrawal rate and lack of interaction between teachers and students. Explain some possible reasons for these problems and suggest some solutions.

Give reasons for your answer and include any relevant examples.

Exemplar 9.1

First and foremost, inadequate monitoring in distance education will cause high withdraw rate. By adopting distance education, teachers and student are no longer sitting in the same classroom in class - students are required to watch pre-recorded video lesson instead. In view of the phenomenon that most parents need to work in daytime, there will not be any authorities to supervise students in classes. As a result, this may contribute to a high withdrawal rate. Offering a tutor for every student is clearly unafford-able. Therefore, assigning after-lesson quiz for students is a way to solve the problem. If all students are required to take a test regarding teaching content after each lesson, they will be more willing to attend online lessons with a view to get a pass. The pupils will attend and concentrate in online classes.

Guiding question	Yes/No	Example/Suggestion
Did the student form new words through the use of prefixes?	Yes	in-adequate pre-recorded un-affordable
Did the student form new words through the use of suffixes?	Yes	withdraw-al educat-ion
Did the student form new words through the use of conversion?	Yes	pass (v.) ⇨ a pass (n.) after lesson ⇨ after-lesson (adj.)
Did the student form new words through the use of compounds?	Yes	with-draw class-room day-time

Exemplar 9.2

Communication between teachers and students wastes much time and will lead to lack of interaction between teachers and students. Students can not only raise their hands and ask questions verbally but also seek help from teachers by visiting the staff room after class in traditional schooling. In contrast, stu-dents can only email their teachers and probably wait for a couple of hours for reply in distance schooling. The long waiting time will discourage students to ask questions and interact with teachers in the long run. The issue can be addressed by launching live lessons in distance education. Unlike pre-recorded videos, students can leave comments which will be seen by the tutor immediately and discuss with the tutor in live lessons. As a result, interactions between teachers and students can be preserved in live teaching.

Guiding question	Yes/No	Example/Suggestion
Did the student form new words through the use of prefixes?	Yes	un-like dis-courage pre-recorded
Did the student form new words through the use of suffixes?	Yes	interact-ion(s) immediate-ly verbal-ly communicat-ion tradition-al educat-ion
Did the student form new words through the use of conversion?	Yes	'students can only email (v.) . . .' (from the noun 'email') 'wait for a couple hours for reply (n.)' (from the verb 'reply') 'The issue can be addressed (v.) by launching (v.)' (from the nouns 'address' and 'launch')
Did the student form new words through the use of compounding?	No	'wastes much time' can be replaced by 'become more time-consuming' Can add the connective 'Furthermore' at the beginning of the paragraph

Exemplar 9.3

Distance education allows students to study wherever they want. But, it also creates problems because many students give up and students and teachers cannot communicate. I reckon that teacher-student miscommunication is the cause of the above problems.

Guiding question	Yes/No	Example/Suggestion
Did the student form new words through the use of prefixes?	Yes	mis-communication 'allows' can be changed to 'en-ables'
Did the student form new words through the use of suffixes?	Yes	educat-ion 'many students give up' can be changed to 'there is high withdraw-al rate'
Did the student form new words through the use of conversion?	No	'students and teachers cannot communicate' can be changed to 'there is a <u>lack (n.)</u> of communication between teachers and students' (from the verb 'lack')
Did the student form new words through the use of compounding?	No	'But' can be changed to 'Nevertheless'

Activity 3: Using Academic Vocabulary

- Read the following question (T2-06) and read Exemplars 9.4 and 9.5.
- Evaluate how well the exemplars are written in terms of using academic vocabulary by referring to the definitions and examples of the related terms. If necessary, use the following guiding questions to help your evaluation:

  o Did the student use a set of more sophisticated and formal words than we would normally use in our daily life?

T2-06

You should spend about 40 minutes on this task. Write about the following topic:

Family-friendly measures (e.g. flexible working hours) should be adopted by companies to ensure the work-life balance of their employees. To what extent do you agree or disagree with this opinion?

Give reasons for your answer and include any relevant examples.

Exemplar 9.4

First and foremost, flexible working hours should be implemented as it can benefit employee while not harming the interest of the company. Imagine that you are an office lady who wakes up at 7 am and return home at 7 pm on weekdays. How can you have adequate time to accompany your children who go to bed at 9 pm? When working hours become more flexible, workers can have discretion over their working hours. Then, more time can be reserved for their family.

Categorise the following words into 'word/expression in a less academic style' and 'word/expression in a more academic style' by putting a tick (✓) in the appropriate boxes. Suggest a more formal and sophisticated word for the latter.

Word/expression	Word/expression in a less academic style	Word/expression in a more academic style	Suggestion (if any)
first and foremost		✓	
implemented		✓	
benefit		✓	
adequate		✓	
accompany		✓	
have discretion over		✓	
reserved		✓	

Compare Exemplar 9.4 with Exemplar 9.4(a).

Exemplar 9.4(a) - words/expressions in a less academic style

There must be flexible working hours as it is good for employees while not harming the interest of the company. Imagine that you are an office lady who wake up at 7 am and return home at 7 pm on weekdays. How can you have enough time to be with your children who go to bed at 9 pm? When working hours become more flexible, workers can work earlier and finish their work earlier. Then, they can spend their evening with family.

Exemplar 9.5

Moreover, childcare money should be given to workers for promoting working efficiency. For employers, the money is worth-spending as employees do not need to worry about their children while working. Thus, they can put more emphasis on work and working efficiency can be promoted. Besides, parents can obtain more leisure time after launching the scheme. This makes working-parents receive other training or further their studies which can also raise their working efficiency.

Categorise the following words into 'word/expression in a less academic style' and 'word/expression in a more academic style' by putting a tick (✓) in the appropriate boxes. Suggest a more formal and sophisticated word for the latter.

Word/expression	Word/expression in a less academic style	Word/expression in a more academic style	Suggestion (if any)
moreover		✓	
money	✓		**subsidy**
working efficiency		✓	
for employers	✓		**From the perspective of the employers, . . .**
do not need to worry about	✓		**. . . employees can stop agonising over their children . . .**
put more emphasis on		✓	
makes	✓		**enables, motivates working parents to receive . . .**

Compare Exemplar 9.5 with Exemplar 9.5(a).

Exemplar 9.5(a) - words/expressions in a more academic style

Moreover, childcare subsidy should be given to workers for promoting working efficiency. From the perspective of the employers, the money is worth-spending as employees can stop agonizing over their children's needs while working. Thus, they can put more emphasis on work and working efficiency can be

promoted. Besides, parents can obtain more leisure time after launching the scheme. This motivates work-
ing parents to receive other training or further their studies which can in turn raise their working efficiency.

Exemplar 9.6

Equal amount of time should be spent by employees on work and family. Working is important to them
because they need the salary to support their family. Also, family is important because people need sup-
port from those who are close to them. So, it is important for the employers to give employees flexible
working hours. It will make the company strong.

Categorise the following words into 'word/expression in a less academic style' and 'word/expression in
a more academic style' by putting a tick (✓) in the appropriate boxes. Suggest a more formal and sophis-
ticated word for the latter.

Word/expression	Word/expression in a less academic style	Word/expression in a more academic style	Suggestion (if any)
equal amount of time should be spent	✓		**strike a balance between . . . and . . .**
Working	✓		**. . . secure a stable job**
important	✓		**it is crucial to . . ./indispensable/it is of paramount importance**
need the salary	✓		**. . . to provide financial support to . . .**
Also	✓		**in addition**
Give	✓		**. . . foster a flexible working environment**
make the company strong	✓		**. . . would empower and motivate the employees to contribute significantly to the company**

Compare Exemplar 9.6 with Exemplar 9.6(a).

Exemplar 9.6(a) – words/expressions in a more academic style

Employees should strike a balance between work and family. It is crucial to secure a stable job to them
because it is their responsibility to provide financial support to their family. In addition, family is indispensable
because people need support from those who are close to them. So, it is of paramount importance for the
employers to foster a flexible working environment. The adoption of such policy would empower and motivate
the employees to contribute significantly to the company.

Activity 4: Using Accurate Vocabulary

- Read the following question (T2-07) and read Exemplars 9.7–9.9.
- Evaluate how well the exemplars are written in terms of using accurate vocabulary by referring to the definitions and examples of the related terms. If necessary, use the following guiding questions to help your evaluation:

    o Did the student use collocations accurately?
    o Did the student spell words accurately?
    o Did the student use part of speech accurately?

T2-07

You should spend about 40 minutes on this task. Write about the following topic:

It is not uncommon nowadays for people to work overseas. Working overseas allow people to experience different cultures and extend their social and professional connections. However, some find it hard to adapt due to nostalgia and acculturation.

Give reasons for your answer and include any relevant examples.

Correct the lexical errors you find in the following exemplars. Focus on collocation, spelling, and part of speech.

Exemplar 9.7

First and foremost, working overseas enables us to experience different cultures and extend our social and professional circles. For instance, you will know more about Japanese cuisine and customs when you are working and living in Japan. In addition, your social and professional networks will be strength by making Japanese friends and aquiring knowledge in a new working environment. You can reap from working in other countries in different aspects.

Type of error	Error	Correction
Collocation	Extend . . . social and professional circles	Expand . . . social and professional circles
Spelling	aquiring	acquiring
Part of speech	strength (n.)	strengthened (v.)

Exemplar 9.8

In spite to these, some people find it difficult to fit into a new environment and reluctant to leave their hometown because of homesick and acculturation. I understand that foreign workers may miss their family and do not want to follow foreign cultures. I reckon that these difficulties can be eased. For curing homesickness, you can cook Chinese dishes by yourself, call your family when you miss them, even go home on holidays. For acculturation, I prefer to adapt to local culture and do not violent local customs. If you could not, you should still treat local culture in respect.

Type of error	Error	Correction
Collocation	in spite to	in spite of
	difficulties can be eased	difficulties can be overcome
	Treat . . . in respect	Treat . . . with respect
Spelling	violent	violate
Part of speech	because of homesick (adj.) . . .	because of homesickness (n.) . . .

Exemplar 9.9

All and all, not only do we gain experiences when living in different cultures, but we also expand our social and professional circle. Though we will still face some challenges, it is believed that these challenges can be overcomed and we will be hugely benefited by working overseas.

Type of error	Error	Correction
Collocation	all and all	all in all
Spelling	overcomed	overcome

Activity 5: Peer Evaluation

Based on your understanding of the assessment standards of 'lexical resource', complete the evaluation form for Exemplar 9.10 written by a university student.

In the evaluation, identify problematic aspects of vocabulary use in relation to (1) **variety**, (2) **difficulty**, and (3) **accuracy** by responding to the guiding questions.

T2-08

You should spend about 40 minutes on this task. Write about the following topic:

The number of slash workers (people with multiple careers) is on the rise. It is less likely for young people these days to settle on one job for a long time. Why would young people want to be slash workers? What are the social consequences of having more slash workers?

Give reasons for your answer and include any relevant examples from your own knowledge or experience.

Write at least 250 words.

Exemplar 9.10 (paragraph 1)

The number of slash workers is rising (Q1) in recent years. Youngsters would like to be (Q2) slash workers because they want to broaden their horizon (Q3). There are bad impacts (Q4) brought by slash workers such as (Q5) shortage of full-time workers and low salary tax revenue.

Questions for paragraph 1:

Q1.   What is a more formal and academic word to replace 'rising'?

Escalating/skyrocketing/increasing/on the rise

Q2.   What is a more formal and academic expression to replace 'would like to be'?

Opt to be/prefer to be/are inclined to be

Q3.   What is the spelling mistake of 'horizon'?

Horizons (the expression is 'broaden one's horizons' which means to enrich one's understanding about something)

Q4.   What is a more formal and academic word to replace 'bad impacts'?

Setbacks/drawbacks/pitfalls/disadvantages

Q5.   What is a more formal and academic expression to replace 'such as'?

Namely/including

Exemplar 9.10 (paragraph 2)

First and foremost, youngsters want to be slash workers because they would like to broaden their horizon (Q1). Take my friend Jack as an example, he works as an English tutor, a secretary and a photographer at the same time. Having several jobs allows him to experience both flexible and regular (Q2) workplace cultures. Being slash workers can also (Q3) enable Jack to broaden their horizons (Q4) by offering him more opportunities to make new friends. He meets colleagues in each job and able to encounter people in different backgrounds (Q5).

Questions for paragraph 2:

Q1. The same expression 'broaden one's horizons' has been used in the first paragraph. Can you suggest another synonymous expression?

. . . because they would like to explore different possibilities in life

Q2. The collocation between 'regular' and 'workplace cultures' is wrong. Can you suggest an alternative to 'regular'?

A formal workplace culture

Q3. What is a more formal and academic word/expression to replace 'also'?

Moreover/Furthermore/Additionally, being slash workers enables. . .

Q4. The same expression 'broaden one's horizons' has been used in the first paragraph. Can you suggest another synonymous expression?

. . .enable Jack to expand his social circle by offering him more opportunities to make new friends.

Q5. In the expression 'in different backgrounds', the collocation between the preposition 'in' and the noun 'backgrounds' is wrong. Can you suggest another preposition?

From/with different backgrounds

Exemplar 9.10 (paragraph 3)

The social consequences of having more slash workers are shortage of full-time workers and low salary tax revenue. When full-time jobs become less appealing for (Q1) youngsters and the full-time places (Q2) remain unchanged, a shortage of full-time workers may emerge in the labour market. Also (Q3), income received from some of the part-time jobs will not be reported to the authorities. As a results (Q4), many slash workers can avoid salary tax and salary tax revenue may become less (Q5) in the long run.

Questions for paragraph 3:

Q1. The collocation between 'appealing' and 'for' is wrong. Can you suggest another preposition?

Appealing to somebody

Q2. What is a more formal and academic word to replace 'places'?

(Job) vacancies

Q3. What is a more formal and academic word to replace 'also'?

Moreover/Furthermore/In addition/Additionally/Besides

Q4. What is the spelling mistake in the expression 'as a results'?

As a result

Q5. What is a more formal and academic word to replace 'become less'?

Reduce/dwindle/lessen/decrease/diminish

Exemplar 9.10 (paragraph 4)

In conclusion, wanting (Q1) to broaden their horizons (Q2) would be a reason (Q3) for young people to become slash workers. Disadvantages of the glowing (Q4) number of slash workers may lead in (Q5) full-time worker shortage and a drop in salary tax revenue.

Q1. What is a more formal and academic expression to replace 'wanting'?

Having the desire

Q2. The same expression 'broaden one's horizons' has been used multiple times. Can you suggest another synonymous expression?

Familiarise themselves with a broader range of knowledge and understanding

Q3. What is a more formal and academic expression to replace 'a reason'?

A contributing factor

Q4. What is the spelling mistake of 'glowing'?

Growing ('glowing' means emitting light)

Q5. The collocation between 'lead' and 'in' is wrong. Can you suggest another preposition?

Lead to/result in

Activity 5: Writing Practice

Based on your understanding of 'lexical resource', replace the italicised words with more formal words in the following paragraph of T2-30. Please note that occasionally, the change of words would entail the change of sentence structures. Modify the sentence structures if necessary.

T2-30

You should spend about 40 minutes on this task. Write about the following topic:

   Some people favor the use of private cars as they bring people much convenience. However, some people think that private cars cause air pollution which is harmful to the environment. Do the advantages of using private cars outweigh the disadvantages?

   Give reasons for your answer and include any relevant examples from your own knowledge or experience.

   Write at least 250 words.

It cannot be *denied* that using private cars can *save time* when we go outside and it is *easier* for us to *go* to different destinations. However, the public transportation is also *good*, because it can help mange our commuting time and it is *cheap* to go around *different destinations*. It has similar functions as driving cars. For example, the underground train follows a routine schedule and there is *no* traffic *jam*, especially in peak hours.

Answer:

It is undeniable that using private cars can be time-efficient when we go outside and it is more convenient to travel to different destinations. However, the public transportation, which has similar functions as driving cars, has certain merits as well. To demonstrate, it can help commuters better manage their time and it is economical for them to travel to various locations. Taking the underground train as an example, it follows a routine schedule and we can avoid the traffic congestion, especially in peak hours.

Answers to Chapter 10
Task 2: Grammatical Range and Accuracy

Check Your Understanding

In Activity 1 in Chapter 6, two important aspects of the 'lexical resource' domain were defined and discussed, which are (1) structure variety and (2) sentence accuracy.

Check your understanding of these two aspects of the 'grammatical range and accuracy' domain by indicating whether the following statements are 'True' or 'False':

1　We have to use both simple and complex sentence structures in Task 2. [**True**/False]
1　Complex sentences are formed by a combination of an independent clause with one or more dependent clauses. [**True**/False]
2　Comma splices, run-on sentences, and sentence fragments will not affect the accuracy of sentences. [**True**/False]

Activity 1: Understanding the Assessment Standards of 'Grammatical Range and Accuracy'

Since the assessment standards of this domain in Task 2 are identical to those in Task 1, refer to Activity 1 in Chapter 6 for definitions of keywords of the assessment standards.

Activity 2: Structure Variety

- Read the following question (T2-19) and read Exemplars 10.1–10.3.
- Evaluate how well the exemplars are written in terms of using a variety of sentence structures by referring to the definitions and examples of the related terms.

T2-19

You should spend about 40 minutes on this task. Write about the following topic:

It seems that people over 40 are difficult to find a satisfactory job. What are the causes? Are there any possible solutions to this problem?

Give reasons for your answer and include any relevant examples from your own knowledge or experience.

Write at least 250 words.

Exemplar 10.1

Firstly, (1) people over forty generally work for a long time. (2) Most of them have ample experience. They have a great CV. Therefore, (3) they always aim high when they are looking for a new employment. (4) They cannot accept any position because they find the salary too low. (5) They may have many job requests but there are few jobs which can satisfy them. It is why they are difficult to find a satisfactory job.

Categorise the underlined sentences into three types: (1) simple sentences, (2) compound sentences, and (3) complex sentences.

Sentence pattern	Sentence number
Simple sentence	**(1), (2)**
Compound sentence	**(5)**
Complex sentence	**(3), (4), (5)**

Exemplar 10.2

Firstly, (1) people who are more than 40 years old have been working in the workplace for a long time. It is depressing to be in a job for a long time. (2) They lost the power to work when they are old. When they were young, (3) they had the incentive to work, they wanted to get promotion, or the boss recognized their effort. However, when they get older and do not get promoted, people get lost in front of work. Also, (4) people will be dissatisfied with their work.

Categorize the underlined sentences into three types: (1) simple sentences, (2) compound sentences, and (3) complex sentences.

Sentence pattern	Sentence number
Simple sentence	**(4)**
Compound sentence	**(3)**
Complex sentence	**(1), (2)**

Exemplar 10.3

Secondly, (1) people feel dissatisfied with their job. People think that busy working can affect health, family and life. In some cases, some people choose to divorce because their partners are too busy working. From the above, it is shown that long working hours can make people dissatisfied with their work. (2) Long hours can affect people's health. They lack time to rest. In some serious cases, (3) people spend all their time on work. They lose the chance to meet their friends.

Sentence number	Instruction	Rewritten sentence
1	Combine the two sentences with a subordinating conjunction 'which' to form a complex sentence	**People who think that busy work schedule can affect health, family and life feel dissatisfied with their job.**
2	Combine the two sentences with a subordinating conjunction to form a complex sentence	**Long hours can affect people's health because they lack time to rest.**
3	Combine the two sentences with a coordinating conjunction to form a compound sentence	**People spend all their time on work and they hose the chance to meet their friends.**

Activity 3: Sentence Accuracy

- Read the following question (T2-20) and read Exemplars 10.4–10.5.
- Evaluate how well the exemplars are written in terms of using a variety of sentence structures accurately by referring to the definitions and examples of the related terms.

T2-20

You should spend about 40 minutes on this task. Write about the following topic:

When it comes to children's leisure activities, they prefer to stay indoors for computer games rather than go outside for sports.

Discuss the view and give your opinion.

Give reasons for your answer and include any relevant examples from your own knowledge or experience.

Write at least 250 words.

Exemplar 10.4

(1) Being more comfortable, the first reason why children love playing computers and stay indoor is because it is too hot outside. (2) Because of the influence of global warming. the scorching sun and suffocating air lead to the fact that city dwellers would like to get into an air-conditioned room, (3) only few, if any, people would like to stay outdoor and enjoy playing sports. (4) Therefore it is not difficult to understand why children these day enjoy playing computer games more. Who would opt for suffering and sweating under the sun instead of playing computer games with comfortable air conditioners operating 24 hours? A similar circumstance is noted in physical education lessons. (5) Most of the girls chooses to sit aside under the shade of building to wait until the end of the lesson instead of going to play sports and games even they are bored and dull. (6) The major reason they would like to sit aside is because of they hate sweat and being hot.

Match sentences (1) to (6) with the six types of errors described in Chapter 6. These error types include: comma splice, run-on sentence, sentence fragment, faulty parallelism, subject-verb disagreement, and misplaced modifiers. Rewrite a grammatically correct sentence for each.

Sentence number	Error type	Rewritten sentence
1	Dangling modifier	Being more comfortable, children love playing computers and stay indoor because it is too hot outside.
2	Sentence fragment	Because of the influence of global warming, … the scorching sun…
3	Comma spice	.Only few, if any, people would like to stay outdoor and enjoy playing sports.
4	Run-on sentence	Therefore, it is not difficult to understand why children these days enjoy playing computer games more.
5	Subject-verb disagreement	Most of the girls choose…
6	Faulty parallelism	The major reasons why they would like to sit aside is because of sweating and being hot.

Exemplar 10.5

Firstly, (1) doing outdoor sports are good for the children's health. The majority of the students have packed schedules. Other than the normal school time, (2) many of them may need to attend various tutorial lessons and participating in extra-curricular activities after school. Therefore, they spend most of their time doing indoor activities without sunlight. (3) However, it is reported that suitable sunlight is good for health, especially for the kids who enter puberty, their bodies are growing every day. It is believed that absorbing enough sunlight and sweating can foster children's physical growth. Therefore, from the perspective of physical health, doing outdoor sports is better than playing computer games.

Secondly, much money is spent on computer games than sports. It is believed that money is involved in purchasing electronic games. (4) Other than the games themselves money is also paid to buy the extra tools which help play the games. (5) The specialized chairs and joysticks. Also, the more time you spend on the game, the more likely that you will pay more. It is reported that thousands of dollars can be lavished on playing one single video game. In contrast, doing sports is mostly free of charge. (6) Being free of charge, people who can afford the time do common sports like running and swimming. Therefore, doing outdoor sports is better than playing computer games.

Match sentences (1) to (6) with the six types of errors described in Chapter 6. These error types include: comma splice, run-on sentence, sentence fragment, faulty parallelism, subject-verb disagreement, and misplaced modifiers. Rewrite a grammatically correct sentence for each.

Sentence number	Error type	Rewritten sentence
1	Subject-verb disagreement	Doing outdoor sports is good for the children's health.
2	Faulty parallelism	Many of them may need to attend various tutorial lessons and participate in extra-curricular activities after school.
3	Comma splice	However, it is reported that suitable sunlight is good for health, especially for the kids who enter puberty because their bodies are growing every day.
4	Run-on sentence	Other than the games themselves, money is also paid to buy the extra tools which help play the games.
5	Sentence fragment	Other than the games themselves, money is also paid to buy the extra tools which help play the games, including the specialised chairs and joysticks.
6	Dangling modifier	Being free of charge, common sports like running and swimming are affordable to most people.

Activity 4: Peer Evaluation

Based on your understanding of the assessment standards of 'grammatical range and accuracy', complete the evaluation form for Exemplar 10.6 written by a university student.

In the evaluation, identify problematic aspects of sentence use in relation to (1) **variety** and (2) **accuracy** by responding to the guiding questions.

T2-21

You should spend about 40 minutes on this task. Write about the following topic:

Women's status has improved dramatically both in the society and in the family as a result of the development of the society. However, they still face the problem of inequalities. What are some of the inequalities? What measures should be adopted to solve the problems?

Give reasons for your answer and include any relevant examples from your own knowledge or experience.

Write at least 250 words.

Exemplar 10.6

Women have long been underestimated with their capacities which causes gender inequality in the past decades. They were unreasonably treated in the society and also in the family. (1) This situation has been improving with liberal education and social movements, yet, there are still room for improvement.

In the social aspect, take Hong Kong as an example, ladies enjoy equal job opportunities as gentlemen. (2) Both genders could have fair competitions they could take legal action if they have evidence showing the recruitment is unfair. Sex discrimination is less serious comparing to the past because of improvement in legislations. However, there are still discriminations in job applications (3) if the employer knows the applicant is pregnant or birth to baby. This could hardly collect concrete clues demonstrating there are sexually unfair treatments as employers could find many other excuses, such as there is physical workload or overtime work. Women applicant might not be treated fairly in this sense. This could be solved with a clear job advertisement with listed duties which prevents any arguments about eligibility.

(4) Another social point of view. people treat divorced men and women differently. People usually believe women should only marry a man once in a life. (5) If the women is divorced, people would still have the traditional thoughts, saying that the women are 'unwanted' and no one would think the men are 'unwanted'. Unfortunately, this faulty belief could hardly be changed. This concerns how others perceive divorced women who are pursuing a second marriage, especially the parents and relatives of the men. These ridiculous thoughts create a burden for divorced women and put them under stress and pressure which affects their personal and social life. (6) This problem could hardly be solved by media or education, it takes time to improve.

Wives are still facing inequalities in family as they are often labelled as 'housewives' and they are relying on their husbands. (7) Having an unscientific belief, the wives are perceived as merely helping with the housework and children's work, which barely have any economic contribution to the family. According to a Japanese study, if we calculate a housewife's workload in the family, they could earn a fortune. Wives' contributions are usually minimized when compared to those of husbands. This biased interpretation reveals the unbalanced family role and expectations of the spouses. Similar to the previous problem, it could hardly be solved.

To conclude, the society is changing and is becoming a better place for men and women. (8) An equal treatment regarding to sexes. This requires the effort of the entire society with the willingness to change which might take a few decades. (441 words)

Q1. Match sentences (1) to (8) with one of the six types of errors described in Chapter 6. These error types include: comma splice, run-on sentence, sentence fragment, faulty parallelism, subject-verb disagreement, and misplaced modifiers. Rewrite a grammatically correct sentence for each.

Sentence number	Error type	Rewritten sentence
1	**Comma splice**	This situation has been improving with liberal education and social movements; yet, there are still room for improvement.
2	**Run-on sentence**	Both genders could have fair competitions – they could take legal action if they have evidence showing the recruitment is unfair.
3	**faulty parallelism**	… if the employer knows the applicant is pregnant or will give birth to baby.
4	**Sentence fragment**	From another social point of view, …
5	**Subject-verb disagreement**	If the women are divorced, people would…
6	**Comma splice**	This problem could hardly be solved by media or education because it takes time to improve.
7	**Dangling modifier**	Having an unscientific belief, people perceive that wives are merely helping with the housework and children's work, which barely have any economic contribution to the family.
8	**Sentence fragment**	Equal treatment should be given to both sexes.

Q2. Give one example of compound sentence used in the exemplar.

These ridiculous thoughts create a burden for divorced women and put them under stress and pressure… (para. 3)

Q3. Give one example of complex sentences used in the exemplar.

This concept influences how others perceive divorced women who are pursuing a second marriage, especially the parents and relatives of the men.

Activity 5: Writing Practice

Based on your understanding of 'grammatical range and accuracy', try to rewrite the paragraph of T2-33 with complex sentence structures and correct punctuation.

T2-33

You should spend about 40 minutes on this task. Write about the following topic:

Electric cars are becoming more popular nowadays because they are more environmentally friendly. Moreover, electric cars have become an emblem for tech-savvy people.

To what extent do you agree or disagree with this opinion?

Give reasons for your answer and include any relevant examples from your own knowledge or experience.

Write at least 250 words.

Second, electric cars are a popular choice among car lovers. Especially those wealthy ones. They represent status and power. For example, you own an electric car manufactured by Tesla. You will be highly regarded in your peer groups. Because you embrace technology to enhance quality of life. Moreover, people will hold the perception that you are technology-savvy. For instance, you will definitely impress your friends. By showing them how you can control your electric car using a touchscreen.

Answer:

Second, electric cars are a popular choice among car lovers, especially those wealthy ones because they represent status and power. By owning an electric car manufactured by Tesla, for example, you will be highly regarded in your peer groups as someone who embraces technology to enhance their quality of life. Moreover, people will hold the perception that you are technology-savvy. For instance, you will definitely impress your friends by showing them how you can control your electric car using a touchscreen.

Index

Bold pages refer to tabular content and *italicized* pages refer to figures

Milton Keynes UK
Ingram Content Group UK Ltd.
UKHW031513120124
435922UK00020B/849

9 780367 258375